# Petticoat Whalers

# PETTICOAT WHALERS

## Whaling Wives at Sea
### 1820 – 1920

## BY JOAN DRUETT
### ORIGINAL ILLUSTRATIONS BY RON DRUETT

University Press of New England
Hanover and London

University Press of New England, Hanover, NH 03755

© 2001 by Joan Druett

Originally published in cloth by
Collins Publishers New Zealand in 1991.

University Press of New England paperback 2001.

Printed in Hong Kong                    5 4 3 2 1

ISBN: 1-58465-159-8
Library of Congress Card Number: 2001090498

# Contents

# Author's note

Some readers might associate the word 'whaler' with the men who were left on the beach in so-called shore-whaling gangs, to row out into the bays as the migrating whales arrived on the coast. It is true that these men were commonly called 'whalers' – but this book is not about them. The 'whalers' of my story are the ships, the windjammer whalers which sailed the open sea and called into port only to recruit (take on fresh water, firewood and provisions). The men who lived and worked on the deep-sea whalers were called 'whalemen'. . . and this book is about those whalemen's wives who lived at sea for years on end with their menfolk. The account is based on the journals, letters and reminiscences left by these remarkable women; a list of these writings can be found at the end of the book.

The quotations from the whaling women and their husbands, sons, daughters and shipmates are given as they wrote them down, always allowing for some difficulty in transcription where the writing was wild or the manuscript damaged. While the writers seldom underlined ships' names, they are printed here in italics, according to convention. Where the writer underlined for emphasis, I have again used italics. Otherwise the punctuation is changed only when necessary for clarity. Spellings are also unaltered, except when wrong spellings could be misleading. I have resorted to the subtly condescending insertion *sic* (thus) as seldom as possible. While there are no footnotes within the text, detailed chapter notes are given at the end of the book to help those who want to learn more of this fascinating aspect of maritime history.

# 1

# A *disgraceful drinking riot*

*Ngatangiia, Rarotonga, Cook Islands.*

IT was very hot. It was the middle of the day and we were sweaty from cycling along the road which runs around the island. I would like you to picture the part of this road that we reached at noon. The road is narrow and potholed, and follows the contours of the beach about exactly. On the landward side the ground is densely cultivated: banana palms and Wellingtonia trees loom over the ditches; taro plots and pawpaw, orange and avocado plantations terrace the land as it rises towards the lush mountain at the heart of Rarotonga. On the other side there is a ribbon of coral rubble between the road and the sea, which hurts the eyes in the glare of the sun. That littoral part is very bare: straggly mallows and thin casuarina give only a grudging shade. Over there a huge old tree once grew, but it's no more than a tangled skeleton now, felled by a recent storm. Knotted roots reach up against the pale sky. Creepers and weeds grow thickly over the stones beneath it, half-hiding potholes and trenches. Beyond the rubble: the sand and the sea. At noon, in the heat, this part of the road is deserted – usually.

On this particular day in May 1984, however, we saw a young man working in the full blaze of the sun, hacking away at weeds in the scrabble at the foot of the fallen tree. It was very hard work and seemed pointless, and yet he was still there next day and the day after that. Why such dogged determination? It was impossible not to ask. He'd had a dream, we were told. An ancestor ghost had come to him in this dream and had bid him clear that bit of land, apparently because it was a graveyard.

We found this unbelievable. Rarotongans do not neglect their ancestors' graves; an unkempt grave is unknown there. The explanation, however, was simple. Once, long ago, a sailing ship had called with a dead sailor on board, and the captain had asked permission to bury the lad on shore. The *Pa Ariki* of that time was reluctant to give permission for this, for the tradition until then had been that only Rarotongans could be buried on the island. However, she thought long and hard about it and decided that this particular patch should be set aside as a burying ground for foreigners. For as long as the ships had kept on coming, more boys had been buried there and the graves were maintained by their shipmates. Then the ships had stopped calling, and the burying ground had been left neglected – until the young man had his dream.

He worked on until the place was cleared and then he went away, leaving raked rubble and heaped weeds behind him. We explored the potholed rubble at once, eagerly, but found nothing more than a few bleached bones and broken illegible monuments. Again it was noon, and very hot. The shade cast by the scoured roots of the deadwood tree beckoned seductively. So I went over to rest there. . .and in the hole where the tree had grown I found a grave with a tall upright headstone. The wording on the stone was as clear as the day it had been carved. It read:

TO
the Memory of
Mary-Ann, the
beloved wife of
Captn A:D Sherman
of the
American Whale
Ship Harrison
WHO
departed this life
January 5: 1850
Aged 24 Years

A woman on a whaler! It was quite incredible. The whaling ships that plied the Pacific last century were small, dirty, over-filled with rough men; the missionary Luther Gulick called the ships 'the most disgusting of moral pesthouses'. It surely wasn't possible that the young wife of a whaling captain should have accompanied him on voyage; to me, it simply did not sound right.

The Pacific and Indian oceans were inarguably dangerous, for a start. It was little wonder that Mary-Ann had died. 'Here in this Urn, From Malabar,' begins the inscription on a legendary Nantucket gravestone, 'The Ashes Lie of Jonathan Barr.' Jonathan went a-whaling because he 'sought a Higher life afar' – and perhaps all the boys who shipped on the whalers that set out from Nantucket, New Bedford, Hobart and Hull were after some kind of stirring adventure. Instead of going home to boast about it, however, large numbers of them left their bones on exotic islands like this one, or their corpses were given ceremoniously to the deep blue sea, or perhaps, like Jonathan Barr, their remains were packed up and 'Travelled Homeward in a Jar'.

For the boys, the adventure was worth the risks – or so said the raunchy tales that were brought home by the swaggering survivors. Away from home and the restricting influences of law, order and public opinion, the Indian and Pacific oceans were a man's world indeed. The drinking bouts, for instance, were legendary. It was traditional for seamen to get on a spree when in port and the whalemen did it more flamboyantly than most, whether the place they were roistering was Honolulu, Tahiti, Sydney Town or Kororareka in the Bay of Islands.

## The crews

'WANTED! *Fifty Able-bodied Young Men* (Americans preferred), to go on a whaling voyage,' began an advertisement in a New York periodical. It then ran on to list the advantages of going a-whaling: 'Excellent chance to see foreign lands,' it promised, and, 'Only warm climates visited.' The whaling trade, the paper went to pains to point out, offered rapid promotion – 'The chance of a lifetime. No previous experience necessary.'

The first young men to ship on whalers might or might not have been naïve enough to believe such tongue-in-cheek nonsense, but on the whole they were almost certainly inspired by the spirit of adventure when they made the decision to sign ships' articles. The raunchy tales certainly beckoned any reasonably red-blooded lad, and, to the unseasoned, battling huge whales could well have sounded like some capital game.

Two weeks at sea would have been enough to disillusion even the most starry-eyed greenhands. 'Poor fellows...' wrote Captain William Phelps to his wife in 1840; 'they little knew for what hardships and privations they were exchanging the comforts and endearments of home, of the cold midnight watches, the frequent drenchings with rain and spray.' The overcrowded conditions, the dirt and discontent and unexpected boredom were bad enough for a start, and could be made unbearable by the 'kind' attentions of a half-mad skipper or a sadistic mate. It is little wonder that so many men deserted at the first Pacific port that offered a good chance of getting away.

'Money easily made,' the advertisement declared further. As on pirate ships, the men on whalers were paid not by wage but by a share of the profits – the 'lay'. The shares were small: a greenhand might sign on for a two-hundredth share, while a boatsteerer might be offered one ninety-fifth of the profits. The proposition seemed attractive, nevertheless, for everyone knew the value of oil. And the advertisement was right in one respect, for the chances of promotion on whaling vessels were indeed very good, because so many men deserted or died – and captains and mates were given a quarter share or even more.

In practice, however, that system which had sounded so democratic and fair at the start of

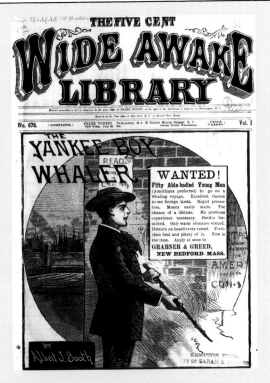

the voyage proved to be nothing more than blatantly callous exploitation. The owner was the man who calculated the value of the take when the ship got home, and he never used the gross market price as the basis for his sums. Secondly, the costs of the voyage were subtracted from the total before the lays were worked out – and those costs, unlike the estimated value of the cargo, could be (and usually were) inflated.

As well as that, each seaman was charged for his initial fitting out (ten or more dollars, plus the agent's fee of about $25). Then there was his share of the cost of the medical chest, which worked out at about a dollar and a half, plus the price of any medicine he'd been given on voyage. If he'd been sick the days 'off' were deducted against his lay, and then the owners' agents might have advanced money to the sailor's family at home, so he had to pay that back plus interest (usually 25%).

And then there was whatever he owed to the so-called 'slop chest'. This was a store of clothes, tobacco, soap and so forth that the captain carried on board ship, on behalf of the owners, to sell to the men. The prices of these goods were extortionate, as generally happens when there is a captive market. Captain George

Pomeroy, who opened the slop chest on the *George Howland* in April 1858, wrote with unmistakable anger (in a beautiful and remarkably misspelled copperplate hand), 'Fited ought the Crew yesturday...with a passel of Miserable clothing which the oners being Moral Quackers Charges almost dubble for...

'I feel moar Remorse Selling these things than the oners do at recieving the money for them for I can see how badley the men are ronged,' he growled. The men, however, spent their credit readily, and because of that iniquitous slop chest many seamen, whose lay for a four years' voyage might be as little as $200, ended up in debt to the owners, and were forced to ship out again at once, instead of holidaying for a few precious weeks at home.

It is not at all amazing, then, that the calibre of the men who were willing to sign on a whaler deteriorated quickly. It is not surprising, either, that the captains and their wives surveyed the men that the agents of the owners had sent them with deep misgiving. 'It is remarkable how many unfit and incompetent men find their way into sea service,' Clara Wheldon mused in October 1864 on the *John Howland*; 'mostly, however, through the outfitters on whom we are dependent for our men.'

The crews, as Mary Brewster noted in 1848, were always made up 'of a mixed up mess'. Country boys who had scarcely ever glimpsed the sea arrived on board completely gulled by unscrupulous agents who were prepared to promise anything to get a lad to sign. 'Food?' one legendary fellow exclaimed. 'I'll tell you, food, for why, but if you find that the food and yer stomach do not agree, then you go see the cap'n, for he keeps a cask of pies especial, for sad 'n hungry greenhands.'

Other men arrived in the forecastle stunned, drugged or drunk: drunken students were easy prey, and as early as 1845 Mary Brewster noted that one of the boys, 'Frank', was a medical student who had been snatched by an agent while on a spree. 'Many from all classes drift into sea life as a last resort,' Clara Wheldon opined. What is certain, however, is that by the 1840s it was so difficult to fill the berths of a whaling ship that the captains were pleased to get whatever men they could, of whatever calibre they might happen to be.

In New Zealand, oddly enough, British law encouraged hard drinking. The logkeeper of the whaleship *California* noted with some disbelief in Mangonui, 17 January 1850, that liquor had to be bought in bulk, for 'the law forbids everyone to sell less than two gallons'. In mission-dominated places like Lahaina, in Hawaii, and Papeete, in Tahiti, the preachers sternly forbade the sale and use of liquor, but that made little difference to the rough and ready whalemen. If there was no grog available, they simply smuggled it in. In April 1843 the Lahaina missionary Dwight Baldwin noted that the mate of the *Governor Troup* had fallen 'down the after hatch of his ship' and had died of a broken neck, the cause of his fall being 'that cursed fiery plague', alcohol. 'If devils go to hell,' he demanded, 'won't all rumsellers be there too?' – and if his wish were granted, Hades would have bulged with grog-smuggling whalemen as well.

The captains were often no better than their men. When the Reverend Daniel Wheeler visited Tahiti in 1835 he was scandalised to find that even the so-called 'temperance' ships, many skippered by Nantucketers who were Quakers like himself, smuggled large amounts of liquor on shore. It was landed in 'the supposed empty casks which are sent on shore for water', he recorded with horror. Wheeler shuddered for 'the awful and woeful consequences' for 'the daughters of Tahiti', and so did all his fellow preachers.

The wild drinking led to some epic brawls, which were certainly no sight for the eyes of a respectable wife. One such fracas occurred in Dunedin on Christmas Day, 1848. The whaling crews in port got drunk, and fought and threw things about. The *Otago News* described it as 'a little disturbance in our usual quiet town' but the Reverend Mr Burns declared it 'a disgraceful drinking riot at Watson's [hotel]'. Another such brawl occurred in Tahiti on 11 January 1846, as told (more or less) in the present tense by Dan Baldwin, third mate of the Yankee whaleship *Charleston*:

> 'Some of our men Get drunk on shore and make much noise and fight a few Battles with other ships' crews for the honor of their Ships. One was a bloody battle. I saw it from the ship. One drunken man got another down and aimed some tremendous blows at his head with his fist. His vision not being very accurate instead of hitting the head aimed at, he smote the ground and started the skin off his hand and shed much blood.

'I hope the French will not claim damage for Injury sustained by the island,' commented Dan, with typically puckish humour. The Tahitian missionaries would not have found it funny: they were no more pleased than the Reverend Burns was to have such an 'overwhelming torrent of iniquity' (as Daniel Wheeler put it) in their midst. They did their best with preachings of hellfire and the Blue Laws of New Haven, but too often the battle was a losing one. It seems evident that they could well have welcomed the revolutionary idea, if the respectable wives of the skippers had started shipping along. However, it seems equally obvious that the men would have hated it – and that includes captains, for many of the skippers roistered as wholeheartedly as their men.

Some of them, indeed, were most notorious drunks. One hard drinker was the skipper of the Rhode Island whaler *Balance*. In February 1845 he anchored in the port of Apia, Samoa, and found Captain Smith of the New London whaler *Hibernia* already there. Smith was waiting, it seems, for some like-minded company. The two reprobates got together and carried two barrels of rum on shore. Then they drank the lot in a matter of days. The *Balance* put to sea in March, with the captain 'verry bad and raving mad', according to the third mate, John Curnin. Then the captain set the crew to tacking the ship 'about thirty times' so that she puddled about in circles that were as drunken as he was. 'From all appearances,' Curnin noted gloomily, 'we bid for a bad voyage.' The ship had to put back to Apia after only three days, as the captain was 'out of his mind on account of drinking so hard'. It is surely obvious that the *Balance* did not carry a wife: if there had been, Captain Smith of the *Hibernia* would have considered it highly unsporting.

Captain Charles Bonney of the *Lewis*, 1853, was so addicted to the demon grog that he was usually incapable of running a ship: during one monumental bout he consumed five gallons (23 litres) of the fiery stuff. Even the most cowed wife, surely, would have put a stop to such intemperance, so it seems little wonder that Mrs Bonney stopped at home. And then there was Captain Reuben Swain of the Nantucket ship *Globe*, whose boozing exploits were the stuff of legend and fable. Swain didn't like to drink alone, so he kept a monkey, 'Mister Joe', for company in his revels.

The sessions were not always amicable. According to one of the many stories told, after several weeks of rugged weather Captain Swain offered to dry the men's stockings at his cabin stove. The crew gratefully handed the sodden socks over — and a short time later a reeking stench of burning wool filled the air. The monkey, it seems, had lightheartedly tossed all the socks in the fire. The men heard a bull-like roar of fury, and next thing Mister Joe hurtled up over deck and into the rigging, squealing and shrieking every inch of the way. The captain blundered topsides in hot pursuit; he had a pistol gripped in each shaking fist; the crew as one man dived for cover.

Swain was most surely the substance of the most stirring kind of tavern gossip. He wore a green eyepatch in an attempt to fix his constant double vision, and many was the time (or so the men claimed) that he set out from the deck for his cabin below, and made that cabin in just one step. Mrs Swain, obviously, was also waiting dutifully at home for Reuben's return: Mrs Swain, like Mrs Bonney, would have been a confounded encumbrance on voyage.

The pompous husband and righteous citizen who became a randy goat once he'd doubled the Cape or the Horn might be regarded as a legend, but it's a fable well grounded in truth. However — and this must be admitted — the temptations were persuasive. Back home in London, Hull, Nantucket and New Bedford, sex was hedged about with ironclad bans, so that the first whalemen in the Pacific found the sight of naked maidens as they played about in island lagoons both strange and refreshing.

The discovery that sex was offered as a simple friendly gesture was even more amazing. When the American whaleship *Tiger* anchored in Hawaii, April 1846, one of the seamen, Perkins, noted in tones of wonderment that, 'In spite of all the missionaries can do, they cannot make [the islanders] respect the marriage vows nor that they must be married before that they may have

# Whaling captains

Standing, left to right: Captains W.A. Beard; Gifford; Swift; Childs; Stall; Rodney French; Wood; Michael Cumisky; James Willis; Thomas Bailey. Seated, left to right: Captains Martin Mallory; Brownell; Swift; J. Howland; Worth; B.T. Tilton; William Taylor; Shubael Brayton; Chadwick.

'Sat 11th [June 1859] my 34th birthday and still a sinner,' wrote Captain James Willis in his logbook – and so were they all, but to varying degrees. Willis himself (second from right, standing) was far from being a 'reprobate': he was a devoted husband who carried his family on the ship *Rambler* in 1852.

Others were all too apt to drop the semblance of righteous respectability once safely in the Pacific: as one wife observed, they were men who left their souls at home. Rodney French, for instance, standing in the pride of place, sixth from the left, was a most worthy and estimable fellow at home, with thoroughly admirable anti-slavery views. At sea, however, he was rather different. By repute he singlehandedly killed between 40 and 50 pirates, and according to rumour he ran his ship as a 'blackbirding' slaver, stealing natives from a whole host of Pacific Islands, and then selling them off to plantation owners.

Some of the captains were drunks, and others were sadists, and it made no difference what town or country they came from.

Captain Hill of the English whaler *Japan*, 1834-7, had such an ocean-wide reputation as 'a dear boy for the girls' that whole villages were emptied of females when his ship was raised.

Unlike the skippers of merchant ships and men-of-war, the captains of whalers all started in the forecastle. They arrived in the after cabin by means of a series of promotions, in a process they called 'going through the hawse-pipe'. This was practical, for a man had to know how to do all the jobs of the complicated ship-cum-factory before he was fit to command it. However, it meant that they began their careers very young, and in a very rough manner. The men developed to suit. First of all they had to be powerful enough to cut huge chunks of blubber from unwieldy carcasses, and then they had to be aggressive enough to keep an oversized crew in some kind of order.

Whaling skippers were also very competitive. Whaling was a hazardous and chancy way to make a living, and it was every man for himself. Josiah Richmond of the *Daniel Wood* in 1860 was one of the many who would stoop to all kinds of devious tricks. A brother captain, John Deblois – who was extremely fond of his wife Henrietta – was doing very well, so Richmond sailed up and asked him what the devil he was doing harassing the whales when his wife was waiting in port. John Deblois was completely fooled and sailed off hastily, and was understandably angry when he found he'd been gammoned.

connection with the men. There is not a "pookapa" [virgin] over nine years of age in Heloe [Hilo]. Every female is open for the desires of sailors.

'They even seem to think the offers they give to every one who enters their huts a part of hospitality,' he added bemusedly.

Charles Murphy, third mate of the whaleship *Dauphin* in 1822, described the scene as the ship arrived at some farflung atoll, in neat and often-quoted verse.

> 'The graceful damsels from the shore,
> As soon as we were moored
> Came paddling off in their canoes
> While others swam on board.
>
> And now our decks with girls are filled
> Of every sort and kind
> And every man picked out a wife
> The best that he could find.
>
> 'Twas here the girls, including all
> (To speak it rather dryly)
> The sailors' amorous wants supplied
> And think they are hon'red highly.'

This ditty presents an engaging picture — but surely not one that many whalemen would wish their wives to witness. As it happens, the truth was rather more sordid, unsuitable in the extreme for a respectable woman's viewing. The whaleship *Covington* called at Ocean Island (Kure Atoll, Hawaii) in 1861, and one of the men, Alfred Peck, described things the way they really occurred.

'We could see canoes coming loaded with natives both men and women. Just before they reached the ship the women jumped overboard and swam for the ship and the canoes reaching the ship about the same time the men jumped up into the chains and politely assisted them on board by pulling them up the chains by the hair of their heads and then marching them up to us would point at them and say "Tobak". As for modesty that was all left on shore as it was of no marketable value on board of a ship. The men were entirely naked while the women had nothing but a bunch of reeds or rushes fastened around their hips and hanging down halfway to their knees and they were in the market for anybody for a piece of tobacco an inch square which they would hand to their husband (if they had any such institution) or father or whoever it might be who would receive it with evident delight. While the women were occupied in their traffic the men would be going around amongst the crew with hats and mats and strings of coconuts.'

Such distasteful 'traffic' was certainly not confined to Ocean Island. 'Byron's Island' (lat 00"37' S. long 175"29' E. in modern Kiribati) was raised by the ship *Ann Alexander*, on 30 January 1848, and, 'When the decks were washed off there was several canoes came alongside and two Ladies. One of them could satisfy all hands easy enough, at least she did several and wanted more for a head of tobacco a piece,' wrote the second mate in his journal. It is little wonder that Captain Sawtell of the *Ann Alexander* never carried his wife to sea: even if he kept himself apart from such business, the mere thought of what a strong-minded Yankee housewife would have to say about such doings on her newly washed decks was enough to discourage any man, surely.

Other skippers left their wives at home for the simple reason that they succumbed to the island girls as readily as most of their men. In February 1850 the Connecticut whaling bark *Cavalier* arrived at Ponape in the Caroline Islands, and Captain Dexter out-rivalled his men in promiscuity, taking the girls into his cabin two at a time. When he tired of those he took on new ones, passing the old girls on to the officers, who, in their turn, passed them on to the men. On 26 March 1850, 'There is now more than half of our men sick, most of them with syphilis. . . It appears as if the Ladies fever [syphilis] had been innoculated into the larboard [port] watch,' a seaman, William Wilson, recorded: 'the mate is but a shell, a mere wreck, and most of his men are diseased.'

According to Wilson, Captain Dexter got thoroughly riled up about the debauched state of his crew, complaining bitterly that 'we are half drunk the other half fucked to death'. This seems outstandingly illogical, considering that it could well have been the old salt himself who passed on the disease to them all. However, it seems that Dexter's conscience, weather-beaten as it must have been, was niggling away and souring his mood. 'The old man told us not to blab and tell that females had been aboard the ship,' Wilson recorded. 'He was afraid of talk — that it would reach the ears of the owners.'

Dexter must have worried about the females at home as well. Indeed, it must have been difficult for skippers like Dexter to face their families when they at last got back. Infidelity was bad enough, but venereal disease would have been very hard to explain away. The reader of this remarkable journal can't help but wonder what Mrs Dexter had to say when the old customer finally arrived home. . . and what Mrs Daggett said when the *Globe*, with her husband in charge, arrived home from voyage in August 1850. Captain Daggett was quite unwell, for, as the mate slyly noted in the logbook, 'Some young lady in Maui gave him what he could not buy at the stores.'

The islands did not, of course, hold a monopoly on the business. In July 1844 the *China* was whaling off Akaroa, New Zealand, and, 'A female a Passenger that a schooner was taking to Otago Bay came on board with the third mate,' wrote one of the men, Reuben Ashley. 'It blew so hard,' he added dryly, 'that she could not leave the ship (that is if she had had the inclination) so she slept on board all night.'

Apparently the captain, William Potter, condoned all kinds of dubious goings on, for, on the 15th, 'a boat which went on shore with some of the crew came off last night (rather late) and upset the boat alongside, there was a hell of a row for some time. . .they lost all the spirits they brought with them about 4 Gallons in two kegs. . .the woman had not gone on shore at 3 PM this day [was] in the Cabin all day.' What she did to pass away the lagging time is debatable: the following line is scratched out heavily. What is certain is that Mrs William Potter was not on board that ship.

When the Sydney whaler *Australian* was in Cloudy Bay in the spring season of 1837, Captain Rhodes invited girls on board, writing, 'The ladies at the Bay were very condescending, and took lodgings on board the ship, to the great satisfaction of the sailors.' Even more famous (or notorious)

# Prince Edward Sherman

Born in Dartmouth, New Bedford, in 1829, Prince Edward Sherman was most probably raised in the same household as Mary Ann, the girl of the Rarotongan grave: his grandfather, Zoeth, was her guardian. Prince was also Abner Sherman's cousin once removed, for Abner's father Jireh was Zoeth Sherman's brother.

Like all his male kinfolk, Prince went to sea a-whaling. He shipped first at the age of 15, in 1844, on the New Bedford whaleship *Brighton*, but, unlike his more solid brethren, Prince, it seems, did not like the business. He went on a second voyage in the same ship in 1847, but deserted at Lahaina on the island of Maui in Hawaii. For a while he wandered the wide Pacific, finally ending up in Whangaroa, New Zealand.

There Prince met a most flamboyant fellow, Henry Davis Snowden, who happened to have a young daughter, Sophia. Henry Davis (the 'Snowden' had been dropped to conceal his identity) was in high standing with the Whangaroa Maoris, and all because of a favour his father (an ex-convict, living in New South Wales) had done for the Maori chief Hone Heke.

Some years previously Heke had travelled to London, where he'd been lionised by the society matrons and also much favoured by Queen Victoria, who presented him with many gracious gifts, including a complete suit of armour. Such things, while interesting, were not of much use to the Maori chieftain. However, when Heke called into Sydney on his way home, Snowden cooperatively swapped the goods for useful items — such as guns and powder.

It is little wonder, then, that when Henry Davis Snowden dropped hurriedly into Whangaroa (to escape his creditors in Sydney) he was welcomed by the local tribe. He settled down to buying much land, which he (rather mysteriously) paid for with Spanish gold doubloons, and then he set up a double life, trading openly in provisions and secretly in guns.

He also smuggled runaway Australian convicts into the country. It is little wonder, then, that the British were keen to catch him out in his nefarious doings. One day they nearly succeeded: a man-of-war glimpsed him as

he was sneaking his small craft *Helen* into Whangaroa, and set off at once in hot pursuit. Henry evaded capture by fleeing up a winding creek, and then found himself trapped when the narrow stream shallowed. The British ship was too large to follow him up the stream, but the captain knew his topography: he ordered the anchors dropped at the entrance, and was prepared to lay in wait there for as long as it took for Snowden to give up and sheepishly come out, along with his illicit cargo.

Henry was too smart for that, however: he talked the Maoris into digging a channel into the next creek, and so he, his ship and his cargo got away Scot-free.

This, then, was Prince Sherman's father-in-law — for he married 18-year-old Sophia Snowden in 1859. It is traditional for sailors to dream of giving up the ocean and buying a farm, and that is exactly what Prince Edward Sherman did in New Zealand. After all, how could he lose? He had excellent advice, and the shrewdest of backing — from Henry Davis Snowden himself.

than Cloudy Bay was Kororareka in the Bay of Islands, which for a few busy years was known as the 'whorehouse of the Pacific'. The trader Eagleston called there in April 1834, and recorded that the women were 'fond of visiting ships. The price of one, from a chief's daughter or sister down to the lowest breed,' he wrote, 'is one shirt for the time the ship remains in the Bay.'

Such bargains were, for many, impossible to turn down – though some of the arrangements were strangely formalised, as if to add a mite of decorum to the business. When the *Columbus* of Fairhaven lay at anchor in the Bay of Islands, February 1838, 'Two marriages took place this day between 2 of our crew and 2 beautys of this country,' the logkeeper (Holden Wilcox) recorded. 'I wish them much Joy,' he tartly added.

Four days later (on the 14th) 'one young man reported himself sick with the New Zealand fever [sic!].' Despite the possibility of venereal disease, however, the 'marriages' proliferated. 'One of our boatsteerers got married today, the 3rd time since our arrival here, but how long he and his new companion will agree the Lord only knows, I don't.' Then finally, on the 19th, 'All our young men what had got married since our arrival here, got divorced by mutual consent and their late spouses with all their children and dunnage either went on shore or on board of some other ships to obtain new employment.'

One can confidently guess that any respectable female visitor to the Bay would have been horrified by such extempore arrangements. Indeed, many men were scandalised. John Dyes, who visited the Bay of Islands in November 1840, wrote, in a letter to *Sailors' Magazine*, that when he was in port he saw, '*The ships filled* with *nativewomen* dancing all day Sunday. The American ships are just as bad as English and French...' he protested, 'and in many cases outstrip them in some of their vices afloat in the harbour.' John B. Williams of Salem, the second American Consul to the Bay of Islands, substantiated this in even more forceful phrases. 'Merciful Heavens!' he wrote in his journal. 'When a ship arrives her decks are almost instantly lined with native women – a floating castle of prostitution. [But] how can it be different when the Master and Officers set the example?'

Such scenes as the Bay of Islands presented then were a long, long way from what young Mary-Ann Sherman had been accustomed to, in the smoky, busy, prosperous town that was New Bedford, Massachusetts. Sailors might stagger drunkenly on Merrill's Wharf and gather in the taverns of Centre Street and Union, to roar the raucous nights away, but a respectable girl would have seen very little of that. The very idea of a modest young woman living on one of those 'floating castles of prostitution' was unthinkable...surely.

I looked at the grave again. Ron said, 'There were wives on merchant vessels.' That was true. The sailors called such vessels 'hen frigates' or 'petticoat ships'. But it still seemed difficult to believe that there were ever such ships as 'petticoat whalers'.

I re-read the inscription. Men were tough in those days, and so, by God, were their women. Women had faced the untamed frontier, and had contrived

# New Bedford

In 1602 Bartholomew Gosnold, the English explorer, landed first on the future site of New Bedford, Massachusetts. He traded with the Indians and went away, and the place was left alone by foreigners until 1652. In that year a group from the Pilgrim Colony at Plymouth arrived to purchase land – for which they paid the Wampanoag Indians the immense sum of 'thirty yards of cloth, eight moose skins, fifteen axes, fifteen hoes, fifteen pairs of breeches, eight blankets, two kettles, one cloak, twenty-two pounds of wampum [tobacco], eight pairs of stockings, eight pairs of shoes, one iron pot, and ten shillings'.

The first township of the district was Dartmouth, where in later years both Abner and Mary Ann Sherman were born and raised. Most of the early settlers there were Quakers, who had come to the Acushnet River in search of religious freedom. It seems logical, then, that the Dartmouth people – like their Nantucket cousins – turned to whaling. They firstly whaled from shore, sending out boats and then towing the killed whales to the beach to be flensed. Then, about 1750, the townships sent out the first deepsea whaling vessels, small sloops of about fifty tons, with crews of about fifteen men. The short voyages were usually profitable: prosperity beckoned, and within fifteen years the town that was to become the

most prosperous port of its size in the whole of the world was established.

The 'fathers' of New Bedford were a Dartmouth Quaker, Joseph Russell, and a Nantucketer, Joseph Rotch. The 'Joseph' venture was outstandingly successful: within a century the whalers of New Bedford were whitening the seas with their sails, and the sky over the city was blackened with the smoke from a multitude of oil manufactories and candleworks. More whalers sailed out of New Bedford than from all the other ports of the world combined; New Bedford whaling employed a whole city of 20,000 citizens and a city-equivalent of 10,000 seamen.

It was a short-lived prosperity, its end spelled out when the first oil well was drilled in Titusville, Pennsylvania, in 1859 – but in Mary Ann's day New Bedford seemed as if it would be rich for ever. The grand mansions built by whaleship owners adorned the wide avenues of County Street, on the hill overlooking the harbour, and Merrill's Wharf was packed with rows of fat casks, covered with seaweed to stop the barrels from drying out and leaking their valuable cargo. In Union Street the stores were filled with exotic goods from all over the world, and the wharves at its foot were filled with ships.

to make a home in the wilderness as well. It would take a special kind of tenacity, however, to make a home on a wooden whaler – but then, I thought, by the year 1850 it was high time some respectable Yankee girls had visited the South Pacific, even if it was for nothing more than to save the national reputation. When John B. Williams of Salem met Mrs Busby, the wife of James Busby, the British Resident in the Bay of Islands, he found with distress that the true nature of decent American women was not known in New Zealand.

'Her Ladyship [was] desirous to inform herself with respect to her sister fair sex, the ladies of the UStates. . .' he wrote, and then rose swiftly and nobly to his countrywomen's defence.

> 'My interrogations bestowed the high honor and respect due to the American ladies. . .It is not to be wondered at, that in this quarter so much ignorance exists with respect to a knowledge of America and American ladies when we see so many ignorant whaling masters demeaning themselves in a manner unbecoming a civilised or rational being.'

The answer to this disgraceful state of affairs seems obvious. The national image could be easily repaired. . .if only the decent, sensible, respectable, demure and pious wives of whaling masters would consent to ship along on voyage. . .

Perhaps.

# 2

# To preserve unbroken the ties of domestic life

'Oh who'd not be a sailor's wife
And brave the Ocean's waves
And sail with him o'er seas of foam
Above the coral caves...

'If along the shores of the Coral Isles
When the moon's soft light spreads o'er sea
I'd bless the hours that are passing then
If he'd but whisper love to me.'
— Mrs William Swain,
*Clifford Wayne*, 1855–8.

IN the northern winter of 1841–2 the Hawaiian cruise of the whaleship *Bartholomew Gosnold* seemed no different from many another. The weather was warm, the scenery beautiful, and there were 'wahines in plenty'. No fewer than 18 damsels lived on board the ship with the men, and 'apear to be contented' – or so an anonymous seaman recorded. Occasionally some of them left, 'after bidding us all a long adieu and heaving many a sigh — for they seem to be very much interested in our wellfare,' he added rather coyly, but — perhaps because every girl 'received a presant of some kind' – those who left were soon replaced by others who were equally eager to be pleasant.

Then, on 17 April 1842, complications arose. The *Bartholomew Gosnold* anchored off Koloa on the northern island of Kauai, and the ship's captain, Abraham Russell, went on shore to pay some calls. And there he fell in love.

The recipient of this sudden passion was Miss Susannah Holden, a nineteen-year-old girl who hailed from Hillsboro, New Hampshire. Susannah lived with her brother Horace, who was twelve years older than herself, and his wife, Mary. Horace Holden was a famous character, as he had been on the whaler *Mentor* of New Bedford when that ship ran onto a reef in the Palau Islands on 21 May 1832. Eleven men died, including the first mate, but Holden was one of the lucky ones who survived.

The blessing was mixed, however, for when he and a few others tried to sail from Palau in a whaleboat, they were captured and enslaved by the natives of Tobi Island, south-west of Palau, and 'for two years afterward were subjected to unheard of sufferings'. Among other things, the islanders forcibly tattooed the chests and arms of the captives. This was nasty enough in itself, but, as Holden noted, 'the worst of the nightmare was the way the onlookers laughed whenever the pain grew too intense for [me] to bear in silence'. After his rescue Holden published a best-selling book about his terrible experiences. Then he moved to Kauai to raise silkworms with the proceeds. The silkworms failed, but he later did quite well with sugar.

For the skipper of the *Bartholomew Gosnold*, meeting such a wellknown personality must have been an interesting experience. It seems that Captain Abraham Russell found Susannah's charms even more interesting, however, for the day after that he invited the family on board the ship for dinner. The crew's consternation can only be imagined, but the panic involved in getting the 'gals' out of sight must have been something like a scene from French farce.

In the event, however, Susannah wasn't capable of noting much: 'Mr Holden, his Wife and boy, and Miss Holden' arrived, but they enjoyed themselves 'but poorly, for they were seasick by the time they had got cleverly on board; however they stopped till dinnertime,' the journal-keeper added, 'but eat nothing.' Then family, sweetheart and captain went back on shore and the men were able to bring the 'gals' out of hiding. Despite the fright the girls were all 'in good heart but rather down in the mouth to think they have got to leave us so soon,' as the Hawaiian season was nearly over. Finally the crew 'set our ladys on shore and took a parting kiss,' and Captain Abraham Russell returned on board, alone and disappointed.

His intentions were perfectly honourable: he had hoped Susannah would consent to become his wife and come to sea with him. That she had turned him down seems not at all surprising. Quite apart from the fact that a young lady who had contrived to be seasick on board a ship that was lying quietly at anchor was not likely to breathe the hoped-for yes, prior to that year of 1842 only a very few remarkable females had consented to go on whaling voyages.

Within months, however, Susannah was given good reason to change her mind. The *Bartholomew Gosnold* spent the northern summer whaling off Japan and returned to Hawaii in November for the usual warm and roistering winter cruise. In January 1843 the ship anchored at Koloa again, and Captain Russell went on shore to resume his courtship. It was interrupted on the 18th, when a storm blew up that soon 'increased to A gale'.

Within hours the ship was in mortal danger. The officers set the ensign 'half mast, union down', but the seas ran so high that it wasn't possible for Captain Russell to get back on board to take charge.

Instead Abraham and Susannah were forced to watch as the ship was driven 'nearer the beach, and that A solid mass of rocks, and the waves adashing down upon them as though they would crush to atoms all that came within their grasp' — as the anonymous seaman put it in his journal. The missionary Cochran Forbes was another to witness the awesome scene. 'The sea ran so high & the wind blew in such violent gusts,' he wrote in his diary, 'that they cut away the mizen mast about 4 o'clock about the same time she parted her starboard cable & soon after that all hands deserted her, So heavy was her motion that they could scarce stand or keep any one position on board, and they gave up all hopes.'

The men were lucky to get to shore at all. It was late afternoon on the 19th and they had been battling the storm for more than twenty-four hours. The ship was abandoned 'within two ship's lengths of the rocks'; if the remaining anchor had dragged or another chain parted they (as the anonymous journal-keeper put it) 'must all be hurled into eternity'. It was a solemn moment. Captain Russell, perhaps in a mood of despair, turned to Susannah and once more proposed marriage.

*And she said yes*! Her motives can only be guessed. Perhaps she realised in that moment of danger that she loved him; perhaps she was impelled by pity...or perhaps as she watched the ship grind towards destruction she was struck with the thought that marriage to Russell might not, after all, involve submission to the sickening sea.

Once the word was said Abraham Russell responded with the speed of a harpooned whale. Perhaps he couldn't believe his luck, but he certainly made sure of it. Within an hour — as recorded by Forbes — 'about 5 o'clock Cap R & Miss Susan Holden were united in marriage by me at the house of Mr Holden while the storm was still raging'.

The matrimonial bonds were irrevocably tied...and the gale went away. As Forbes put it, 'the sea fell and the ship once more rode easy'. Against all odds, the *Bartholomew Gosnold* was saved, still seaworthy, perfectly capable of another Sea of Japan voyage. To the missionary's gratification, no doubt, the miracle happened on the sabbath. He did not record how the new Mrs Abraham Russell felt about it.

On 24 April 'the Capt came on board with his wife & Reverent Mr Forbes,' noted the anonymous journal-keeper. They sailed for Honolulu and left Forbes there, and then set sail for the whaling grounds off Japan and all the nausea that those rugged seas promised — and, on 25 June 1842, the *Bartholomew Gosnold* 'spoke' (or encountered) the whaling ship *Roman* of New Bedford, and Captain Russell went on board the other vessel to gam. The captain of the *Roman* was Alexander Barker, and the first officer was a man named Abner Devoll Sherman.

The practice of 'speaking and gamming' was peculiar to the whalemen. The custom probably developed because the ships congregated in certain seas at particular seasons, anticipating the migratory patterns of the whales. 'Gam' is a Nantucket word, which originally meant a group of whales — what is today called a pod or a school. Then it became applied to a group of whaleships which had hauled aback to exchange visits, and gradually the word was given to an activity which was social indeed. The voyages were so long that any chance to meet and talk was appreciated greatly, and as well as this there were letters, news, whaling hints and gossip to be exchanged.

Consequently when the lookouts in the topgallant masts called out, 'Sail ho!' there was great excitement on board — as described by the steerage boy on the whaleship *Hannibal* in 1849.

"'Where away?' cries the captain.

'Three points off the lee bow, sir.'

'What does she look like?'"

If the answer to this was, 'A whaler, sir,' signals were exchanged in a flurry of flags. Then the leeward ship would lay aback, waiting with her sails pulling against each other to hold her to a near standstill, while the windward ship ran down, aiming at the other's waist, amidships. It was a flamboyant and nervewracking process, and required a skilled hand at the wheel. However, at the very last moment, just as collision seemed inevitable, the moving ship would brace up so that she slowed and sheered past the stilled ship's stern.

The two captains would be standing on the quarter deck, or on top of the 'hurricane house' that sheltered the helm, and they talked while one ship slid by the other. It is a testimonial to whaling seamanship that for those few moments the two ships were so close that the skippers could often hail each other in natural voices, without recourse to speaking trumpets.

"'Ship ahoy,' says the stranger.

'Hello.'

'What ship is that?'

'The *Hannibal* of New London.'"

This was the start of an oddly formal conversation, with the same ritualistic questions about identity, port, oil taken and so on asked each time, even if the captains happened to be brothers or had seen each other just days before. Then one would invite the other for a social call on board his ship — a gam. If this was accepted (and it usually was), the captain of one ship would take a boat and go on board the other, and the first officer (mate) of the visited ship would take a boat's crew of his own and go to have his own gam with the other vessel's first officer.

It was an excellent system that ensured that both vessels had visitors. It also meant that the captain's wife (if there was one) found herself entertaining the visiting officer while her husband was on board the other ship. It was an odd social situation: as a future whaling wife, Henrietta Deblois, put it fourteen years later when her husband had first gone off to gam, 'I am expecting the mate here. It seems very funny.'

When Abner Devoll Sherman arrived on board the *Bartholomew Gosnold*, Susannah Holden Russell could well have felt the same uncertainty. It must have been difficult for her to know how to behave in this, a man's game in what was very much a man's world. It was highly unlikely, too, that Susannah had ever met her guest before. Abner Devoll Sherman, first mate of the *Roman*, was 28 years old, fair-haired and blue-eyed; he was five feet one and three-quarter inches (156.8 cm) tall and had been at sea almost constantly since his first voyage in 1832; he hailed from South Dartmouth, in New Bedford, Massachusetts; he was overdue for a command of his own...and to Susannah Russell he was almost certainly a perfect stranger.

The situation could be complicated still further by the way her guest behaved. The whalemen started their careers young, and Mr Sherman, who had shipped first on the *South Carolina* at the age of 17, was no exception. He was the product of four generations of whaling — his great-grandfather

Fortunatus took a 75 ton whaling sloop to the Davis Straits in 1768 — and a whaleship was no place to learn fine manners.

Conversation might have been difficult for him as well, for Mr Sherman must have felt a great deal of curiosity concerning Mrs Captain Russell. In a word, he must have wondered why the devil she'd agreed to sail. While Susannah could well have been the first whaling wife he'd encountered at sea, he certainly would have heard of the species — for those few enterprising females who had taken up life on a whaling ship had caused a great deal of chatter.

One of the first was a Nantucket woman, Mary Hayden Russell, who

## Eliza Williams

Eliza Williams was 32 years old and five months pregnant when she first sailed on her husband's whaleship *Florida* in September 1858. She was a small woman, who in true romantic tradition could walk upright beneath her husband's outstretched arm, but she owned a courage beyond her size. Her son William Fish Williams reminisced in later years that when a man was horribly wounded in the face after a gun exploded on board ship, strong men couldn't bear to hold the patient's head while the captain sewed him up, and his mother had to take over and 'finish the job'.

Her courage was very necessary, for Eliza Azelia Williams of Wethersfield, Connecticut, was one of those women who went whaling because of wifely duty. She married Thomas Williams in April 1851, and he sailed off as master of the *South Boston* exactly 12 weeks later. Their first son, Stancel, was two years old when Williams returned. When he sailed off again, as master of the *Florida* in October 1854, Eliza was six months pregnant with another son, Henry, who was three years old when his father got back.

It is perhaps little wonder, then, that Captain Williams carried Eliza along when he sailed next, on the same vessel in late 1858. It is hard to tell how she felt about it, for Eliza was a reticent and ever-loyal wife. She certainly had cause for complaint, for not only was she forced to leave her two little boys in the care of family and friends, but she was a home-lover, totally unused to the troubles and dangers of a life at sea. As she put it in the first entry of the journal she kept on that first voyage, 'that dear word home; how many tender associations are connected with that one word and center about the heart, causing it to throb every time it is brought to mind; there we have left Dear Friends, parents, and Children, Brothers and Sisters, all near and dear to me.'

However, despite homesickness and seasickness, Eliza Williams never uttered a word of complaint, merely looking forward to the day she got home. But her 33 months on the *Florida* were by no means her last. She accompanied her husband on all of his voyages from then on, sailing out of New Bedford and then San Francisco, voyaging the southern Indian Ocean and all parts of the Pacific, up to the Arctic north, bearing three children at sea and surviving two shipwrecks.

in 1823 boarded her husband's ship, the London whaler *Emily*, and voyaged through the Indian Ocean and the south-west Pacific towards the Sea of Japan. According to the letters she wrote on board to her daughter, Mary Hayden Russell's reason for sailing was a strong and righteous sense of wifely duty: when her husband bade her to pack up and go she obeyed without question, and this despite the advice of her friends, who 'stated many objections'.

That advice was well meant. Not only was sea-life rough and monotonous, but the whaling grounds of the South Seas fishery were definitely dangerous. Seas were scarcely explored, reefs were uncharted and savages were undeniably savage. As late as January 1851, the news reached Hobart that the Tasmanian whaler *Flying Fox* had been wrecked on an uncharted reef off Sydenham Island in the Kingsmill Group (in modern Kiribati) and the natives had swarmed onto the wreck, intent on plunder. According to some accounts the master of the vessel, Captain Brown, was knocked on the head and his wife was carried off as a slave, to meet 'a destiny worse than death'. However, it seems that Mrs Brown was spared this nasty fate, for her husband dressed her in dungarees and passed her off as a man.

Mary Hayden Russell, who was the perfect embodiment of the puritan wife and mother, must have found the prospect of this kind of adventure highly alarming. However, she kept her silence and survived the voyage with unblemished dignity, even when her husband was threatened near New Guinea: 'one of the natives siez'd a spear and pointing it at your dear Father with his body crounch'd would have darted it,' she penned; 'had he [Captain Laban Russell] not instantly siez'd a musket and presented it.' The native, as fully expected, 'drop'd his spear and salam'd the boat' and Mary then, with marvellous calmness, noted down a detailed description of his clothes before inviting him down into the cabin for a glass of muscatel wine.

Such unshakeable equanimity is the stuff of fable and legend, surely. One would think that Mary would be much admired back in London and Nantucket once the story got about — but not so. People were more likely to tut. In the first part of the century going to sea on one's husband's whaler was considered extremely unladylike. This strange public attitude was probably caused by the 'daring' behaviour of other early whaling wives. One such was Louisa Fearing Gibbs, the wife of Captain Stephen Gibbs of New Bedford, Massachusetts. Her son Benjamin (who became a wife-carrying master himself) was born in 1820, on board ship. 'I used to hear them tell about her going to sea with Capt Gibbs,' an old whaleman, Murdock, reminisced, 'and that she was quite as good a seaman as he, and she used to go aloft to look out for whales and would look out for the ship when the boats were in the chase.'

This kind of behaviour was not merely eccentric; it was positively indecent. Properly raised females did not indulge in such masculine behaviour; tomboys then were not considered cute. Women were supposed to be demure, peaceable, poetic and pious; they were supposed to stop at home and keep the home fires burning; they were supposed to look after elderly parents, the farm and children; they were meant to budget and pay the bills and wait in dutiful patience for the lord and master to return.

When the explorer Captain Benjamin Morrell of Stonington, Connecticut, arrived home from voyage in 1829, he found to his consternation that his wife Abby Jane had abandoned patience. 'My wife had informed me,' he penned, 'that during my late absence she had made up her mind to accompany me on my next voyage, be it to whatever section of the globe it might, even to the icy regions of the antarctic circle.'

> 'So much had she suffered from anxiety of mind on my account, during the last twelve months, that she assured me she would not survive another separation. "Only take me with you, Benjamin," was her constant reply to all my expostulations against the measure, "and I will pledge myself to lighten your cares, instead of adding to their weight".'

This put Morrell in quite a quandary. He listed his objections to the plan, firstly citing the views of ship-owners and their 'mean avaricious apprehensions of the lady's food abstracting some $50 from the net profits of the voyage'. He also mentioned their fear 'that the husband would neglect his nautical duties, by attending more to the comforts of his wife' than his duty to the ship. 'And how little must they know *you*, Benjamin,' she exclaimed with disarming loyalty, 'who could for a moment suspect that you could neglect your duty on my account?'

Then Morrell admitted his real objection: 'the fear of slanderous tongues, which might injure my professional character'. Her family sided with Morrell unreservedly, no doubt along with all the other prim citizens of Stonington. However, Abby Jane prevailed: she won him over with a week of relentless weeping. Two days before sailing he agreed to take her. 'She threw herself on my bosom,' the complacent husband recorded.

However, he was speedily mortified by her presence on board. In October 1829, just six weeks after sailing, Abby Jane and eleven of the men fell ill of what he called 'the intermittent fever', nowadays known as malaria. He didn't even have his diagnosis right, for it was, in fact, an even more dangerous disease, cholera — but that was the least of his problems.

'My situation was now truly deplorable and appalling,' he wrote on 28 October. 'The prospect was gloomy in the extreme. . .

> 'Had she not been on board I should certainly have borne up to the first port under our lee. . .But I reflected that some slanderous tongues might attribute such a deviation from my regular course solely to the fact of my wife's being on board. That idea I could not tamely endure. . ."No! perish all first!" I muttered with bitterness, as I gloomily paced the deck at midnight.'

Morrell then medicated the patients himself with 'blisters, friction, and bathing with hot vinegar', rather than put into port at St. Jago (in the Cape Verde Islands) and risk 'the unfeeling sarcasms of those carpet-knights, on whose delicate frames the winds of heaven are not permitted to blow too roughly'. Two men died but the rest recovered, and Morrell's reputation was safe.

Obviously, if anyone had asked Abby Jane Morrell why she'd decided to go on voyage, her answer would have been a blushing affirmation of love, and the hearer, most probably, would have found this romantic. If Abner

# Benjamin and Abby Jane Morrell

Captain Benjamin Morrell jr. was an explorer who specialised in discovering new whaling and sealing grounds for his Connecticut brethren. In May 1824, at the end of his first voyage, he arrived in Salem with unusually depressed spirits. He should have been eagerly anticipating his reunion with his wife and family but instead, as he recorded, he was oppressed by 'A vague indefinite idea of some impending calamity'. A letter from his home town of Stonington confirmed his worst fears: 'My wife and two children – comprising all my little family,' he wrote, 'were no more!' They had been dead for quite some time.

He was by no means the first or last seaman to arrive in port to learn such tragic tidings. Morrell took it badly at first, but then his father advised him to put the tragedy behind him: 'A speedy second marriage,' he exhorted, 'would restore your happiness.' Benjamin saw the sense in this, but was too busily involved in preparations for a second voyage to do much about finding a suitable replacement. There was plenty of time...he wasn't sailing until 19 July; then July arrived and the 18th was upon him, and still he'd done nothing about it.

However, as he mused later in his memoirs, he did have a pretty little cousin, 'a sprightly, amiable little girl'. The only trouble was her age, for Abby Jane was just fifteen, not quite old enough to wed. 'Two years hence, if I return in safety,' Benjamin meditated, 'I shall find Abby Jane a full-blown flower, instead of an opening bud...If I live to come back,' he decided, 'and Abby Jane is still free, I shall certainly seek to win her. But two years is a long time,' his thoughts panicked then. The 'full-blown flower' could well have been plucked by another, luckier, man by the time he returned.

Connecticut sailors were resourceful by nature, however. Benjamin found a neat answer to his dilemma. He married little Abby Jane and thus legally claimed her, right there in her stepfather's parlor. Then, with a 'chaste parting kiss' on the cheek, he 'committed' his 'virgin bride to the care of her friends' – and sailed away to the Pacific, the Galapágos and the Isthmus of Darien. It was nearly two years before she saw him again.

Sherman had been rude enough to ask Susannah Holden Russell why she had agreed to sail, she could well have said the same thing — for she was unlikely to admit that a mischievous Providence had tricked her into believing that her suitor's ship was safely wrecked.

Wifely devotion was a very good reason for shipping along, one that was given by many whaling wives later on, and it was one that Abner Sherman could have found attractive, for he had a sweetheart at home. Wife-carrying was a privilege reserved for captains, but Abner was due for a command of his own, so taking Mary Ann on voyage could be perfectly possible. . .if somehow he could bring himself to ignore the 'unfeeling sarcasms' of the gossips back home.

Then, when the ship *Roman* was on the way home from that Sea of Japan season, another whaleship was spoken. This was the *Uncas*, Captain Charles Gelett, who invited the captain of the *Roman*, Alexander Barker, on board to dine. Gelett later gave an account of this in his memoirs. To his surprise, as he remembered it, Captain Barker of the *Roman* 'requested permission to ask the blessing at the table, to which I consented. This,' Gelett went on, 'was followed by a conversation between us, wherein he informed me that a number of captains of his acquaintance had reformed their lives, and that he had united with a Christian Church at New Bedford'.

The captain of the *Roman* was certainly an enthusiastic convert, in high standing with the missions at Honolulu and Lahaina. The Lahaina missionary Dwight Baldwin called Barker 'an exceedingly pleasant young man' and went on to state that the whole crew of the *Roman* (presumably including Abner Sherman) was pious. However, Alexander Barker was not content with that; he was an evangelist as well, with a burning need to urge others to see the Light. He spoke at length and with stirring eloquence. 'The news deeply impressed me,' Gelett wrote, 'and having had pious parents I began to reflect upon my obligations to myself and the men under my command.'

It was the start of quite a character change for Gelett. The conversion begun by Barker was completed by the Hawaiian missionaries and Gelett became an extremely pious man. Then, when the *Uncas* arrived back home in New Bedford in April 1846, his wife Jane announced, like Abby Jane Morrell earlier, that she 'had resolved to accompany' him on the next voyage, because she couldn't bear another long separation from her husband.

Charles Gelett, like Benjamin Morrell earlier, was taken aback. However he readily agreed to take her — and it seems reasonable to guess that his new piety helped. A righteous conscience was a very good antidote to the unfeeling laughter of 'carpet knights' and perhaps he felt, too, that the presence of a decent woman on voyage could do nothing but good for the moral state of the ship.

There had been a precedent for such a philosophy. Back in July 1844 the wife of an English Pacific trader, Mary Wallis, had resolved to sail on her husband's bark *Zotoff* in a one-woman campaign against the dire 'effects of heathen intercourse' on the crew of his ship. On 9 August 1846 the *Zotoff* dropped anchor at 'Pleasant Island' (Nauru). 'Our decks were completely filled with native men and young girls,' Mrs Wallis expostulated in her journal, 'who stole everything they could lay their hands upon...

> 'All that they brought was sold for tobacco, and I was almost stunned by the vociferous cry of the girls, of "Captain's woman, give me chaw tobacco." They placed no value upon cloth, which was offered them, although they wore nothing but a "*leku*," made of grass. The whole conduct of this people was boisterous, rude, and immodest in the extreme. The girls came on board for the vilest of purposes, but stated that their purposes were not accomplished, as the sailors were afraid of "Captain's woman."'

And so Jane Gelett was allowed to sail on the *Uncas*, for perhaps the same high motives: Gelett, in his newfound piety, could well have reasoned that the presence of his proper and reticent wife would bring more decency and order on board. Jane sailed from New Bedford on 27 August 1846 — and suffered most terribly with seasickness. It was an awful penalty to pay for her devotion. 'She was really so seasick that I feared she would not live to reach Fayal [in the Azores],' her husband mused in his memoirs. Nevertheless (with true Yankee grit and courage) he carried her on about the Horn and into the wide Pacific.

The fact that he was pious, then, could have helped Abner Sherman in his decision to carry Mary Ann on the *Harrison*, when he was given command of that ship in May 1845. Loneliness was yet another factor that could have helped him make up his mind. Up until the 1840s most Pacific voyages lasted about two years, but so many whales had been killed that the hunted species were growing scarce, and so four or more years were needed to fill up the ships with oil. It was the owners, not the skippers, who made fortunes out of whaling, and most captains couldn't afford to spend more than four or six months at home between voyages. As one whaleman — Charles Robbins — put it, 'The stay in a home port is shockingly short,' and courtships were correspondingly swift. Captain George Smith of Edgartown, Martha's Vineyard, proposed to Lucy Vincent two days after he met her, and this was by no means unusual.

The weddings were as hasty as the courting. In June 1855 the *Vineyard Gazette* reported three weddings, all held on a Monday at dawn and solemnized by the same reverend, Sanford Benton, in rapid succession. He walked rapidly from one house to another to gabble off the vows, gathering up a trail of wedding parties as he went. One of the grooms was Captain Shubael Norton, who sailed off in command of the whaler *Cleora* just eight days after this. It was almost three years before his bride, Susan, saw him again, so it seems little wonder that the decision was made for Susan to ship along when he took out his next ship, the *Splendid*.

The voyages were so long and the spells between voyages so short that the stay-at-home wives and seafaring husbands must have felt as if they were scarcely acquainted, and this was a good reason, too, for the wife to go a-whaling. Lydia Beebe of Nantucket had lived with her husband John for six months 'in the six years of our married life' when she sailed with him on the *Brewster* in 1863. When Betsy Morey (another Nantucket woman) sailed on the *Phoenix* in 1855, she confided in the first entry of the journal that she kept on board that 'It is just nineteen Years to Day since we wer

Marraid.' Betsy had no children, which meant that there had been a lot of lonely waiting while her husband Israel was off whaling in the wide Pacific – and so it seems little wonder that despite her age (43) she agreed to sail when Israel proposed the notion.

Israel was asking a lot of her, for the *Phoenix* was headed for the icy waters of the northern Pacific and the Arctic beyond. However, it is not surprising, either, that husbands like Morey decided to try out this wife-carrying idea.

All the whalemen complained about feeling out of touch with home. Because of the distances involved and the length of the voyages, communications were very poor. An old Nantucket joke tells of the captain who, when he received a letter from his wife saying, 'Dear husband, where did thee put the cradle?' replied in a suspicious growl, 'Dear wife, why do you want the cradle?'

'Dear husband, never mind the cradle,' came the answer. 'Where did thee put the crib?' This yarn held a good deal of wry truth. Captain Benjamin Wing of the *Good Return* did not know he was a father until the baby was eight months old: 'Oh that I could be there with you and our sweet little Laura as I understand you have named her,' he wrote in reply to the news, in November 1852; 'you must kiss her about twenty times a day for me.'

Many letters, when they did arrive, held sad tidings. In September 1864 one whaling wife, Elizabeth Stetson, was visited in port by Captain William Gifford, of the whaler *Charles and Edward*. He had a letter which he had just received and was afraid to open, for the envelope was bordered in black. When Elizabeth opened it she found it contained the news of the death of his only child. Captain Gifford was so stricken he sold his ship and travelled home.

'Jennie sat in her chair a few days ago thinking very deeply,' wrote Hannah Blackmer of New Bedford to her husband Seth, in a letter dated 17 November 1864. 'All at once she looked up at me and said, "Papa will never see me a little girl again, will he?"'

'Everyone is asleep and it is so still I can hear my heart beat,' wrote Ruth Post to her husband, Captain Francis Post, in September 1850:

> 'it seems as if I must hear you speak, as Frank said last sabbath morning when we was all taking a look at your likeness, he said now let me take it, he looked at it very earnest for a moment and then raised his eyes, Ma, said he, pa is going to speak to me, he has got his lips open now, I will put it to my ear I can hear him whisper if he don't speak loud.'

And so the reasons for taking a wife along on voyage mount up: reassurance, companionship, sharing children, the ties of domestic life preserved. However, the vital factor that helped Abner Sherman make up his mind to take Mary Ann on voyage could well have been the memory of that gam with Mrs Captain Abraham Russell, on board the *Bartholomew Gosnold* in June 1843. If the picture she presented of a demure helpmate on board ship was pretty enough, the temptation to follow Abraham Russell's example could well have been overwhelming.

As it happened, it was a very poor example. The *Bartholomew Gosnold* arrived in New Bedford in September... and Abraham Russell deserted his wife. He abandoned Susannah and their infant son Charles in the bustling, unfamiliar port, after just two years of marriage. What happened to her after that is unknown, but her fate was surely a miserable one. She couldn't in all conscience go home to New Hampshire, for her mother, a widow, was too poor to take in two more dependants, and Horace, who would have taken her into his home at Koloa, was the whole breadth of a continent away.

Abner Sherman did not know that, however, and neither did Captain

## Azubah Cash

During eleven years of marriage the Nantucket wife Azubah Cash had been with her husband William not quite 26 weeks, so it is perhaps little wonder that she sailed in 1850 on the *Columbia*, along with a ten-year-old son and despite the fact that she was pregnant. For a prim and properly pious Nantucket Quakeress, in fact, Azubah was surprisingly adventurous.

She first met William in 1835, when she was just fifteen. Azubah was a seamstress in a local shop, and her eye was taken by a young seaman who came in to be measured for a suit. She was as resourceful as any whaleman or whaling wife: when the suit was finished she stowed a note into one of the pockets. It read, 'I hope I meet the dashing young man I made these clothes for!' The young man (at that time only 19) was William Cash, and they married in July 1839. In November William sailed off, as second mate of the *Ganges* of Fall River. It was the start of the usual whaling on-and-off marriage: by 1850 he scarcely knew his wife and son – or so Azubah impatiently decided. She insisted on sailing, and did so in October.

She did not begin to write a journal until 13 March 1852, but when she did, it was nothing more or less than a 'baby book', a record of the growth and development of her second son, William Murray, who was born in August 1851, in Hilo, Hawaii. 'When 4 months old he began to put things in his mouth to eat, and at 5 months and 2 days his first tooth cut through…He will be 7 months if he lives a week longer and he creeps about nicely and gets up by things and tries to go along by things a little. He is a healthy and active little thing at present and I hope will continue to be. A.B.C. [Azubah Bearse Cash],' she noted in that first entry, at the start of a most remarkable document.

'I hope we shall be able to bring him up in a proper manner, to know and to love the commands of God and fear to disobey them,' wrote Azubah, and she certainly did her best. Despite all the difficulties of bringing up a baby on board ship, the little boy thrived. Like his mother, William Murray Cash enjoyed his life at sea: 'The little thing gets to the foot of the stairs very often and looks up very wishful for he is so fond of going on deck,' the proud mother wrote in May 1852. He had trouble teething and went through the usual childhood illnesses, including ringworm. Life on board a pitching ship was more dangerous than at home: he fell and broke his collar bone at the age of 14 months, but recovered swiftly. Like all toddlers, he had screaming tantrums 'when things do not suit him, and I have to use the rod', wrote Azubah. Little Murray was 'mischievous withal', but nonetheless enchanting, and the Christian upbringing prevailed. 'Has gone to bed pleasantly,' his mother recorded in August 1853, 'after repeating after me his little prayer Now I lay me down to sleep etc. So ends the day. A.B.C.'

Frederick Fish of the Fairhaven ship *Columbus* who, when he met one of the earliest whaling wives, Mary Brewster, at sea in January 1846, was most surely impressed by her feminine example. Mary recorded that he 'Seemed very freehearted and candid says he means to get married and next cruise bring his wife.' The compliment, of course, is unmistakable: it is little wonder that she wrote this down. It was by no means the only time that Mary Brewster influenced a skipper by presenting an 'endearing' scene of domesticity.

When she met Captain William Tower, master of the whaleship *Moctezuma* on the whaling ground in July 1846, Mary noted that 'he was very much surprised to see a lady on board'. Tower seemed embarrassed too,

## Mary Brewster

On 4 November 1845 a petticoat whaler sailed from the small village port of Stonington, Connecticut, with one of the earliest and most remarkable whaling wives on board. This vessel was the whaleship *Tiger*, and that trail-blazing wife was Mary Louisa Burtch Brewster.

Mary was born on 22 September 1822, the sixth child of Samuel and Polly Burtch. Her mother died when she was five years old, and it seems that she was raised by Deacon Robert S. Bottum of Stonington, and his wife Malvina. Mary married William Brewster, a man nine years her senior, on 23 March 1841. He sailed off on 1 July to New Zealand as master of the *Philetus*, and Mary, like multitudes of whaling wives, stopped at home and waited, counting the weeks until he returned.

None of the wives found the waiting easy, but Mary Brewster found it harder than most, for she was obsessively in love with her husband. 'Oh what is there which will fill this aching void,' she wrote once when he'd left her; 'nothing but the presence of the dear object of my heart and affections. He truly is the bright star of my affections, the center of all my thoughts,' she further declared. It is little wonder that she made up her mind to accompany him on voyage. William's reaction is unknown: he probably agreed to take her because he was an easy-going man who preferred to avoid trouble if he could. Instead Mary's opposition came from her adoptive family.

That opposition was violent: Mary's foster mother disowned her when she sailed.

'She who has extended a mother's love and watchfulness over me said her consent would never be given,' Mary angrily recorded in the

first page of her journal;

'in no way would she assist me and if I left her she thought me very ungrateful and lastly though not least Her house would never be a home for me again if I persisted in coming – Well thank Heaven it is all past and I am on board of the good ship *Tiger* and with my dear Husband.'

And so she was, for good or ill. The *Tiger* returned home in April 1848, and 14 weeks later was off again, still with the captain's wife on board. Despite constant seasickness Mary Brewster never regretted her decision to accompany her adored William...and, because of her pioneering example, dozens of her whaling sisters took up a remarkable existence, at the mercy of the winds and gales and the turbulent (and nauseating) waves.

and 'made many apologies for his dress which caused me to notice it more particularly,' she added, 'and looked well enough save a little dirt which whalemen must expect'. Her tolerance evidently gave him much food for thought, for next voyage he carried along his wife, Betsy.

Mary Brewster gammed with Betsy Tower on 18 December 1847, off Cape Horn, and was delighted to learn that her happy influence was bringing such women to sea. 'At 8 this evening spoke ship *Moctezuma* of N- Bedford — Capt. Tower,' she wrote.

> 'Husband went on board but soon returned for me as Mrs Tower was on board; accordingly I was not long in preparing myself for the opportunity offered for a change of scene. So went on board and passed the evening till nearly 12 o'clock. I was happy to meet with a female acquaintance and was pleased with Mrs Tower. . .Mrs T. said a number of ladies were out this season with their husbands — I am glad they are following the late fashion.'

As more wives sailed the numbers snowballed, for precisely the same reason. Charlotte Wyer, who voyaged on the ship *Young Hero*, gammed with her uncle Morslander in September 1853, and wrote, 'He seemed very glad to see me, and I was certain that I was to see him, he played the Fiddle for us, and we had a very pleasant time. . .he thinks he shall not come around here again without taking Aunt Mary Ann.'

And so it went. In effect, the example provided by the early female sailors had made the practice of taking one's wife to sea respectable. The prospect of domestic comfort in the cabin and stateroom became so enticing for the lonely captains, in fact, that some spent a great deal of time, ink and paper in trying to persuade their wives to agree to go on voyage.

'It would be a great pleasure to me to have your sweet company here,' wrote Benjamin Wing wistfully to his wife in 1852, but when he returned home in April 1855, to see his three-year-old daughter for the very first time, his wife Emily still refused to sail. 'I suppose it is best as it is,' he sighed in a letter in November, outward bound:

> 'it seems hard to be sepparated so long having to sleep alone every night and deprived of your company days I suppose it is useless to tell you how verry glad I should be to see you but must forbear.'

Other husbands were less forbearing: they simply ordered their wives to sail and that, it seems, was that. Wharton's Law — that 'the wife is only servant to the husband' — was still valid then, and the women were given no choice. One such was Eliza Brock, who sailed from Nantucket on the *Lexington* on 21 May 1853. She left three young children behind, one a seven-year-old, William, and she missed home and family most pitifully. 'Farewell my more than father land,' she wrote at the start of her journal;

> 'Home of my heart and friends adieu
> Lingering beside some foreign strand
> How oft shall I remember you
> How often o'er the water blue
> Send back a sigh to those I love
> The loving and beloved few
> Who grieve for me; for whom I grieve.'

And her attitude throughout the voyage did not improve: Eliza Brock, sadly, was a martyr to homesickness. She had a long wait to see home, friends and family again: the voyage did not end until June 1856.

Another unwilling sailor was Almira Gibbs, who kept a journal on the *Nantucket* of Nantucket from June 1855 to August 1859. 'When I get home,' she decided in November 1855, 'I think I shall stay and lett them that wants to a whaleing, it is no life for me' — but nevertheless she found herself carried off on a second voyage, on the *Norman* in 1860. It was a voyage that killed her, for she died of some tropical disease in Valparaiso in 1864. Her husband, Richard, it seems evident, was a domestic Jehovah, but no doubt he thought

## Harriet Peirce

On 12 October 1848, on passage in the southern Indian Ocean, Mary Brewster, captain's wife on the whaleship *Tiger*, noted in her journal that they had spoken a ship — the *Dartmouth* of New Bedford, with Captain Abraham Peirce in command. 'Capt. Peirce came and spent the afternoon with us, which visit we enjoyed very much,' she penned. Then, on the 18th, they spoke the *Dartmouth* again, and it was William Brewster's turn to go on board the other ship for a gam. 'Poor me remained alone,' Mary mourned; she would have loved to pay a call herself, but because of the social strictures of her time it was not 'proper' to visit a ship that did not have a hostess on board. 'Hope to see some ship with a female on board so I can have a change,' she sighed.

Abraham Wilcox Peirce, it seems, wished for a change as well: he found the domestic scene on board the *Tiger* so beguiling that he took up the wife-carrying practice himself. The *Dartmouth* sailed as far as Pernambuco and then returned home without completing the voyage, for Peirce was sick, and then, when he was given command of the *Kutusoff* in 1851, he carried his wife Harriet (Durfee) Peirce along with him, together with their daughter, another Harriet.

The venture, it seems, was successful, for the family — which by this time included another daughter, Sarah — travelled another time, to Honolulu on the whaling bark *Emerald* in 1857. Young Harriet kept a journal on this voyage, a charming document that is largely an accounting of her baby sister's doings: 'The baby is so full of mischief it takes me all the time to look after her,' ran her first entry, on

20 July 1857; 'She scatters her things all over the cabin and I do not think she will have many by the time she gets to the Sandwich Islands.'

On 22 September, 'The baby is two years old today and knows most all her letters,' penned this proud sister. Little Sarah Peirce was certainly intelligent. Abraham Peirce and his family settled in Hawaii, where he invested in property, and after graduating from the missionary school at Punahou, Sarah became the first female student to enrol at Boston Medical School. Male outrage at this scandalous departure from tradition meant that she was expelled within two weeks, but at length Sarah was readmitted, and graduated near the top of her class.

he had good reasons.

And what were Mary-Ann Sherman's reasons for sailing on the *Harrison* in May 1845: did she sail for love, or did Abner give her no choice? Whoever made the decision, he or she was still defying convention then, for when Mary-Ann sailed it was still unusual, eccentric — and scandalous — for a woman to voyage on a whaler. Only five petticoat whalers cleared the ports of New England in that year of 1845: five, out of a fleet of 302.

When nineteen-year-old Mary-Ann Sherman sailed from New Bedford on 21 May 1845, she was a bride of just four months. Interestingly enough, Abner's brother Wanton married another Mary-Ann — Marianna Almy — the day after Abner and Mary-Ann were wed. Wanton was also a whaling master; he took out the *Nimrod* on 27 May, just six days after the *Harrison* had cleared port...but Wanton did not take his Marianna on voyage.

The reason seems obvious. Marianna Almy Sherman was a respectable girl from a prominent and prosperous family. She did sail with Wanton the voyage after that, in 1848, which is a telling indication of how wife-carrying had become fashionable in the meantime. However, it is reasonable to assume that if Marianna had gone on voyage in that year of 1845, the two families would have raised a commotion.

Mary-Ann Sherman, by contrast, had no special standing whatsoever: she was illegitimate. Until Abner married her, she did not even have a name. She had been raised by Abner's uncle, Zoeth, and her mother was probably a servant, for a seventeenth century Puritan edict was still upheld in the old New England families, that the master of the servant was responsible for the consequences of that servant's moral lapses. Bearing this in mind, it seems equally reasonable to guess that no one in the Sherman lot would give a damn whether Mary-Ann sailed or not. They could well have been pleased when she went.

Not so. When Mary-Ann sailed the family did not just disown her: that was not enough to express their condemnation. They went the whole road and declared her dead — and put up a gravestone to prove it! Mary-Ann Sherman has two graves: one is the grave in Rarotonga that bears the true date of her death, 5 January 1850. The other, in the Elm Street cemetery, Padanarum, New Bedford, declares her death year as 1845, the year that she sailed on the *Harrison*.

# 3
# This floating prison

'Poor mortals to never know when we are well off, but I wanted to come so as to have a home, and I am not sorry, for I flatter myself I have been a little help to Wms, though I am not sure that he would admit it. *Men* are so *independent*, you know.' – Lucy Ann Crapo aboard the bark *Linda Stewart*, writing to her sister, Ruth Ellen Mosher, on 20 June 1880.

THE sun shone brightly and the wind frisked free on 25 June 1856, when Henrietta Deblois first embarked on her husband's bark *Merlin*. The start of a whaling voyage was a thought-provoking time for all the wives, particularly the first-time sailors; they were all very conscious that they would be away for four or more years, if not for ever. However, Henrietta Deblois, loving wife, dutiful home-maker, school teacher, church supporter and respected citizen of the town of Newport, Rhode Island, had more reason than most to feel afraid.

John Deblois, by contrast, was exultant. He had waited many years for this moment, for he was a devoted husband and had openly resented the long whaling voyages that had kept him from Henrietta's side. Back in November 1847 he had mourned in a letter to her, 'It will be 24 months in 6 days since I left my all. When I think how long I have got to stay in this floating prison it makes me hart sick.' At that time he was mate of the ship *Ann Alexander*, and when he had sailed, in 1845, he and Henrietta had been married for just forty days.

Henrietta, it seems, felt lonesome too: 'Do come home as soon as you can,' she wrote in November 1848. 'And if you go again take me with you.' It was not usually possible for mere officers to carry their wives, but 'I have no Doubt,' she penned, 'if you do go again you will go master.'

She was right. When John left New Bedford next, on 1 June 1850, he sailed as skipper of the same ship, *Ann Alexander* – but Henrietta did not sail with him. The reason is revealed in a note sent to her by the first officer of the *Martha*, one Thomas J. Lee. 'Shall tell your Dear blois,' he wrote, 'how lonly his Dear wife was that day he sailed and left her in my care to see her safe home to her sainted Mother.' Duty kept Henrietta shorebound. She was an only daughter, and seemingly the sainted old woman could not be left to cope by herself.

## Charles and Rachel Chase

Whaleship owners, on the whole, tended to be doubtful about the wife-carrying fashion. When Captain Philip Howland commanded the bark *Mary & Susan* for the owners Knowles & Co. in 1864, he wanted to take his wife Patience along, but instead they made him sign an agreement that Patience was 'to be allowed to join him at the end of two years if the Ship has one thousand Barrels of Sperm Oil in that time'. Those thousand barrels eluded him, and Philip Howland never saw his wife again: he died at sea in November 1866.

The owners thought they had good reasons for such a heartless stand. For a start, women ate up expensive provisions. Many believed, too, that good whaling time would be wasted in dancing attendance on the skipper's wife and taking her sightseeing ashore. They also argued that her husband would be less likely to take risks if his wife was watching — and it was certainly undeniable that the men who took the most risks took the most whales. In 1866 the firm of Swift & Allen blamed Lucy Ann Crapo for the bad luck the *Louisa* was suffering, and another captain, Peter Gartland, wrote to them angrily, saying, 'You speak of the *Louisa* doing nothing because he had his Wife how can that be when a ship sees Whales 9 or 11 times in a season and does not get some Oil I dont think it should be lade to the Woman.'

'They seem to think it so dreadful a thing for a woman to go on board a vessel, that I wish they could know how much difference it really does make to a voyage,' Luce Ann Crapo wrote angrily to her sister Ruth Ellen, from the bark *Linda Stewart* in October 1880. 'I know I shall never get any credit for the oil I have been the means of bringing to this ship, and I do not care for it but I do think it is hardly fare that Wms should have to sacrifice on his lay, that I might come, as I am told was the case, 1 bbl in 100, though that,' she added sarcastically, 'might be considered cheap boarding.'

Obviously, a great deal of ill-feeling was engendered by the issue. However, the real problem was one that many wives expressed as well: a wife had no function on board a whaler. No matter which way you looked at it, she was nothing more than a passenger, and, in the last few decades of windjammer whaling, many owners came right out with this objection. Whalers were not packets, they ruled, and therefore their whalers did not carry passengers.

This would have stumped many a skipper — but not men of the whaling variety. The solution, as they saw it, was simple. They simply signed their wives on as crew.

Charles Chase was one of these resourceful ones. The crewlist for the 1908-10 voyage of the *Andrew Hicks* reads, in part:

Rachel A. Chase Assistant navigator,
Master's wife,
Marion A. Chase Master's daughter,
Albert E. Chase Master's son.

As it happened, it was lucky Henrietta did not sail. On 20 August 1851, in a famous encounter with a furious bull whale, John Deblois lost his ship. The whale attacked two boats and bit them to kindling, and then rushed the *Ann Alexander* and went through her side like a cat through wet paper. Six months afterwards he was taken by the *Rebecca Simms*, with John's marked harpoons and a large amount of splintered wood in his hide and

## The old Nantucket

'The sail proved to be the *Nantucket*, Captain [Richard] Gibbs,' wrote Henrietta Deblois of the *Merlin* in May 1858. 'They came on board and spent the day. Had a delightful time. Very pleasant people. Under God, I am indebted to Capt. G. for the safety of my husband.'

'We spent the time very pleasantly,' Almira Gibbs agreed in her journal. Her husband's rescue of Captain John Deblois, after Deblois had lost his ship *Ann Alexander* in a famous encounter with a ferocious bull whale, had certainly been providential, but she omitted to mention how she felt about it — even though, the hazards of whaling being what they were, the positions could easily have been reversed. Indeed, back in September 1856, when her own husband was hauled overboard from his boat while fastened to a similarly pugnacious 'fish', she merely observed that he 'lost his hat and one shoe'.

Almira Gibbs embarked on the ship *Nantucket* in June 1855, just four months before her thirty-ninth birthday; she and her husband Richard had been married fifteen years, and had a thirteen-year-old son, Richard C., who sailed with them and carried out sea-duties just like one of the seaman (though probably without pay). Almira herself was not exempt: when the steward was sick her husband ordered her to take over the job, and she dutifully obeyed him, though she didn't like 'the station' one bit.

Almira went a-whaling with no romantic illusions at all — which was lucky, for the old ship (built in Nantucket in 1837) was slow and uncomfortable, especially in rough weather: 'rather too rugged for comfort or anything else,' she wrote in June 1857. 'I can hardly walk about, I fetch up sometimes where I start for and sometimes somewhere else.' At night it was almost impossible to sleep. 'Got up and dressed

and went up on deck to see how it was,' she penned; 'and I found it blowing merrily the old ship down to it jumping all she new I found it blew just as hard with my being on deck as it did when I was below,' she added in her characteristically dry fashion, 'so I thought I could as well stay below and make the best of it.'

The whales proved scarce and wild, so she had to make the best of it for an unusually long time. They did not raise the shores of home until the afternoon of 7 August 1859. Block Island was sighted at two and a pilot was taken on board at four...and he ran the ship ashore at the southwest end of the Island of Nashawena. 'So ends a long voyage,' wrote Almira, phlegmatic to the finish. 'Saved our oil but lost the Ship after carrying us safely over thousands of miles by water we left her upon the Rocks.'

'The whale...bit them to kindling.' The powerful sperm whale was quite capable of counter-attack. *Ann Alexander*, under Captain Deblois, had two boats destroyed by an angry whale, which then sank the whaleship itself with a blow of its head.

head, to give away his identity. The ship did not last nearly so long: the old vessel foundered, leaving John and his crew puddling about in two frail boats, 2,000 miles from the nearest land.

With characteristic good luck, however, John was rescued within two days by Richard Gibbs of the ship *Nantucket*, and he and his men were taken to Paita, Peru. John paid for his passage home by selling the story to the papers. At that time *Moby-Dick* – an epic story of a ship sunk by a whale – was in press. 'Ye Gods...' exclaimed author Herman Melville when he heard the account; 'I wonder if my evil art has raised the monster.'

What Henrietta said when her husband arrived at the door can only be guessed: she, unlike Melville, had not heard the news, and – what's more – she failed to recognise John at first, for the monster had knocked out his front teeth. Surely she was frightened. When John was given command of the *Vigilant* soon afterwards she stopped behind again, and it would seem that this time she had two good reasons for that decision.

Small matters like wrecks and manic whales did not shift the determination of whaling skippers, however. When Richard Gibbs sailed on the *Nantucket* again, in 1855, he carried along his wife Almira, who did not seem at all enthusiastic at the prospect. John would have loved to do the same. 'When I get a lone I wish Mother had a nother daughter or somboday that we should not been a fraid to let her be with so you could come with me. I know I shall grieve all of this voyage to think I have come with out you oh my Dear wife,' he wrote in July 1852, and then, rather tactlessly, added, 'I wold pland for you to meat me if anything shold happen to our Dear Mother.' Then, in 1856, when John Deblois was given command of the new bark *Merlin* after nearly eleven months at home, fate took a further hand in the couple's affairs. The sainted mother expired. In an exultant rush, the pugnacious whale quite forgotten, John carried his beloved Henrietta to sea.

Whether Henrietta was pleased is hard to tell. As the perfect embodiment of the proper Victorian wife, she did not give vent to any undutiful feelings.

# John and Henrietta Deblois

'Ant you going to wash me this morning? Oh, I hav just got thrue. I have wash shave and put on som clean closes comed my head and I think that I look smat enofe to be call Capt De Blois but I shold rather hear my Dear Wife say com old Scott les we go to Church.' — letter written to Henrietta Deblois by her husband from the ship *Ann Alexander*, dated 23 August 1850.

His name was John Scott Deblois and he was born on 25 November 1816, the eldest son of a family of eight — which may explain why he ran off to sea at a very young age. He worked on coasting sloops for some years until, at the age of seventeen, he shipped on a whaler as the cooper's assistant. John was an ambitious man who wanted to rise to the top in the whaling business, but had to talk his way into the after cabin, for, being a small man, he was considered too light for the makings of an officer. However, determination had its way, and in 1845 he was appointed first mate of the *Ann Alexander*. He sailed in November — reluctantly, for he was newly married to his sweetheart, a schoolmistress, the former Miss Henrietta Tew.

The match is one of the romances of whaling. John loved Henrietta so much that in the days before sailing he would hide little notes in her gloves and stockings, for her to find in the lonely days and nights ahead. 'Dear Wife God bless you,' read one, and another, 'O my Dear Wife do pray for me, your husburn, J.S. Deblois.' His devotion was as true as his spelling was erratic — and there was a very good reason for his odd style of prose.

John had started life at sea so young that he had spent little time at school, and so he paid a shipmate to teach him how to read and write. 'I am ashaim of my spelling,' he wrote once to Henrietta, but this did not prevent him from writing her hundreds of letters throughout his whaling career. Only once did he allow his lack of lettering to hold him back. In part, his obituary, published in the *Newport Mercury*, 5 December 1885, reads:

'He was highly esteemed by all who knew him and without being consulted he was unanimously elected Alderman of the 3rd Ward in this city in April 1864, but declined to serve, not even qualifying for the position.'

Henrietta, who — in a different age — would have been admirably well-qualified for such an honour, died two years before him.

Instead she settled down to being as outwardly happy as possible. However, like so many of her whaling sisters she kept her mind firmly fixed on home, keeping a journal for her friends to read afterwards and writing long letters to her pupils, describing the vessel and daily life on board the bark.

'My dear Friends,' she wrote on 20 November 1856, 'as you had no opportunity of seeing the Barque I will try to describe her to you. In the first place,' she penned, 'she is 108½ feet [33 m] long.' (Most of the whalers were as small as this: the *Merlin* was 348 tons, while the slightly larger *Harrison* made 371 tons displacement.) 'She carries four boats,' Henrietta wrote, 'one of which is on the Starboard, the other three on the larboard [port] side.' This, too, was typical. Whalers could be easily recognised from a distance by the boats that were slung along the sides, ready for lowering in an instant if whales were raised. The other distinguishing feature of whalers was a brick furnace built aft of the fore mast — the tryworks — which held huge cauldrons for boiling whale blubber into oil.

More important to the wives, however, were the two cabins below which were allotted to the private use of the captain and his wife. They were tiny: the area of the two rooms combined would have been smaller than Henrietta's bedroom at home.

The first was the captain's stateroom, which Almira Gibbs called 'the sleeping room'. On the *Merlin* this room measured six by ten feet (approx 2 m by 3 m) and held a number of closets and lockers: 'on board Ship,' Henrietta explained, 'every inch of room is of importance.' It also held a three-quarter sized 'swinging' bed, which was suspended on stone-weighted gimbals. As Henrietta put it, the bed swung 'with the Ship so that you are not sensible of the motion'.

The wives who had a swinging bed usually appreciated the luxury. Some were not so fortunate. Elizabeth Marble's first voyage, in 1857, was on the bark *Kathleen*, which was very poorly fitted out. Her husband John and the mate, his brother George, 'boath say she is the ugliest ship they ware ever in,' she recorded, and it is probably poetic justice that the old bark, like the ship *Ann Alexander*, was finally sunk by a whale on St. Patrick's Day in 1902. Elizabeth had to make do with an old-fashioned extended berth: she and John took out the board base and replaced it with canvas, as it was so very uncomfortable, and then she spread various pastes on the canvas in a constant battle with the hordes of bedbugs and roaches, but to little effect.

Still others made their own arrangements, hoping to improve on what the owners had provided. When Captain William F. Joseph skippered the *California* in 1899, and carried his wife Anne — who was four feet eight inches (121.9 cm) tall, and known by the crew as 'the doughnut lady' — he installed a bed of his own invention, hung from the ceiling on chains. During a storm the bed spun, trapping little Anne inside it like a fly in a metal web. When her husband finally heard her cries for help and investigated, he thought for a moment that she and the bed had been spirited away, for the tautening chains had drawn it up into the ceiling. Anne was so terrified by the experience that once she got home she never embarked on a voyage again.

Some of the women made curtains for the bed, to try to give a more domestic appearance to the sleeping quarters. In June 1855 on the *Cape Horn Pigeon* Almira Almy and her little girl Sissy spent a day 'fitting curtains for her [Sissy's] bed'. The experiment was successful. Next day Almira recorded that they had 'finished Sissy's curtains and put them up, she is much pleased says it seems like a home bed'. Children weren't easy to accommodate, considering the lack of space. Mostly they had trundle beds, which were stowed under their parents' bed in the daytime. Babies slept with their parents, or had a little 'sailor's cot', which hung from the ceiling on ropes.

A short corridor off this stateroom led to the captain's 'head', or water closet. This also held a wash stand with a locker beneath, which was triangular in shape to save space. 'The washing apparatus,' wrote Henrietta Deblois, 'is like Steamboat fixings, water let into a marble basin, and a pipe to let it off'.

Another door led to the second part of the captain's private quarters, a narrow 'transom' or 'after' cabin, with a huge upholstered horse-hair sofa which ran across the stern. This was the captain's sanctum. As an old whaleman – Murdock – put it, it was 'the reception room, the sitting room, the parlor, the library, the business office, the directors' room, the jury room, the supreme court room of the ship. Nobody could enter therein without permission from the captain' – except, of course, for his wife. It usually measured about six feet by eight (1.8 m by 2.4 m) and held a remarkable amount of paraphernalia.

'In the after cabin we have a green Brussels carpet with a tiny red flower sprinkled all over it,' wrote Henrietta Deblois, 'a blk walnut sofa, one chair, a small mirror with a gilt frame – over this is the Barometer – at the side of this hangs the thermometer. Under the mirror is a beautiful carved shelf...a beautiful little landscape done by our cousin Kate hangs over the Sofa. A Melodeon [harmonium] Music books work baskets and bags, give this room quite a home-look.' She forgot to mention the captain's chart table – a solid affair – which was a major part of the furnishing as well, along with the chair that went with it. In later years women like Lucy Smith carried a sewing machine, too.

Two more doors led out of this cabin, one door to a narrow stairway (the companionway), that led up to the deck, and the other to the main, or 'forward', cabin. Henrietta Deblois once called this the 'eating cabin', for that is what it was.

This forward cabin, on the *Merlin*, measured '8 by 10 feet [2.4 m by 3 m]. It is our dining room,' she wrote, 'and contains an "extensive" table of black walnut and what sailors call a "Scotchman" to keep the dishes from falling off when the vessel rolls. There are two long seats (similar to the seats in the [railroad] cars) fastened to the floor each side of the table – at the head the Capt. has an armchair.'

More doors, on the port side of this room and in the forward partition, led to other parts of the ship. 'Out of this room are two staterooms on one side where the mates sleep,' described Henrietta Deblois. 'At the end is an entry one side of which is a stateroom where sleeps the fourth mate Steward & Cabin boy – on the other side a nice large Pantry – further along is

# Bark Kathleen *sunk by a whale*

## *as related by the captain* Thomas H. Jenkins

'Having been requested to give an account of the sinking of the Bark *Kathleen* by a whale,' related Captain Tom Jenkins at the start of a speech he'd been invited to give to the New Bedford Board of Trade, in May 1902, 'I will do the best I can, though I think that those who have read the papers know as much or more about it than I do.

'We sailed from New Bedford the 22nd October, 1901, and with the exception of three weeks of the worst weather I have ever had on leaving home, everything went fairly well till we arrived out on the 12-40 ground...'

There, about 1,000 miles off the coast of Brazil, they raised a very large whale. He was a tempting prospect, and Captain Jenkins ordered that the ship be tacked to follow the sperm whale's course. They steered different ways, losing him in a rain squall and then finding him (or his twin) again, in perfect weather.

Jenkins ordered all four boats lowered, and the mates found a big school of sperm whales, all playing about. Mr Nichols the first mate got one, and soon all the other three boats were busy harpooning — and then times got even more exciting, for Captain Jenkins went aloft with a spyglass, and 'saw sure enough a large whale not more than five hundred feet from us, coming directly for the ship.'

Mr Nichols' boat was not far off. 'I told him there was a whale, a big fellow, trying to get alongside and to go and help him along and he did help him along.' Instead of sheering off or sounding when menaced with harpoons, however, the big whale kept on running, directly for the ship. Then he hit, 'forward of the mizzen rigging and four or five feet under water. It shook the ship considerably when he struck her,' Jenkins reminisced; 'then he tried to come up and he raised the stern up some two or three feet so when she came down her counters made a big splash.'

Then the whale lay still, apparently stunned. However, he had done his damage, for the ship was rapidly filling with water. Captain Jenkins set signals for the boats to call them back, and then he went down into the cabin.

**BARK SUNK BY WHALE.**

Strange Accident to the Kathleen on the "12-40" Grounds.

Just Returned to New Bedford, After Their Ship Was Sunk by a Whale.

Plucky Mrs Jenkins, Wife of the Master, Arrives Home in New Bedford and Tells the Story of the Thrilling Events of Last St Patrick's Day.

Mrs Jenkins was sitting on the transom sofa, reading. 'Hey,' he said. 'Didn't you feel that bump?'

'What bump?' said she.

'Never mind that,' he said. 'The ship is sinking.'

As Captain Tom remembered it, he told her to get some warm clothing as soon as she could, but not to try to save anything else. 'Well,' he told the Board of Trade, 'the first thing she did was to go for the parrot and take him on deck. Then she got a jacket and an old shawl.'

Then, along with her husband and nineteen men, Millie Jenkins got into Mr Nichols' boat, the other three boats being still obliviously whaling. Five minutes later the ship rolled over to windward. Baling madly every moment, Mr Nichols, his boat's crew and his unweildy complement of passengers paddled until they found the others. The other men were most surprised, the captain remembered, to hear that the ship had gone. Night had fallen in the meantime, and everything indeed looked dark. However, as he said, it was a beautiful moonlit evening, and at nine next morning they raised a large steamer.

'We got alongside,' Captain Jenkins reminisced, 'and she was way out of the water.' He craned his neck to look up to the deck and he said, 'Millie, do you think that's too high for you to climb?'

'Tom,' she said, 'I could climb that side if it were twice as high.' And she picked up her skirts and did so.

the steerage where the Boatsteerers Shipkeeper and Cooper live. For'ard is the Forecastle where the seamen live,' she added. 'I cannot take you there as I have not been there myself but am told it is very nicely fitted up.'

All these rooms – except, perhaps, for the pantry – were masculine territory. Below decks forward of the dining cabin was strictly off-limits for women. The forward cabin was a comfortable enough room for eating and relaxing, however. The big table made a place where the wife could lay out patterns and cut out sewing, between meals. The trouble was that she had to share it with three or four officers, who used it for eating and relaxing as well. Because of the cramped conditions, there was no separate dining area for the captain and his wife.

A whaler was necessarily over-crowded. A merchant vessel of similar tonnage could be sailed by nine or ten seamen, but thirty or more hands were needed to man a whaler's boats and work the ship when the boats were down and chasing whales. These men, as in men-of-war, were divided into ranks. There was an officer in charge of each boat, along with a harpooner (called 'boatsteerer' on American vessels) as a kind of second-in-command. Then there were the common oarsmen and the tradesmen such as cook, steward, carpenter and cooper. In effect, each whaling vessel was more like a village than a ship.

The qualities looked for in whaling officers were leadership, seamanship and courage when faced with a whale, not social airs and graces. This meant that while some were amiable company at the dining table, other men proved difficult.

'Without exception, I think him the nearest to a *savage* of any one I ever met,' declared Lucy Smith concerning Mr Holmes, the first mate of her husband's bark, *Nautilus*. Mr Luce, first officer of the *Merlin* on a later voyage, when Harriet Allen was on board, developed a mysterious illness just two months after sailing, in September 1868. He threw fits and seemed delirious. Then, on 7 October, the truth came out. The steward 'informed us of the nature of the disease. . . It is a great *surprise* to us,' Harriet mused. Mr Luce's condition was finally controlled by 'a general throwing overboard of bottles of whisky'.

Obviously, the best stance a captain's wife could take when dealing with such men was one of dignified reticence. However, some of the wives were so desperately lonely that they made the very human error of being too friendly when they first met the officers and then regretting it later. When the bark *E. Corning* sailed in November 1860, Elizabeth Stetson, the captain's wife, decided that 'Mr Hammond our second mate seems to be a very smart man', and, 'Our third officer Mr Silva (a Cape De Verd Portuguese and Black) looks very pleasant'. By 24 September 1861 she thought the junior officers *'disagreeable, despicable* men. I detest them', she wrote, and proceeded (in her journal, at any rate) to give them spiteful nicknames. 'Hateful old Chubbup,' she wrote on 28 September, 'I wish he was out of the Ship, Old blatter.' The men fought with each other as well as with Elizabeth, and life about the table must have been thoroughly miserable.

Elizabeth's most colossal blunder, however, was to fall in love with the first officer, Mr Williams. Will Williams was an Englishman, 29 years old, ten years her junior. It all began when he was hurt badly in an accident on 5 January 1861, less than two months after sailing. A cask, 'Swang over and got away from those who were holding on, and struck against Mr Williams, took him in the Groin, jammed him against another.' As was usual, the captain's wife was put in charge of nursing the invalid, and Elizabeth certainly did her best. She sat up all night with him when he was delirious, and then, when he was put into hospital in Talcahuano, Chile, in February, she visited him three times a day.

'Have my cup of coffee in the morning,' she wrote on the 14th, 'then go to see *Brother Will*, for he is my brother, no brother could be thought more of.' On the 18th, 'Hot Coffee, then to Willie; wash and comb his hair; rub his teeth, rub his hip, clean his nails, and comfort him with *talking*.' On the 20th she finally admitted the state of her feelings. 'I hope that Charles [her husband] does not *mind* if I do love Willie so much,' she penned, 'how can we help liking one another, he commenced with gratitude, I with pity, both akin to love.'

Charles Stetson seemed remarkably understanding — or perhaps he knew his wife too well to be worried. After they sailed she wrote to William every day and dreamed about him constantly. Then in November he was well enough to rejoin the ship, and Elizabeth was overjoyed. However, as the months dragged by even he fell out of favour, as she discovered first that his temper was bad, then that he sulked when corrected, and also that the smell of the pipe that he smoked made her vomit. At Paita in September 1864 he bought her a peace-offering (a chamber pot!), but matters remained unmended.

Such complications were to be avoided if humanly possible. Separating the captain's family from the officers was ideal, if it could be managed, and because of this many captains built a little deck cabin for the private use of their wives and children. This room was commonly set in the so-called 'hurricane' house that sheltered the helm, and because of this it was usually called the 'room in the house'. It was very small, about six feet (1.8 m) square, and was as over-furnished as the transom cabin, with a divan, cushions, a chair and table, and often a stove for heating flat-irons and water. Many wives kept pot-plants there as well, as a green reminder of land.

Despite its minute size the room in the house was greatly appreciated, not least because of the blessed privacy that it offered. When Mary Brewster had finished 'regulating' her room on 1 October 1847, she felt exceedingly complacent, for 'I have no occasion to go below and am entirely separate from the officers.' It meant that she and her husband William could 'take our meals at our own table and when seated imagine we are keeping house; here I am with my husband alone,' she gloated, 'and we are both making great calculations upon our enjoyment.'

One would think that the officers would make 'great calculations' too, at the prospect of having the dining cabin to themselves. However, illogically, the room in the house also provided occasion for complaint. One of those who begrudged a wife and family that little bit of extra room was the third mate of the *Eliza Adams*, 1872-5, one Abram Briggs, who disliked Mrs Hamblin, the captain's wife, exceedingly.

'The Carpenter to work making the house on deck larger,' he carped. In his opinion it was too big already. And – what's more – 'the carpenter has put a long window in the forward part of the house, so Mrs Hamblin can set down & look whats going on on deck, who goes over the bows, or to the Urine barrell,' he griped.

In a word, Mrs Hamblin could view the men as they relieved themselves. It was certainly a public act. The urine barrel was used for one function (except for men with venereal disease) and the men scrambled over the bow and squatted in the nets that were slung there, for the other. So many men...and just one woman. In Hollywood terms the idea of thirty sex-starved men alone with one female in the middle of the trackless sea implies the most sensational of goings on, but in fact nothing could be farther from the truth.

To the average whaleman – which category almost certainly included

## Jane and Daniel Worth

On 17 October 1869 Harriet Allen of the *Merlin* noted that a 'Fine Brig' was in sight. This was the *Para*, commanded by Captain Daniel Worth, who habitually carried his wife Jane (pictured here together). 'I was afraid at one time would speak her,' Harriet confessed. 'Did not feel *equal* to entertaining Mrs W.'

Jane's reputation, it seems, was questionable. 'I hear so much about Mrs W I am curious to see her,' Harriet admitted, 'though from chance observations I fancy we shall not suit each other *too well*.' Jane Worth, it seems, was 'not *highly* educated' – and some of the women who came from old whaling families were as lacking in social airs and graces as many of their men. For the next two days Daniel Worth did his utmost to catch up with the *Merlin*, and then, on the 19th, he finally managed the trick. David Allen reluctantly hauled aback, and Captain Worth came on board to gam.

To Harriet's relief Jane Worth was not on board the brig – she was 'in Mahé with her organ lessons' – but Daniel Worth made up more than a little for her absence. He had come on board after 'some crochet patterns' that Harriet was supposed to be carrying for Jane. Harriet did not have them, but he took some convincing of that. 'All his conversation, or nearly all,' she wrote, 'was concerning his wife.'

Daniel was a devoted husband, certainly. He

married Jane Harding of Holmes Hole, Martha's Vineyard, in 1852, when he was twenty-three and she was only seventeen. She sailed first on the bark *Gazelle*, in 1862. 'Capt's wife sick nearly all the time,' recorded the fourth mate in his private journal; 'does not

Mr Will Williams of the *E. Corning* – the captain's wife was as sexless as the traditional mother-in-law. Instead of lust she was much more likely to inspire constant and continuing resentment – and nothing was resented more than the fact that she ate up food. 'You would look with wonder,' griped young Abram Briggs, 'to see the grub go to her while In bed, enough for two ordinary women.'

John Perkins, a seaman on the *Tiger* when Mary Brewster was on board, asserted in January 1846 that Captain Brewster was mean with the food because he 'has his wife aboard & therefore wishes not to get out of potatoes, mollasses, sugar, butter &c.', while the fourth mate of the *Gazelle* 1862-6 declared that Mrs Worth was 'the most hoggish and greediest female that ever existed.'

It must be remembered that whalemen were very young (Elizabeth Marble recorded on the *Kathleen* that 'there are not but four on board registered over 18 years old') and adolescence plus sea air gives a young man an appetite. The food itself was certainly nothing wonderful. 'Our food is of a kind that

agree with her to be on board of a ship though every attention necessary is administered by all hands.'

That 'attention', to that young man's constant and continuing resentment, involved giving 'Her Majesty' lots of good food, while he, with hard work to do, was constantly going hungry: he almost became accustomed (or so he declared) to waking up each morning with 'a peculiar sensation about the abdomen only known to such as have been bordering on starvation'.

'We sit down to the table to eat half cooked duff and the worst kind of molasses with a scanty supply of meat,' he carped in December 1864, 'while those at the head of the table are a gourmandizing on fresh meat soup and sundry other eatables. Cake is made and put away for their use until mouldy or likely to spoil, then is thrown overboard.' The coffee caused another gripe: 'One kind has to be made for the Capt. and wife and mate, another for the three inferior officers.'

There is nothing like injustice to get a person riled up, of course, but Mrs Worth's manners seem to have been as lacking as her sense of democracy. 'We often hear etiquette spoken of among us,' the young man loftily penned in March, 'saying this one is ignorant of it in one way, and some in another. Not being very well posted myself, of course, it is not right for me to accuse anyone. But my idea of it is that it implies grace, good manners, and

politeness. It often happens that those who observe others are the very ones that break these rules most.'

This outburst, as he told it, was caused by a lamp. The young man was seated at the table and writing by lamplight, when 'the landlady of this lordly tabernacle' leaned over and took the lamp away, without a single word. 'If that is one of the rules of etiquette,' he opined, 'then I for one hope always to be ignorant.' The atmosphere of simmering resentment in the cabin must have been very depressing, particularly as the months and years of voyage dragged by on leaden feet.

Jane, according to gossip, did no better in port. Harriet Allen heard more news in May 1870: 'Mrs W has created a sensation in Mahé,' she wrote. Curiosity, obviously, was growing apace. Three weeks later Harriet went on shore at Mahé herself. 'One of the worst features of Mahé is that there is no accommodation for strangers,' she commented, 'except the hotels which are full of man of wars' men generally and are neither more nor less than drinking saloons.' Because of this lack of accommodation she was forced to offer to share her rooms with Jane Worth. 'Hardly know *what* to do,' she agitated when Daniel asked the favour.

Then, on the 25th, she finally met the subject of all the talk. 'So I have seen Mrs W,' Harriet penned, and then added, devastatingly, 'My first impression is that she is *very pretty* – seen in the evening with her hat on.'

I am entirely unused to,' observed John Perkins on the whaleship *Tiger*, and it is certain that Mary Brewster found it strange as well. The menu was based on hard sea-bread ('biscuit'), salt beef, salt pork, dried beans, onions and potatoes, together with whatever items were picked up or caught as they sailed along. It was served either boiled (in salt sea-water) or fried. 'Lobscouse' was salt beef cooked up in a stew with vegetables; 'hash' was ditto with crushed hard bread. The sailors' treat was 'duff', a stiff flour and water pudding, sometimes with a few raisins mixed into it, boiled in a bag and then served with molasses. When another Elizabeth, Elizabeth Waldron, sailed on the *Bowditch* in 1853, Thursday was Duff Day — 'Duff Day has come round again,' she wrote in April. 'I dare say that all of them forward thought of it this morning. I can't say that I love it dearly.'

Elizabeth Waldron liked very little of the food, which is not amazing. When Elizabeth Marble sailed on the *Kathleen* in 1857, that old ship was particularly poorly provisioned. 'I am sick for the want of something decent to eat,' she wrote with evident passion. 'I believe we have nothing on board of the ship that is not eather wormy or stinks except hard bread, I believe that is good so far.'

She could have been over-optimistic. John Perkins of the *Tiger* watched a cask of hard bread being opened in December 1845 (just one month after sailing), and noted that it was crawling with 'little black bugs'. Earlier when a different cask was opened it was found that the bread was wormy. 'But the worms taste no different from the bread,' he philosophically commented, so hopefully Mary Brewster did not notice.

The molasses was the poorest grade of blackstrap, and had salt water mixed into it to keep it from fermenting, and pea-soup was generally loathed, because of the worms that floated to the top. 'And our water is salt and stinks to,' wrote Elizabeth Marble, 'and the tea and coffee is worse than the water, what drink I have used I have had to drink water with lemon syrup in it and the water keeps me distressed all the time.' The coarse bread and fatty meat kept them all flatulent, and many of the women suffered cruelly with colic. Lucy Ann Crapo 'ate a hole through the plate of my teeth, so I have given up my hard bread.' It is little wonder that some wives, like Lucy Ann herself, became enthusiastic fishermen, for ever dangling a line over the stern in the hope of catching a 'fresh mess'.

The chances of success were small, however: fish could usually be caught around a wreck or a floating piece of wood, or even when sailing across another ship's stern, but at other times it was a wasted effort. It was much easier to catch porpoises or dolphins, by harpooning them as they played about the ship's bow. The women had very mixed feelings about this cruel practice, especially as the porpoise was fabled to change colours while dying. As Henrietta Deblois put it, in October 1856, 'The colors were all that I had imagined, yet the idea of the sufferings of the poor fish took away the pleasure of seeing the beautiful colors.' The next time she was called to see a dolphin dying, she refused to go and watch.

To complete the semblance to a village, the whaleship carried livestock on board, and the care of these — as at home — often became the province there leave of me at 12 N or at Noon, it was a heartrending sceen few but those that have experienced the same can imagine the agony of mind that is felt at a seen like the above.'

Another man to experience 'the same' was Obed Swain, when his wife Harriet was forced by ill health to leave the *Catawba*, on 11 April 1855. 'At 6 pm Obed bade us farewell, to embark again on the Ocean,' she wrote. 'Of my feelings I will remain silent.' Her husband, however, waxed eloquent (and to the devil with the fact that he was writing in the official logbook).

'First Part commenced with fine weather,' he wrote; 'at 5½ PM left the shore for the ship leaving my Dear Wife at the House of Capt Hillman's feeling as I never felt before the look she gave on parting I never can forget.' Harriet took a coastal steamer to Panama, and then crossed the Isthmus by the newly built railroad. 'Trubbled in my sleep about crossing the Isthmus,' Obed wrote on April 17, and then, on the 25th, 'two weeks since I left my Dear Wife at Payta but it seam as more like two years —

'Absence
'If in absence I were forgot
If lapse of time destroy the tie
That binds the heart to one dear spot
I then should wish that I might die

'Ere I could know that those I loved
Because with them I could not be
Because from them so far removed
Alas had ceased to think of me

'But 'tis not so, no, God forbid
I've that for which I wish to live
Of which I would not be thus rid
For all that worlds or world could give

'Tis simply this: — that those so loved
Altho' with them I cannot be
Altho' from them so far removed
Yet still, O still, they think of me.'

And then, on the 26th, obviously still troubled in mind, he wrote, 'Dreamed of seeing Harriet in good health but not able to speak to her.' That dream was prophetic. The voyage did not end until 31 May 1857: when Obed arrived home his wife Harriet had been dead for 22 days.

# Obed Swain

On April 28, 1857, Mrs Lawrence of the *Addison* spoke Captain Freeman of the *Tybee*. Captain Freeman had brought his wife to sea, Mary Lawrence recorded, but Mrs Freeman was so prostrated by seasickness 'that he was obliged to send her home from Valparaiso. He says it seems very lonely on board now,' she added, 'more so than if he had not attempted to take her. I feel sorry for him,' she penned — and, indeed, many men suffered greatly when they were separated from their wives by the vicissitudes of the voyage.

Often the partings were brief, but poignant for all that. Captain Michael Baker of the *Gazelle* left Eleanor for a spell on Norfolk Island in October 1860, and, 'Oh this has been a bad day for me,' he wrote in the journal she'd left on board, 'how lonely.' Even sadder were the separations when the wife had to leave the ship for home. 'This day all that I hold deer on this wide world have lift me,' wrote Captain Elisha Fisher of the *Trident*, 2 October 1863; 'yes my own Dear Wife and Two children took of the wife. Hens and pigs were supposed to be kept in pens, but in fact roamed freely. Some skippers even allowed them in the cabins: on 13 December 1880 Captain Almon Stickney's wife Mary recorded (perhaps, incredibly, with a giggle) that 'one of the pigs had three little ones, Almon brought one below and put it in the bed with me.'

Lucy Ann Crapo had a goat and kid on the *Louisa* in 1866: 'The kid is getting troublesome, making raids on the pantry, to devour the Steward's broom,' she noted. It also invaded her stateroom and ate newspapers, 'but I hope he will do better,' she joked, 'as his last lunch was a portion of Beecher's sermon whose remarks are always applicable.' There were other drawbacks. Captain Herbert Colson carried sheep on the *George and Susan* in 1878, and when, in April, lamb arrived on the table, his wife Mary wrote plaintively, 'I do hope we shall never have another animal on board this ship for I get fond of them and they of me and then they either die or are killed.'

'We had rice for dinner,' wrote John Perkins on the *Tiger* on 21 November 1845. One of the pigs got into it before the men had a chance to collect their food; 'however I was quite hungry & made a hearty meal'. Cockroaches and rats also fouled the food and water. David Baker, who carried his wife Mary on the *Ohio* 1858-62, reminisced to his daughter that eggs had kept on going a-missing, and that he had blamed the cook. Then one afternoon when he was resting on the transom sofa, he saw one rat backing along a shelf towards its hole, dragging another rat by the tail. That second rat was lying on its back and an egg was cradled on its stomach.

> '*Ginger Cookies*. 1 pt. of molasses, 1 cup sugar, 1 of butter, ½ cup water, 1 tsp. ginger, 1 of saleratus and flour.' – receipt in the book that Almira Gibbs kept on the *Nantucket*.

It is little wonder that many of the women's journals include lists of recipes ('receipts') for flour and molasses-based breads and cakes. Cooking up treats could be difficult, however, for the woman's greatest enemy on board was very often the steward. The cook, who prepared food for all hands in a deck galley, was the fellow in charge of the stove, but the steward, whose domain was the pantry off the forward cabin, was in charge of the cabin table and the food that was put upon it. This personage was often older and better educated that most; he was often a man who had 'come down in the world' (usually on account of the demon drink) and he had an unshakeable sense of his own importance. Anything domestic that the captain's wife might wish to do was an intrusion on his cherished territory. In December 1861 Elizabeth Stetson's steward told her that he wished she would not interfere, that 'he'd be thankful if I would let things alone. *Impudence!*' she fumed.

'Our steward is worse than nothing,' Elizabeth Marble wrote on the old *Kathleen* –

> 'For if he was not hear I could try to get something to eat myself but as it is I can't stomach to be in the pantry to do eney thing it stinks so I have made them apels into pies. . .and they would have gorn very well if I had had clean dishes to eat out of but I do not think we have had a dish washed as it should be since we left home. When he takes them from the table he takes his dish cloth and gives them a whipe around and then they are ready for the next time.'

Elizabeth Marble, like her stronger minded whaling sisters, took over much of the fancy cooking even if it meant a quarrel. Henrietta Deblois dominated her steward with no apparent effort. 'The officers like my bread better than the steward's,' she stated firmly, October 1856, and that, it seems, was that. It was more difficult, however, if the wife was ill, or wanted to fix something small for herself.

'So you think of going to sea, do you?' wrote Lucy Ann Crapo in reply to a letter received from her sister, Ruth Ellen Mosher, on 11 October 1880. Well, she said, 'be sure to provide yourself with some sort of a convenient spirit lamp, or such as you can make a cup of tea, or fix a little medicine if needed hot, for you cannot always get hot water from the galley which will be agreeable, more especially if you are nauseated...I have a small tea kettle in which I send water to the galley and have it heat[ed] but in the night I would have to hold it over the lamp, which is not easy when the ship is rolling and tumbling about.

'And I would have a few necessary dishes that is a cup, saucer, one or two plates knife, fork and spoons, to keep in your own apartment...' she added, 'as only one steward has been a good dish washer.' The lack of hygiene was an even greater threat to health than the badly cooked food. Elizabeth Stetson suffered shockingly with erysipelas ('Saint Anthony's Fire'), a dangerous skin disease caused by streptococcal bacteria. 'Erysipelas in my face and body, all over me, Oh dear,' she wrote in January 1862. She took laudanum at nights to dull the pain and help her sleep.

'Not very well today,' wrote Henrietta Deblois on 3 November 1856. 'Laid awake most of last night from pain; after three o'clock got up and pitched about (for it was very rough), until I found my way to the medicine chest. Made up my mind that *home, dear home*, was the best place for a sick woman. Plenty of bed, plenty of room and a steady floor is so much easier for one to wait on one's self. Never mind!' she added. 'I will make the best of it. Four months gone already.' Brave words, for a whaleship was a poor place indeed to be ill.

While French ships and many English whalers carried a surgeon (of a sort), very few American or Colonial vessels bothered with such an extravagance. The fellow in charge of the doctoring was the skipper, who was armed with a medical chest. This held instruments plus lots of little phials, each of which was marked with a number. The numbers were put there because there was no guarantee that the skipper could read fancy Latin labels. The firm that provided the chest included a book, which informed the captain which numbers to use and how much and when. According to an old Nantucket yarn one captain who ran out of bottle number 11 made up the deficiency by using equal parts of 6 and 5 — but this could well be merely legend, for every skipper had his own pet remedies, which he used far more readily than anything thought up by a so-called professional.

'Remedy for Piles,' wrote the master of the *Good Return* (1844-7) on the flyleaf of his journal; 'take twice a day 20 drops of Balsam Copavia on sugar and a light dose of salts daily and use mercurial ointment on the fundamental extremity' — and then he signed the receipt 'John Swift, MD when necessary.'

Susan Veeder, the captain's wife on the *Nauticon* in 1851, treated herself even more drastically: when she had a headache she 'put a blister on the back of my neck.' Blistering was achieved by laying on a blister plaster, which was coated with mustard, burgundy pitch or some other caustic substance, which then was allowed to react on the skin. From the modern perspective it seems very strange that anyone should try to cure a headache like this, but Susan announced to her journal next day that she felt much better. Perhaps the pain of the blister was so intense that the headache seemed paltry by comparison.

Other 'cures' relied heavily on emetics, rum and enema injections. It is odd how each age has its tabu topics of public conversation. In Henrietta Deblois' time undergarments were unmentionable and a woman in an interesting condition was 'sick', never pregnant. However, she and her whaling sisters and whaling brethren had a preoccupation with bowels and testicles that would have most of us blushing today. In November 1853 Elizabeth Waldron 'had a round turn, it came upon me all of a sudden, I was in terrible pain, very sick at my stomach and faint as death.' Her husband Nelson treated her with 'a large mustard plaster [read 'enema'] for my bowels' – and it worked.

Because of the coarse food, toothache was a common complaint and most skippers became adept at drawing teeth, though on the *Cicero* in December 1880 Mary Stickney, the captain's wife, 'tried to extract a tooth for Will Winslow but failed'. The *Tiger* was badly damaged during a tremendous storm in the Arctic Ocean, August 1849, but Mary Brewster felt not the slightest fear: 'One can't think of any greater trouble,' she confessed, 'when they are half crazy with a toothache.'

Setting broken limbs was commonplace for whaling captains. On 18 March 1823 Mary Hayden Russell was sitting on the deck of the *Emily* admiring the sunset, when she 'heard a scream from my dear little Charles, who had the minute before left my side.

> 'Before I had time to inquire the cause his brother brought him to me with his arm broken just above the wrist joint. Such an accident on the land would have been distressing, but what were my feelings when I saw the child writhing in agony and no surgeon on board...His dear father with that fortitude and presence of mind that seldom forsakes him took him immediately below and with a man to steady the arm set it and splintered it up.'

The captains could stitch and amputate with the same blithe expertise: in July 1856 on the old *Nantucket* Almira Gibbs recorded that one of the men cut his foot 'quite bad the Capt. sewed it up and did it up and now he is doing very well.' However – as we have seen – the job of routine nursing was usually handed over to the captain's wife.

'The best part of the day I have spent in making doses for the sick and dressing sore hands and feet,' wrote Mary Brewster in July 1846; '5 sick and I am sent to for all the medicin. I am willing to do what can be done for any one particularly if sick...' Then she added, 'a whaleship is a hard place for comfort for well ones and much more sick men.' Mary knew exactly what she was talking about, for while she enjoyed splendid health as a rule, when the ship pitched and tossed she was always most tediously seasick.

'Old Swell on and seasick,' wrote Elizabeth Stetson, that most experienced mariner, on 16 November 1860; 'Eat and then vomit is the order of the day.' The first few days of leaving port were the worst for everyone, captains and men as well as wives. However, while the men recovered swiftly, the women did not, perhaps because of the lack of fresh air and activity. Mary Brewster ruefully recorded on 4 December 1845, one month out from home, that she had been seasick all the time, 'and not able to sit up but have been confined to my bed'.

'Hardly able to crawl,' wrote Henrietta Deblois in September 1856, eleven weeks after sailing. John tried to cure her seasickness by giving her glasses of water straight from the sea. The remedy worked — sometimes. She always tried to put a brave face on her voyage, but it is interesting to look at her choice of words when she recorded, on the 25th, that she had been three months out: 'and hitherto,' she wrote, 'the Lord hath sustained me.' At home she would have used the word 'preserved'.

'I sit here on deck,' she wrote earlier that month, 'and think of distant friends and times long passed, and I feel that there are many who think of and pray for me.' There were many months of prayer ahead, for the *Merlin* did not arrive home until 19 June 1859. Then, when John took the same ship out again, almost exactly 12 months later, Henrietta was not on board. It wasn't the way he had meant it to be, for in his estimation the previous voyage had been a resounding success, but nevertheless he sailed alone.

Henrietta had made some promise to meet the ship in some port or other, but she never got around to leaving Newport. Apparently her sense of wifely duty did not allow her to refuse outright to go on voyage, so instead she put him off with the vaguest of excuses and prevarications. John's letters over the next few years make poignant reading, for his distress and bewilderment are so very apparent.

While what Henrietta did seems cruel, it seems very odd that John — of all people — did not guess her true reasons. In that letter he wrote to her back in 1847 on the doomed *Ann Alexander*, he had called the ship a 'floating prison', and when one considers the years of confinement, the terrible food and rough company, the comparison is very apt. As it was, after John Deblois returned home to Newport in 1863 he never went whaling again.

Life at sea did not look so bad all the time, however. There were amiable officers, respectful men, stewards who were eager to please, and on some days the sun shone brightly, and the ship lay still on a tranquil sea. There were festivals like Thanksgiving to lighten even the most miserable shipboard existence. Almira Gibbs spent a day 'makeing pies' in preparation for her first Thanksgiving at sea on 29 November 1855: 'We are having a porker killed on the occasion,' she added. 'I don't expect it will be anything extra, however it must answer for us as we have not got any oil.' Whales were all the preoccupation. On April Fools' Day 1853 Elizabeth Waldron dryly noted that 'the Cooper made fools of the men this morning and the whales again this afternoon...' Then she added, perhaps with a sigh, 'a little more bad luck, hope it will be better soon.'

When Lucy Ann Crapo had her thirty-third birthday on the bark *Louisa* on 28 February 1866, she noted that 'I see no flags up' but nevertheless she invited three captains to supper, and served fish chowder, baked fish, huckleberry pies and fruitcake. On American ships, the Glorious Fourth — which Lucy Ann called 'the anniversary of our national independence from the yoke of English tyrany and opression' — was always observed, even in the Arctic. The *Bowditch* was there for the Fourth of July in 1853, and Elizabeth Waldron had 'roast lamb "*alias*" pig for dinner with a top off apple pie, if anybody can beat that I would like to see them,' she declared. Then she added, 'our friends at home have not yet commenced action but while I am sleeping I expect they will be going it *all holler*, hope they think

## Helen Jernegan

As the wife-carrying fad gained momentum, some captains sent for their wives and children, to come and join them in some farflung port or other, and dutiful wives made hair-raising journeys to meet them. They travelled alone or in small groups, some carrying babies and small children, many in shocking health and all of them wearing the most impractical of garments. Helen Jernegan (pictured) was one of these obediently enterprising females.

Her husband Jared was a Martha's Vineyard man, while she was an 'Off-Islander' from Maine. When Helen first met him she was 20 and he was 34, a widower with one son, Aylmer. Then, in 1862, he sailed off as the skipper of the *Erie*, leaving Helen to cope with a close-knit and suspicious community and the hostility of Aylmer's maternal grandparents. As it happens, the voyage was a short one: the *Erie* was dismasted and abandoned off Cape Horn, and Jared was back within six months. Then, on 3 June 1863, he was off again as master of the *Oriole*, and after that, in 1864, Helen received a message which asked her to pack up their baby daughter Laura and bring her to San Francisco. It would cost him a thousand dollars, Jared declared, but it would be worth every cent. 'I shall let you git rite up into my lap just as you used to,' he wrote, 'then I will tell my beautiful little wife how lonely I have been.'

The proposition was for Helen and three-year-old Laura to take the railroad cars for New York, catch a steamer from there to Aspinwall (now called Colon), on the Atlantic side of the Isthmus of Panama, cross over by train, and then take another steamer up the Pacific coast to California. In September 1865 Helen partially obeyed him: she took the steamer from New York, but left Laura behind with 'Aunt Pierce'.

No doubt she'd been worried about the journey across the notorious tract of jungle and marsh that was the Isthmus of Panama. However, 'it was a lovely ride between mountains with beautiful flowers and ferns growing on the sides,' Helen reminisced later. 'The natives came to the cars to sell all kinds of fruit but we were warned not to eat any, as at [that] time there was much sickness on the Isthmus, and we were not allowed to drink any water — but wine was free to any one.'

The steamer from Panama City to San Francisco took ten days...and she arrived to find that Jared was not there. Helen stopped at the Palace Hotel for two weeks, but the owners would not allow Captain Jernegan to take the *Oriole* into that port, so she took another steamer to Honolulu, and finally met up with him there. They then sailed home, taking almost five months. 'A few gales of wind,' wrote Helen, 'but most of the time pleasant, and I enjoyed the sea.'

of us poor fellows away up here in the frozen regions of the North.'

Christmas was apparently not as important on American vessels as it was on the English and Colonial ones, for it was so rarely mentioned in the formal logs, but it was more likely to be celebrated if a woman was on board. Solomon Gray of the *Hannibal* in 1849, for instance, was a tough and uncharitable old customer, but the steerage boy Nat Morgan recorded that all hands were 'treated to fried cakes &c &c by Mrs Gray – [it] being Christmas.' A Nantucket whaling wife, Nancy Grant, once organised a Christmas party mid-sea: all the ships they spoke for some months previously were advised to be in a certain latitude and longitude on the day. It is a tribute to whaleman navigation that eight whalers kept the appointment.

Having children on board made both birthdays and Christmas more exciting. On the bark *Merlin* in 1868 the two Allen children became 'anxious about Christmas' halfway through December, so their mother Harriet set them to making button bags for all hands, and needle-books for the officers. It must have been obvious what was going on, for on the day itself the children's stockings were 'full and running over', mostly with small, painstakingly handmade gifts. One of the Portuguese seamen gave Nellie, Harriet's daughter, a scrimshaw ring, with the shy suggestion that her mother might like it if it proved too big. 'It was too big,' wrote Harriet.

The day set a pattern for the Christmas festivals to come. On Christmas Eve 1869, 'Everybody entered into the spirit of the fun. Those who had no stockings at hand hung up boots, and all were well filled.' It presented quite a challenge to make Christmas 1870 even better – so the children made a panorama. It was a long piece of canvas, wound on two rollers, with pictures drawn and pasted on the strip so that a story was told (accompanied by words) as it was slowly rolled along. Once the children had learned their lines they made tickets, and gave one to each man on the ship, and then they made candy and lemonade to give out to the audience during intermission.

'The panorama,' Harriet recorded at the end of the day, 'was a decided success.' It had to be shown several times, until all the men had seen it, and it proved to be the talk of the forecastle for weeks. 'Sea and sky are tranquil and everything about us suggests peace,' she mused. 'How is it with the faroff restless world?' In France women and children were starving in the Siege of Paris, and Victor Emmanuel's armies were marching on the Forum in Rome, but on one whaling bark in the Indian Ocean it was peace on earth, and heaven in its rightful place.

At all times of the year the grim monotony of whaling life could be immediately enlivened by raising the sail of another whaler, for this meant the chance of a gam, or social visit. 'We have just finished arranging our rooms as neatly as possible,' wrote Malvina Marshall to her family in October 1852, just before her guests arrived on board the *Sea Queen*. She and the steward had been busy, 'taken up our carpet coverings, dusting, wiping the glasses &c &c as we should at home if we were preparing for company.'

Gamming with another petticoat whaler was particularly exciting, for it meant that the woman had the rare privilege of enjoying what she had missed for weeks, months or years — a visit with another of her own sex.

For at least one of those women, however, visiting the other ship meant a ride in a boat, and getting into that boat was a problem. According to whaling legend, the wife was lowered into the boat in a chair. 'Capt [James] Cleveland came on board and brought his chair for me to on board the *Seconet* and pass the day,' Henrietta Deblois recorded on 4 July 1857. Elizabeth

## Laura Jernegan

'On the 29th of October 1868 your father Laura and Prescott and me sailed from New Bedford in the Ship *Roman*,' wrote Helen Jernegan in a memoir intended for her younger son Marcus. 'Laura [pictured] was six years old and Prescott was twenty-two months' — and Laura, like many children, kept a kind of journal on board.

'It is Sunday and a very pleasant day,' her first entry ran on 1 December 1868. 'I have read two story books. This is my journal.

'Goodbye For To Day.'

Helen and the children stopped on shore at Honolulu during the northern whaling seasons. 'It has blown real hard for two days,' wrote Laura on 26 September 1870. 'Prescott cut his foot last night it bleed. I am in Honolulu, it is a real pretty place.' Mama is making a dress for me. Papa is up north where it is cold, he will come back pretty soon. I have two kittens here and one aboard the ship.' Then, when Jared came back, the family went back on board for the 'between seasons' cruises.

'It is quit rough today,' wrote Laura on 10 February 1871. 'But it is a fair wind. We have 135 barrels of oil, 60 of humpback and 75 of sperm. We had two birds, there is one now. One died. There names were Dick and Lulu. Dick died. Lulu is going to. Prescott has got a little dog, its name is Tony. We have not seen a ship since we have left Honolulu. Prescott is playing with Papa. I am in the forth reder, and the fith righting book.'

Next day she recorded that, 'Lulu died last night. It does not blow very hard to day. I am eight years old and Prescott is four.' Jared Jernegan put up hammocks for the children and marked a chalk line across the deck as the boundary they must not cross when playing, because they were forbidden to bother the sailors.

It is often and sentimentally taken for granted that sailors are always fond of children,

but the overcrowded conditions on board a whaler often meant that they were instead resented. However, little girls like Laura left an engaging child's view of everyday life on a whaler. 'Papa has been fixing the sink,' she wrote on the 13th, 'and it runs real nice', and then, on the 15th, 'we saw a ship today it was the *Emily Morgan* Mrs Dexter came on board and we had a game.'

Then, on the 20th, they took six whales. 'Prescott is up on deck seeing the men cut the whale in,' she recorded, while, 'Mama is up in the house reading a book.' Next day, 'the men are cutting in the whales. they smel dredfully. we got a whel that made 75 barrels the whales head made 20 barrels of oil the whales head is as big as four whole rooms and his boddy as long as one ship.' On Wednesday the 22nd, 'the men are boiling out the blubber in the try pots the pots are real large when the men are going to boil out the blubber, too men get in the pots and squis out the blubber and are way up to there knees of oil. when the men at the mast head say there she blows, Papa gives them 50 pounds of tobacco. . .would you like to hear some news,' this well-travelled child asked the reader, 'well I dont know of any.'

Stetson noted on 7 September 1861, 'Cooper making me a chair to be hoisted up and down in.' The chair, according to her, was made out of a barrel, and was attached to ropes that hung from the mainyard.

Whether the chair was used or not is another matter. According to Susan Brock, who spent part of her childhood on the merchantman *Midnight*, she and her mother were lowered in a chair when they made port in Valparaiso. Young Susan thought it tremendous fun, but her mother found the experience so terrifying that she refused to get back on board the ship, and boarded on shore instead. Jamie Earle, who voyaged on the *Charles W. Morgan* as a child, stated that his mother, the New Zealander Honor Matthews Earle, never used a chair. Instead she stepped into the boat while it was still in the davits, and was lowered that way. 'I know jolly well that they never used that gamming chair without getting dunked,' he opined; 'you were in it, and if the thing went under water you were in the chair and you got dunked.'

'My friends at home would be surprised at my *courage* in going and coming from Ships in a small whaleboat,' Henrietta Deblois observed. The gam, however, was well worth any frightening moments. The cooks and stewards and some of the women themselves went to much trouble to prepare a nice meal, and, considering the limited resources, some of the menus were amazing. Malvina Marshall served her guests on the *Sea Queen* 'warm bread and butter, preserved blackberry, cold boiled ham, plum Cake and cheese and coffee'.

However, what was important to the women was the chance it gave for a little dressing up and fuss. It compensated, in a measure, for all the 'endearments of home' that the women sacrificed when they came on voyage — and yet some of them were begrudged even that.

On 4 June 1892 the whaling bark *Josephine* spoke the *Triton*, which had Emma McInnes' bosom friend Mrs Gifford on board, and, 'John gave the order to clear away the starboard boat,' wrote Emma. 'I asked him if he was going to take me, he seemed to think he could not and he was only going to stay a few minutes; he was gone two hours and when he got back he found me crying like a big baby...

'I was so disappointed I could not get over it for a long time,' she confessed. However her tears had worked the trick. John McInnes felt guilty enough to relent next day and take her to the *Triton*: 'Did it seem nice to see a woman and those dear little children?' Emma demanded of her diary. 'Well, it did,' she replied, 'and I had a good time.'

Other wives, however, were too dutiful, weak or cowed to complain. Such a woman was Jerusha Hawes.

It was 5 December 1859, and the weather was calm and smooth. A number of ships, including Jonathan Hawes' command *Emma C. Jones*, had clustered about the whaleship *Florida*, where Captain and Mrs Fish were entertaining Mary and David Baker and Captain and Mrs Hempstead, along with a number of stag skippers. It promised to be quite a party — but Jonathan didn't bother to invite his wife when he lowered the boat. He sailed off without a word, and Jerusha was forced to stop on deck and watch as he went.

The scene she watched must have been a pretty one. It is easy to imagine

## The ship that Mary McKenzie called home

The *Platina* first arrived in New England as a ship (square-rigged on all three masts), in 1847, and sailed out of Westport. Then, when in 1853 she was commanded by Captain David E. Allen (who took his wife Harriet on voyage) she was converted to a bark, with fore-and-aft sails on the sternmost – mizzen – mast. In 1864 the bark was taken over by Otis Hamblin, who also carried his wife, and she –

like Harriet Allen earlier – bore a child on voyage.

Then, in 1867, Captain Amos Chase took over the *Platina*, and carried his wife Louise and their children to the New Zealand whaling grounds. The family became firm favourites with the citizens of Russell: Louisa Worsfold, in her memoir of the Bay of Islands in the later years of the century, reminisced that they were 'very jolly people and loved the children'. Amos Chase was also popular with his crews, 'added to which,' Louisa wrote, 'he was a "lucky skipper" they said – which meant that he had

the ships all laying aback with the sun on their sails, and the little boats converging on one ship, cresting the sparkle of the sea – and even easier to picture Jerusha's drear disappointment. She went below and sat alone with her journal in the transom cabin, and it is certain that she wept.

'This is the second time he has been aboard to gam where there were ladies I would very much like to see, and not so much as invited me to go with him,' she wrote. 'Twice last week he has treated me the same way, and WHY? I know not.

'The tears will come as I sit here alone and think of home but my face shall be all smiles when he returns for I have decided that is the way to make him

a good eye for weather and a knowledge of the habits of whales – This made a big difference to a crew, as they were paid, "on lay" they called it, which meant, that they had a share in the "catch".'

In 1892 the command of the vessel was given to Captain Thomas McKenzie, who skippered her for about the rest of her life. The *Platina* was showing her age, but McKenzie kept her sailing, even as far as the wintery Arctic, right up to the day in 1911 when the old bark was sold, in the Island of Brava, at the huge price of $1,300 – for firewood.

'Mr Riley,' wrote one of the owners of the bark *Platina* on the flyleaf of the logbook for the 1892 voyage: 'Write short logs and mark all whales seen – J.F. Tuck'... and short indeed were those entries, for all six McKenzie voyages.

The owners of the *Platina* were in favour of the wife-carrying practice, obviously, but the logs give little indication that Mary McKenzie was on board, simply because Mr Riley and the first mates who succeeded him followed the owners' logbook-keeping instructions so faithfully. Members of the crew got a mention if they were sick, hurt, drunk, dead, flogged or deserted: in September 1892 the captain 'disrated the steward for stealing rum and getting drunk', for instance, and on 21 May 1894 a seaman named Teddy Thomas fell 'into the forehold      Cut his head and put his shoulder out' and next day 'the Captain tried to put the shoulder in place today but Could Not do it'. However, Mrs McKenzie's doings went perfectly unnoticed. She could very well be ailing, giving birth or dying even, but there was no legal need to note that at all – unless she'd been signed on as a member of the crew. Mary McKenzie had not, so on board the *Platina* she had no legal presence at all.

On 13 June 1910, however, the first mate's entry unwittingly gave her presence away. 'Commenced with moderate breeze,' he wrote; 'at 3.30 a.m. saw a sail on our lee which at daylight proved to be the bark *Wanderer*.' Captain Thomas Jenkins was in command of that vessel, and he carried his wife Millie, and, 'At 9 a.m. gammed her,' the logkeeper of the *Platina* wrote; 'Capt & wife coming on board of us.' This was a sure indication that Mary McKenzie was there to act as hostess, for it was not polite for a wife to visit a ship unless another wife was there awaiting.

Thomas and Millie Jenkins were another jovial couple, it seems. Reg Hegarty, who spent part of his childhood on the *Alice Knowles* (and other whalers) reminisced that when his parents gammed with Jenkins ships, he used to leap onto the Jenkins decks hollering, 'Captain Jenkins of the horse marines fed his horses on pork and beans!' – but that kind of frivolity was not noted down in official logs, neither.

happy and I would not cause him a moment of unhappiness, no God forbid that I should ever be the cause of unhappiness to someone so dear to me. I feel so lonely and homesick but I suppose he does not think – he has never had a wife at sea before – he does not think...

> 'ERROR IN JUDGEMENT
> 'NOT IN HEART.
> Jessie C. Hawes

SHIP  E.C. JONES
[of] NEW BEDFORD [5 December] 1859.'

This is the final entry in her journal. The ship did not make home port for another eight months, but Jerusha's diary stops right there.

# 4
# Blood, grease, sweat and oil

'Whale-fishing, in truth, is not only a very dangerous and laborious, but also a most precarious pursuit.' – Scherzer.

IT was Sunday 11 December 1853, and Harriet Swain on the Nantucket ship *Catawba* had a problem. The vessel was very nearly 12 months out, and only one small sperm whale had been taken, yet when the lookouts at the mastheads raised spouts she felt apprehensive, not happy. Then her worst fears were realised: her husband gave orders that the boats should be lowered from the davits, and then the men sailed off, murderously intent on the whales. 'Wish I could influence them to remain on board ship on the Sabbath,' Harriet confided to her diary. 'But if they see the fish they feel that they must go after them and it is hard for them to think they are doing wrong, I hope they may [soon] feel differently.'

Sunday, according to the Calvinist code of morals of the time, was supposed to be strictly observed as a day of rest, and most women then adhered to this, not least because they worked so hard on the other days of the week. A day when scrubbing and laundering, cooking and sewing could be set aside with a righteous conscience was a valued privilege. As well as that, it was a time for dressing up and making calls and going to church to listen to good sermons and inspiring music, so it is not amazing that Sunday was the day of the week when the seaborne wives felt homesick the most. However, many of the whaling skippers did make the sabbath a day of rest, which pleased their wives mightily. 'It is the Sabbath, and all is orderly and quiet on board; much more so than I expected among so many Men . . .' wrote Eliza Williams on the *Florida*, 19 September 1858. 'All work is laid aside Saturday night and nothing done on Sunday but what is necessary.'

'Another Sabbath, mild and lovely,' wrote Mary Lawrence on the *Addison* in January 1857. 'I think of friends at home wending their way to the house of God and wish I could bear them company. After breakfast I generally dress up a little more than on ordinary days and take a book and go on deck; sit there most of the day.' The serenity of the scene could be shattered most rudely, however, simply by the sound of *There she blows!* The vast majority of captains lowered boats after whales whatever day of the week it happened to be; if it was Sunday the wives just had to cope with disappointment — and once those boats were down they were faced with still more problems and worries.

Ordinary people lived closer to animals then. Horses, of course, were the common means of transport, and every housewife had her coop of chickens. Hogs, steers and sheep were killed and butchered in the plain view of children — but nothing the first-time wives had seen before could have prepared them for the blood and brutality, the huge dangers, the cruelty and waste, the whole immense scale of the killing and flensing of whales.

At first, when the lookouts sang out for whale, the scene was merely bewildering. The men raced about decks collecting the whaling craft and gear and putting them into the boats, while all the time the lookouts hollered from above. 'They are singing out from aloft, a school of Blackfish [pilot whales]. . .' wrote Eliza Williams on the *Florida* in September 1858; 'They are all playing about unconscious of danger, while on board all is confusion. The men are lowering the boats to go after them. It must be sport to them, for they act like crazy men.'

Then, when the boats were down with their sails set, the scene became tranquil. . .for a while. 'What a beautiful sight it was,' wrote Clara Wheldon in a letter of 17 July 1864; 'three little boats each with its oarsmen and one little white sail, the only visible objects on that broad expanse. At first they diverged as though going in different directions, but after an hour they gradually approached each other, and in another hour the combat commenced, and proved successful.

'They were so far away I could not distinctly see the attack, but after a while the spouting of the whale could be plainly seen with glasses,' she continued. 'Captain was at masthead and assured us they were "fast".'

'Fast' meant that the harpooner (boatsteerer) had managed to lodge a harpoon (or 'iron') in the whale's hide, so that the boat had fastened to the huge mammal by a good strong length of whaleline — and this was the moment that the first-time wives fully understood the awful dangers of the chase, because the whales immediately reacted in some fashion.

Some whales tried to get rid of harpoon and line by rolling over and over. This tactic could tangle men in the rope, tearing off limbs or dragging them down to a watery death as the whale sounded. Other whales ran away, keeping close to the surface. The boat was dragged along in what was romantically called 'a Nantucket sleigh-ride', which could take it out of sight from the ship in a nerve-wrackingly short time. Whales of the more aggressive kind turned about and attacked the boats. The sperm whales used their narrow peg-toothed lower jaws to crush boats and men to smithereens, and the huge right whales threshed out with giant flukes, sending men spinning to eternity.

On 15 June 1846, John T. Perkins of the ship *Tiger* was one of the oarsmen in the first boat that managed to get fast to a whale, and that whale killed him with the same smack of the tail that turned the boat into scrap. Mary Brewster watched the other boats pick up the fragments and the remaining men, all of whom had been hurt. To find that one of their crew had been 'Taken from the business of life without a moment's warning' shocked her

## Whaling off the north cape of New Zealand

### — from an engraving made in 1838 by Joel S. Polack

'Tuesday March 6th. . .' wrote Henry S. Potter, the logkeeper of the whaling schooner *Alfred* off 'Munganna' (Mangonui, New Zealand) in 1849; 'at 9 AM Spoke the Ship *Harrison* of New Bedford, Captn [Davenport] went on Board & spread Chances & Steered to East'd.'

If two or more ships were cruising a whaling ground in company, the skippers occasionally joined forces, or 'mated', to improve their chances of getting oil. If one ship in the group (in this case consisting of three vessels, the *Harrison*, the *Alfred* and the whaleship *Mechanic* of Newport, Rhode Island) took a whale, then they all helped process the blubber into oil, and then the fare was shared out between the mated whalers.

It took less than a day for whales to be raised. 'Came in with fine weather,' wrote Potter; 'at 1 PM the *Mechanic* raised A shoal of Whales & lowered her 4 boats & gave Chase.' The *Mechanic* was some distance off, and the *Alfred* made all sail and set off to join the fray. However the Sherman ship was closer: 'at 3 PM the *Harrison* lowered 4 boats & Joined the

*Mechanic's* boats in the Chase,' Henry Potter wrote. The *Alfred* still had some way to make, but finally, 'At 5 PM [we], having got nigh Enough to the Whales. . .down boats & Joined in the Sport,' penned Henry with palpable excitement. Tackling huge bewildered whales was sport for the men, perhaps, but never that for the women who watched and trembled.

The chase was a long one: 'the Whales being Gallied [frightened] they run for it to leward At the rate of 8 Knots & the boats dashed after them in fine Style. At 5:30 the *Harrison* boat struck a 50 bbl [barrel] whale & this Whale took to running,' Potter continued. While the *Harrison* boat was drawn swiftly towards the horizon the boats from the *Mechanic* and the *Alfred* struck and killed another whale. They 'took the whale alongside. . .' but the *Harrison* was not nearly so lucky. Night fell, and at 8 PM the harpooner was forced to cut the line, so that the whale was left to run off and die later of its wounds.

'Cruising about for whales under all sail,' wrote Henry Potter on the schooner next day. The men on the *Mechanic* were busily cutting in while the men on the *Alfred* were watching out for another chance of the whaling kind of sport, but when 'At 4 PM [we] Spoke the *Harrison* [Captain Sherman] had been looking for his whale he lost but saw him not,' Potter wrote; 'don't think he ever will,' he decided.

intensely. She turned to her journal for solace, and wrote down a long prayer. 'How it becomes us to dwell in sober earnestness on our own final end,' she brooded. 'I pray God that this affliction may not pass unheeded and forgotten without leaving a lasting impression on my mind.'

Similarly, Susan Fisher of the *Cowper* wrote to her family in July 1853, saying, 'I am sick and sad at heart today. The day before yesterday we met with an accident that has cast a gloom over all on board the ship, we lost three men...To us to have three taken out of our ship's company without a moment's warning is dreadful to think of, it truly may be said, "In the midst of life, we are in Death".' As Mary Brewster meditated later in her voyaging, 'Death in any form has its terrors, but on shipboard it is much more solemn and gloomy.' The ship may have seemed overcrowded at times, but after the death of even just one man the vessel felt uncannily empty.

How unimaginably awful it must have been, then, for Almira Almy, who kept the official logbook when she voyaged on the *Roscoe* in 1860. She wrote such stirring items as, 'Thursday Feb 2nd First part light winds and cloudy from NE course SSE...' right from the start of the voyage (8 November 1859) until the day following this entry.

On 3 February 1860 her husband William and son George were both drowned, killed by a whale along with six men. There is no entry for that date in the *Roscoe* logbook. That part of the page is left eloquently blank.

It is little wonder, then, that the wives hated to see their husbands go off in the boats. Many skippers shipped a fourth mate and stopped on board to direct the chase from the masthead, but others, like John Deblois, couldn't resist the urge to take part in the battle with the whales. The terror Henrietta Deblois felt when John was down must have been almost unbearable. A huge sperm whale that he harpooned in October 1856 'spouted red blood and made directly for the ship,' she wrote, and then confessed, 'The feeble company on board was most terribly frightened for the safety of the ship.'

No matter how hard she tried, she could not ignore the memory of the whale that had sunk the *Ann Alexander*, back in August 1851: for her, the whales were 'monsters' indeed. In May 1857, she wrote, 'I pray God that all may be preserved, but it does truly need great courage to go and capture a whale.'

Charles Stetson not only lowered, but left his wife Elizabeth in charge of the ship when he was off either chasing or gamming. 'Washed in the morning,' she wrote on 13 August 1861. 'Laid down. Got up and went on deck to take down my clothes and while I was there (Captain Stetson) Mr Sylvia raised whales...Thank God, have got three...*I treated all hands.*' Success did not ease her fears, however: in November, when she saw a boat stoven by an attacking whale, she threw a fit.

The problems that confronted the first-time whaling wives did not stop with fears of accident and death, either. While the yarns told at home might have prepared them for the dangers of the chase and capture, they could not possibly have been ready for the callous nature of the business. They knew perfectly well that they could not go home until the ship was full with whale-oil and whalebone — but they surely did not expect to feel so

Lowering for right whales, an illustration from the log book of the bark *Richmond*.

scrry for the whales.

A cow whale has a very strong mothering instinct, and won't abandon her calf until he or she is dead. The whalemen sought to take full advantage of this by harpooning the baby without killing it, so that its cries and convulsions kept the mother within range of the irons. One whaleman, Ellsworth West, wrote that he once saw a calf being born. He 'ironed the little fellow before he was truly alive,' he casually recorded.

This cruel practice was not restricted to the bays where the whales gathered seasonally to breed, but happened in the open seas as well. In November 1858, in latitude 22.30 North, longitude 24.50 West, Eliza Williams recorded that 'the first Mate came alongside with one [sperm whale], a cow whale. . .This one, the Mate told me, had a very small calf. I must say I was sorry to hear it. The poor little thing could not keep up with the rest, the mother would not leave it and lost her life. He says they exhibit the most affection for their young of any dumb animal he ever saw. This one had a number of scars from fighting.'

The custom was wasteful as well as callous. Not only did the killing or orphaning of a calf mean one less adult whale in future seasons, but often the ploy did not even succeed in its aim. In July 1853 a boat from the *Phoenix* harpooned a calf but lost the cow. 'Poor little creature they kill'd it for the sake of its Mother,' wrote Betsy Morey, the captain's wife, 'and they was unfortunate enough to lose the Mother under the Ice. Oh! it does seem so Cruel.'

Once the whale was dead, however, it was easier for the women to be philosophical about the business. A corpse was a corpse, no matter how huge, and getting oil and bone was the reason for the voyage. Before the products of that whale were safely stowed on board, however, the filthy, hellish, nauseating business of taking the fat off the corpse and then turning the huge masses of stinking, oozing blubber into oil had to be accomplished.

# Cutting in and trying out
## A sperm whale head being cut

Harriet Swain saw her first sperm whale in November 1853. 'Although it was quite a small one it was quite a sight to us *Greenies*,' she wrote. It was a forty barrel whale – roughly 40 feet long; a hundred barrel whale (a rare prize) was fully as long as the ship. The men secured the great corpse to the starboard side, and then the cutting stage – a narrow platform on pivots – was lowered over the whale, and the officers lined up on it. Harriet took a seat 'in the boat where I could see them cut': this was the boat that was slung from the starboard quarter of the ship, and it made a very fine grandstand which was utilised by many of the wives and children for viewing the action.

The officers had long-handled cutting 'spades' which they first of all used to cut off the whale's head. This, in a sperm whale, was divided into two parts, the 'case' and the 'junk'. From the junk came spermaceti, a fibrous fat that was used in the manufacture of candles and fine ointments. The case contained a reservoir of fine, clear, most valuable oil. These two parts were separated, and then a hole was bored into the case, and the liquid was scooped out with a bucket.

## A right whale head hauled up

In place of junk and case and toothed lower jaw, the head of a right whale held great masses of baleen. The mouth of an adult right whale was so huge that it could easily encompass a man – as Tom Williams wished to prove one day in December 1858, when he told his wife to walk into a right whale head that had been brought in on deck. For once Eliza mutinied, for 'it was very wet and dirty from the rain. One cannot imagine without seeing it, how the mouth looks,' she penned. 'Those long slabs of bone, set as thick together in the jaw as they can be...they tell me it is not at all uncommon to see them 15 or 20 feet long...[all with] hair on the edge, making the whole of the mouth lined with hair...

'I could not imagine for what purpose this hair was, till my Husband explained to me...' she wrote. 'The whale moves along with his mouth open and draws in large quantities of [krill] and it is strained through this hair. It seems singular that such fine food should have been formed for so large a fish. These fish are truly one of the wonderful works of God and well may we think that everything in the deep is wonderful.'

According to legend right whales were called 'right' because they did not sink when killed. However, this was by no means always true – as hundreds of infuriated journal entries testify. On 17 September 1871, for instance, Lucy Smith's husband George killed a right whale 'then came on board to take care of the ship, the other boats commenced towing had got but a short distance when the whale sunk,' she recorded; 'they have been trying to sink irons into it [to haul it up] but could not.' Despite such frustrations, however, hunting the right whale was considered worth it – simply because the baleen in their mouths was 'right' for making corset busks, in a time when absurdly tiny waists were all the fashion.

## The first blanket strip being hauled away from the carcass

Once the head was cut off and the valuable parts brought in on deck, the officers concentrated on stripping the blubber from the body. The thick fat was marked (scarfed) with a deep continuous cut that wound about the carcass in spiral fashion, and then a man was lowered by a rope onto the bobbing carcass, to lodge a huge blubber hook into a hole that had been hacked into the head end of the scarf. This was always most suspenseful. The dead whale was like a tremendous greasy log, leaking blood and slime that attracted a frenzy of voracious sharks. When Susan McKenzie was watching her husband and his crew cut in a whale in January 1870 she was horrified to see the fin chain that secured the whale give way, knocking the man on the 'monkey rope' into the water. 'The sharks at the time were very numerous all round the ship,' she wrote, but happily he emerged unhurt.

Understandably, once the blubber hook was lodged, the man on the rope was hauled up swiftly. Then work commenced on the windlass. This drew up the cutting falls, which were attached to the main mast at one end and to the blubber hook in the whale at the other. As the men heaved at the handles the falls creaked and groaned, wrenching at the thick strip of blubber, trying to haul it up off the whale. At the same time the officers on the staging plank jabbed at the junction of blubber and body, hacking away with the razor-sharp spades.

Then at last the fibres began to tear free, so that the long thick 'blanket strip' pulled up and away from the unrolling carcass, like the peel coming off an orange.

## The stage and two shipbound blanket strips

When the blanket strip rose all the way up to the mainmast and could go no further, it was severed with a huge swordlike 'boarding knife' and another blubber strip was started. Cutting blubber was demanding work. 'Fred has been over the stage cutting the whale in since six o'clock this morning,' wrote Sarah Cole one evening in January 1860; 'tonight he is so tired he can hardly speak.'

The process was also disgusting. When Henrietta Deblois arrived on deck during cutting in, October 1856, she found all the crew as 'busy as bees' but, 'I looked everywhere for some person bearing resemblance to my better half, but without success,' she wrote. 'I could occasionally hear orders given in what appeared to be his voice, [then] at last a face appeared above the rail which was quite familiar, excepting the dirt, and the owner of it sprang over it, and such a looking man!'

Henrietta herself found the butchering of the whale so bloody and gross that the sight made her vomit. However, John liked to have her in view, so she dutifully remained on deck. 'Never mind,' she wrote, 'this dirt will bring him clean money' – and then she distanced herself from the awful business by writing in her journal, penning long descriptions of the flocks of birds that gathered about the ship to grab crumbs of meat from the oily pool that slowly spread over the bloodstreaked sea.

## A blanket strip being heaved inboard, captain in charge

Meanwhile the heavy, oozing blubber strips had to be manhandled in over the rail. Despite the arduous nature of the task, it seems that the men worked with a cheerful will – perhaps because they all had a share in the profits of the voyage (the 'lay') and could calculate how much of this giant prize would be theirs. As one whaling wife, Annie Ricketson, put it once, the job was all 'hurrah boys'.

In rough weather, however, cutting in became a nightmare. In December 1855 the *Nantucket* men battled a rugged sea to take a whale to the ship, 'the wind blowing very strong; got it alongside about 4 PM secured it the best that could be, wind still blowing very strong the ship labouring hard with a heavy

swell.' At 10 o'clock the chains parted and the men fought the gale to secure the carcass with lines – and then, at two-thirty in the morning, the ropes broke, so that boats had to be lowered to get the whale back.

'Eight PM,' wrote Almira Gibbs next evening; 'the head is not in yet the wind blowing very strong and a heavy sea thick and looks rainy lightning all over the horizon; can do nothing more with [the head] tonight than make it fast alongside, it has been very hard work.'

The second dawn arrived with more of the same. The men lost the most valuable part of the head despite strenuous efforts, but struggled on to save the blanket pieces. 'It is very rough,' she noted, 'and hard to work on the decks being oily one can hardly stand on their feet.'

## Blubber coming in and being lowered

As each blubber strip arrived inboard it was lowered into the 'blubber room' in the waist, between decks. There it was cut up into large chunks called 'horse-pieces' by a gang of greasy and bloodied men. 'Oh such a greasy mess...' wrote Annie Ricketson on the schooner *Pedro Varela* in November 1881, 'and the sun is so hot.' The oil ran out of the blubber while they were hacking the horse-pieces, because of the heat that was trapped between decks. This made the conditions more treacherous than ever: 'The grease is running on deck and there is a terrible mess of it,' she penned next day, 'and it smells very bad.'

Not surprisingly, she did not go up on deck on the third day: 'have not felt very well,' she confessed.

## Mincing blubber

The horse-pieces, once cut, were handed up to a gang that chopped the fat up thinly but left the piece connected on one edge, so that the chunk resembled a book – the pages of which were nicknamed 'Bible leaves' because of the 'spine' of black skin. This made the piece give up its oil more easily, once it was in the trypots.

'All hands look happy and greasy,' recorded Mary Brewster when the crew of the *Tiger* was cutting in the first whale of the voyage on 18 June 1846. 'Two men between decks in the blubber room with spades cutting it up in pieces. Two more stand by the hatch and take it in tubs; when full drag it forward where stands a man with a mincing board and knife where it is sliced up in small thin slices.' Shortly after

this date a mincing machine was invented, which made the process much easier. 'I have been On Deck...' penned Betsy Morey of the ship *Phoenix* in November 1853, 'and Also saw the Minceing Mashine in Opperation and I should think it was A verry great improvement.'

Once several tubs of minced pieces were ready, the signal was given for another gang to begin the process of 'trying out', or boiling the blubber to extract the oil. This was accomplished in the tryworks, a furnace built aft of the fore mast, with two or three huge cauldrons – or 'trypots' – set into the brickwork. The fires in the furnace were started with wood. The first few horse-pieces of blubber were boiled in fresh water, and soon produced enough oil to keep the process going as more pieces were fed into the pots.

## Blubber on deck

If the whale was large, or several had been taken, the blubber, inevitably, began to pile up on deck, in a welter of grease, slime and blood. It was no place for a woman, for walking anywhere was hazardous.

'Such a pile of blubber as there is on deck now,' Henrietta Deblois exclaimed. 'It looks firstrate,' she penned loyally, 'only I must acknowledge rather dirty.' Inevitably the tarry grease exuded by the raw blubber was tracked into every part of the ship, even as far as the floors of the after cabins. 'Our vessel is the dirtiest place I ever saw,' Lucy Smith wrote irritably on the *Nautilus* in July 1870. Her little boy Freddie was 'in the midst of everything, as dirty as a little pig, then rubbing around me [and] together with what I get from the ship my clothes are too dirty to take any kind of [sewing] work on.'

## A whaleship trying out

Once the oil had been extracted from the blubber, hunks of fibrous connective tissue floated to the top of the cauldrons. The whalemen called these 'scraps', and scooped them out with a sieve and used them as fuel for the tryworks fires once the wood had burned out. This oily mess produced a thick rancid smoke when burning that blackened everything it touched.

The flames produced were very high and brilliant, reddening the underside of the great drifts of smoke, lighting up the night sky for miles. By legend a British man-of-war once hailed a whaler which was boiling oil, demanding to know what the devil they were all about. 'Trying,' replied the sweating whalemen. 'Trying?' echoed the man-of-war commander in astonishment. 'Trying what — to set your ship on fire?'

Another time, when the old *Andrew Hicks* was boiling during the 1908 voyage, Lottie Church noted that a 'steamer came to us and wanted to know if we wanted assistance'. The crew of the *Andrew Hicks* did not. The irritation of the Good Samaritan skipper when he found that the 'ship afire' was merely a whaler about whaling business can be easily imagined.

Perhaps he mumbled, 'Stinking spouter' — for a whaleship in the throes of trying out surely stank most foully, too. 'Had the try works going at half past ten,' wrote Annie Ricketson. 'Everything is greasy and smoky and such a disagreeable smell.'

The explorer D'Urville described the stink as 'a thick nauseating smell of burning fat'. By repute a whaling vessel a-boiling could be seen for fifteen miles day and night, and scented for five downwind.

No female, even if raised on a farm, could have seen anything like the huge shapeless chunks of fat and flesh that were hauled inboard with such fierce labour, or the great clots of black blood that bobbed about in pools of grease. Even those women who lived near the candleworks of New Bedford would never have smelled anything to match the thick nauseating smoke that billowed sluggishly from the tryworks chimneys, or could have anticipated the insidious oozing of the deck planks, as the oil washed in slimy fashion higher and higher up the bulwarks.

English whalemen called the trypots 'boilers' and called the boiling oil 'the stink', which seems hardly surprising. What is astounding is that the American whalemen celebrated the boiling of the thousandth barrel of the voyage by frying up doughnuts in that very same oil. 'At 7 PM boats got fast to a whale at 9 got him to the ship,' wrote Mary Brewster on 26 July 1846. 'Men all singing and bawling *Doughnuts* Doughnuts tomorrow as this will certainly make us 1,000 bbls and it is a custom among the whalemen a bache of doughnuts to every thousand.' On the *Tiger* the cook provided the dough and the men fried it themselves in the seething trypots, but when the *Merlin* boiled out the thousandth barrel in August 1858, Henrietta Deblois took part in the fun.

'Today has been our doughnut fare, the first we have ever had,' she wrote. 'The Steward, Boy and myself have been at work all the morning. We fried or boiled three tubs for the forecastle — one for the steerage. In the afternoon about one tub full for the cabin and right good were they too, not the least taste of oil — they came out of the pots perfectly dry. The skimmer was so large that they could take out a ½ of a peck at a time. I enjoyed it mightily.'

There was little else about the process to be enjoyed. Even those women who rejoiced when the first whales were taken on a weekday were disillusioned, for more often than not the work those whales created carried over to the sabbath, simply because it took so long to process one reasonably large whale. The men on the *Nantucket* took a whale on Saturday 7 December 1855, and so, of course, were cutting in on the sabbath. 'The ship hove to cutting in the whale although it is Sunday all hands are very hard to work...' wrote Almira Gibbs, and then added in justification, 'It is hard work to get whales when we are fortunate enough to get one it must be taken care of as soon as possible and I don't know that it is wrong in such a case if the sabbath day is made a day of toil.'

Taking several whales at one time guaranteed at least one hard-working Sunday. 'Another sabbath has gone never to return,' Lucy Smith penned in August 1870; 'it has not seemed like a day of rest, all hands have been busy boiling out and stowing down...Oh how I long for a quiet sabbath.' Other wives were stricken with unexpected guilt: 'Employed setting up shooks and boiling,' wrote Harriet Bliven on the same bark *Nautilus* nearly five years earlier, in December 1865. 'I took my work and went on deck and Sewed about two hours before I knew it was the Sabbath.'

The mundane worries were perhaps even worse than the spiritual, for there was so much about the process to make a wife feel nervous. Rough weather made an anxious situation almost unbearable. 'I thought it was

impossible for them to work at all with the waves dashing up against the
Ship and those huge monsters moving up and down in the water, sometimes
so covered that you could scarcely see them,' Eliza Williams wrote in
November 1858. 'But they worked on and did not cease. There was a complete
din of noises on deck — the wind, the rain, the Officers shouting to the men.'

Trying out was equally precarious. During rugged weather the boiling
oil slopped over the sides of the cauldrons and into the fire. There was a

## Cleaning whalebone

The business of preparing the products of a
right whale for market did not stop with
coopering and stowing down the oil. The
baleen from the mouth had to be scraped and
cleaned, an arduous and unpleasant and smelly
task. It was worth it, however: as well as being
the stuff that held corsets in shape, whalebone
was used for buggy whips and umbrella spokes;
in industry it was the 'spring steel' of that age.

The bundles of bone had to be taken out of
the place where they had been stored every
now and then, and aired in the sun to prevent
mould. 'We are drying and bundling bone
today,' wrote Adra Ashley when the *Reindeer*

was on the way home in February 1860, 'and I
have been on deck to see it. It looks like a
Forest the slabs standing up against the rail,
their fringing tops swayed to and fro by the
breeze, like the leafy branches of woodland
trees.' Then, on a more practical note, she
added, 'I have also been down into the Steerage
today for the first time. That is at present the
bone room and the Boatsteerers have taken up
their abode in the forecastle.'

The boatsteerers may not have enjoyed
living with the common seamen, but it is
unlikely that any of them would have
complained: the proceeds of the valuable bone,
like the oil, were divided into shares, so that
such a good cargo meant an extra good share
for each man.

shallow tank set under the furnace to contain this, but a crack in a pot put the ship at terrible risk. On 28 July, 1879, when Carrie Turner voyaged on the *Napoleon*, she recorded that she and her husband Charles 'were awakened about half past four o'clock [by men] holowering fire. It frightened me dreadfully,' she confessed. 'Charlie got up and went on deck as soon as possible he found the deck all on fire oil came out of the tripots and set it afire I could see the blaze in bed through one of the lites it frightened me so that I had quite a cry. . . if it had been a strong breeze we never could have saved the ship the men throwed water on and put it out and oh wasent I thankful.'

Stowing down the oil in the hold was equally fearful, especially in a rugged sea. 'Herbert was down in the hole all day,' wrote Mary Colson on 20 December 1877. 'I felt sick and nervous enough.'

'It is very encouraging to get some oil,' she wrote a week earlier, 'but it is such awful hard work. I think this is an awful business any way and I hope we shall get money enough this voyage so we shall not have to come again.' And it was an awful business indeed, far worse than the women at home could possibly have imagined. After two days of cutting in the entire ship ran with grease — and stank most foully, for whales decay very fast once dead, and the quality of the stench matches the size of the carcass. Everything above and below decks became polluted, and it was worse than hopeless to try to keep clean.

'I felt very uncomfortable for several hours to see my things so spoilt and in such a condition,' confessed Mary Brewster in August 1849 after a desperate attempt to dry her clothes after a storm during trying out. It was a common complaint, on a ship that was as dirty as a whaler at work. All the women hated to see their pretty things ruined; many of them struggled against great odds to keep as 'nice' on board as they did at home, and wept when they did not succeed.

The clothes that they wore (in an age when it took ten full yards to make a dress) did not make a hard task any easier. 'I wish you could step on board for a short time,' Susan Fisher wrote to her friends in August 1854 while the men on the *Cowper* were cutting in; 'you would see *doings*,' she promised, ' but you would need Bloomer costume and high boots to be able to get through it.' The tunic-and-pants suit devised by the women's rightist Amelia Bloomer would certainly have been more practical than the voluminous skirts of the time, and a few wives were strong-minded enough to try them: Harriet Bliven made herself Bloomer outfits on the *Nautilus* in 1865.

However, most wives wore dresses, even if they were the shortened 'wash dresses' that they wore at home for doing the laundry, and all of them kept good gowns on board to wear when gamming and when in port. Being a longtime mariner did not make a woman less interested in the latest fad: Elizabeth Stetson tried to wear hoop skirts on board when she found that hoops were all the rage, and the cooper was forever mending them until she got tired of getting stuck in doorways.

When the bark *A.R. Tucker* made port in Barbados in April 1874 Annie Ricketson wanted to go to church but did not, for 'I had nothing that was nice enough to wear,' she sadly recounted. She had been at sea almost exactly three years, and, 'They dress very stylish here.' Being in fashion was one of the things about home that the women missed the most, and however philosophical they might be about dressing on board, they were constantly making new clothes to wear on social occasions.

The wives stored their good clothes in trunks and took them out at frequent intervals to air and iron them, for if they did not take this precaution the sea air ruined them swiftly. In January 1860 Sarah Cole brought all her shoes on deck 'and cleaned the mold off of them and dried them. It is so damp that almost everything molds,' she sighed. 'It is of no use for any one to bring anything nice to sea.'

Lucy Ann Crapo advised her sister Ruth Ellen that 'anything that will not show the dirt, is best for ship. If I want to go again,' she continued,

## Charlotte Jernegan

Nathan Jernegan of Martha's Vineyard, who skippered the *Niger* on the 1852-6 voyage, was a jovial fellow who became as lonely as the rest of them. 'The captain down below playing on a accordeon for the first time,' recorded the third mate, Mr Maxfeld, on 25 October 1852; 'I guess he's homesick tonight.' The ship had been outward bound for just ten days. 'We have a fine ship Capt officers and crew,' Maxfeld decided in December, 'That is some comfort anyhow to drive away homesickness.' Nathan and his men were exceedingly sociable, and delighted in 'A regular Vineyard gamm' which usually involved 'Plenty of gas blowed and Rum drunk'. However, it seemed a very long voyage and it is little wonder that Nathan carried his wife Charlotte along next time, on the same ship, leaving New Bedford in September 1856.

A story told about Charlotte illustrates the peculiar isolation of the whaling folk and just how long they were away from home. When the *Niger* arrived back in New Bedford on 14 August 1860, Nathan went on shore to make his report to the agent. When he at length returned on board Charlotte was waiting impatiently, all dressed up in her best, hoop-skirt and all, eager to get back to Union Street, William Street, and all the smart places that she remembered.

Nathan, however, was slow to move; he looked puzzled and was scratching his head. 'I don't know what it is,' quoth he, 'danged if I do, but the women on shore sure don't look the same.' When Charlotte questioned him further, she learned nothing more, for he

couldn't quite put his finger on it. Once in the carriage and heading up Union Street, however, Charlotte saw the change in a blink. The women, to her consternation, had a different silhouette altogether, for hoopskirts had gone out of fashion.

She was as resourceful as any other whaling man or woman, however. The hoops were swiftly ripped out and tossed over the stern of the carriage. The hack drew up to the Parker House hotel, the steps were unfolded and the door opened with a flourish. Charlotte descended to the street with marvellous dignity – and tripped over the slack in her skirts.

'I would like to have dresses made of dark goods and wear as long as decent, and then leave them ashore and have enough to last no matter how cheap the material, better than to wash.' Everything mildewed, even the sails on the yards, because of the dampness and the so-called *bilge*. 'I am sewing, and the *Louisa* is bilging,' Lucy Ann penned in March 1867. 'The steward trying to clean paint, but it only makes a bad matter worse.'

All facets of personal cleanliness were problematical, because fresh water was so often scarce. Henrietta Deblois took a salt water bath several times a week, while Harriet Allen coped with the corner of a towel soaked in water and rum. However, doing the laundry was the major problem. 'This day had my first experience in washing on Board Ship,' wrote Sallie Smith on 19 July 1875. 'I don't like it mutch,' she admitted — and all the wives would have agreed.

Managing a tub on a rolling ship was bad enough — 'pretty hard work,' wrote Sallie during rugged weather in October, 'the gale washed faster than I did' — but the lack of good soap and fresh water made a hard task horrid. 'I should like some clean rainwater very much,' wrote Almira Gibbs wistfully, but when rain did fall she was not allowed to 'go to washing . . . [for] the Capt thinks once a week is enough and I have to obey orders.'

## Lucy Vincent Smith

Lucy Vincent Smith was a perfect Yankee lady of unblemished rectitude — and no one knew it better than Lucy herself. She was industrious, pious and extremely strong-minded. She first met George Smith on 19 June 1859: two days later, on the 21st, he proposed. They were married on 17 July. She declared she was devoted to her husband — but that didn't stop her from signing him up for a new voyage before he'd even got home from the last one.

Perhaps this was the reason he insisted on taking her along, on the bark *Nautilus* in October 1869. Going to sea did not disconcert Lucy in the slightest, however. 'I went determined to be happy,' she reminisced in her journal, and determined she was indeed. She did have the occasional quarrel with the first officer, Mr Holmes, who, she declared, was 'very ignorant of the rules of good breeding', but on the whole she kept herself happily occupied. She learned to navigate, steered on occasion, and filled in the rest of the time by sewing and mending everything in sight, from sails to shirts, from signals to stockings.

She also kept herself clean, a virtue indeed considering the difficult conditions. Other whaling wives did not manage nearly so well.

And so it seems that Sunday was for rest and Monday was for washing – and that Richard Gibbs was a domestic Jehovah. However, surprisingly enough, the husbands were usually ready to help their wives with the awful job. In September 1860 John Marble and his wife Elizabeth washed, and by the end of the day 'our hands are sower enough I can assure you,' she penned. In between washes Fred Smith, who was an enthusiastic scrimshander, made whalebone clothes pins for Sallie.

There were plenty of ropes about a ship, and a clothes line could be slung just about anywhere. The breeze was a hazard, and some wives stitched the clothes on the line. However the spray often meant that the washing flapped about without getting dry. 'Pleasant but not drying,' Henrietta Deblois recorded. 'Clothes brought down in my room as wet as when they were put out.' There were other hazards, too: 'Lost my purple calico overboard,' she wrote in June 1857. During the previous wash she had suffered the embarrassment of losing 'an undergarment' to the breeze. Harriet Peirce, the captain's daughter on the *Emerald*, recorded on 12 September 1857 that when one of her baby sister's 'aprons fell overboard they lowered a boat and in doing so stove it against one of the cranes. But they did not get the apron,' she added.

'This morning spoke the *Canton*, [Captain] Lapham,' she wrote in her journal in January 1871. Captain Lapham had his wife and daughter on board, so he invited George (pictured right) and Lucy to his ship for a gam. Lucy fetched out a clean dress for her visit but to her surprise, before she'd had a chance to change, Mrs Lapham and daughter arrived at the *Nautilus*, all in a rush.

'I wanted to see how you live,' Mrs Lapham declared. She was a very sad and gloomy looking female, dishevelled in appearance, and her daughter looked little better. They had been four months at sea and had loathed it. 'Do you comb your hair every day?' Mrs Lapham demanded.

Lucy, as she recorded later in her memoirs, felt most taken aback at this. She said, 'Always,' and then added rather loftily, 'But I was going to rearrange it before you arrived.'

'Well,' quoth Mrs Lapham with a martyred sigh, 'I'd hate to tell you when I did mine last.' Then she said in the same accusatory tones, 'You're wearing a white collar.'

'Well, yes,' admitted Lucy. 'I like to wear a collar or a ruching, and I change it every day, and I change my calico dress for a clean one about every week too. In fact,' she pointed out somewhat righteously, 'I did not think the dress I am wearing decent enough to go gamming in, so there is another lying on my bed, but you gave me no chance to change.'

This, as Lucy remembered it, reduced Mrs Lapham to silence for quite some moments. Then: 'Well,' Mrs Lapham declared, 'I hate to say it, but the one I'm wearing now is the one I've worn ever since home, for 'tis the only one I've got round to unpacking.'

'And,' Lucy observed dryly in her memoir, 'it was very easy to believe it, too.'

Ironing was the best means of drying and preventing mildew, but ironing, on a pitching ship, was a hard and dangerous job. Most wives ironed on the cabin table or on a little table in the room in the house, but that longtime mariner, Elizabeth Stetson, knew better: she ironed on the cabin floor.

Recipe for soap

1 lb castile soap
1¼ lb soda
6c worth borax
add 5 pts water and let it simmer till it is all dissolved, take it off and add 9 pts water cold and let it cool. – Almira Gibbs.

Washing and ironing when the ship was boiling or cutting in were, obviously, so doomed to failure that the tasks were best abandoned until the whole awful process was over – which meant that the laundry might be neglected for weeks. Even more daunting, however, was the task of cleaning up the ship, once the trying out was done.

This was a job for the entire crew. First the decks were scraped with jack knives, and then holystoned with bricks and sand, the sand mixed with lye from the tryworks ashes. Then tubs of salt water were hauled over the bow to rinse down the planks, which were afterwards squee-geed with mops made of rope-yarn. When dry, the decks had to be swept again, for the spun-yarn broke up and left shreds between the planks.

Meantime the grease-sodden whaling clothes were soaking in the urine barrel. The dungarees were then dropped overboard on lines, and towed behind the ship for a good rinsing, and, after that, they were boiled up in the trypots in salt water and ley. Finally, as Mary Brewster described it, 'the rigging [was] hung full, a few garments floating which had taken flight overboard to save more washing' – and then . . .

And then, the ship settled down into the same old routine, cruising about, looking all the time for another of the whale kind.

'A whaleman's life is a hard life,' Sarah Cole philosophised in January 1860; 'it is either all work or all play.' It was a strange existence, for when there was no whaling business going on and storms kept their distance, there was very little to do on board ship. Merchant vessels sailed as fast as they could, and when they arrived at a port the voyage was done and that job was over. Not so on a whaler. Like the aircraft of today that fly slowly back and forth, searching for lost shipping, a whaling vessel cruised a whaling ground, sailing to and fro in an endless search pattern, quartering the sea in the hunt for whales – and when whales were nowhere to be seen, life became mindlessly boring.

Theoretically, the men had shipwork. Whaleships were so over-manned, however, that the routine jobs that could easily be accomplished by a dozen men had to be stretched to occupy thirty, and despite all the 'make-work' that the officers could devise – such as pulling pieces of old rope apart and then spinning the fibres into rope-yarn – there were still many empty hours to be filled.

'The watch employed in loafing what could find nothing better to do,' recorded Dan Lincoln, steward of the ship *Coral*, in November 1847. The men sang and talked and read and traded stories, and occupied themselves with the traditional sailor crafts of macramé and modelling. The whalemen developed another kind of handiwork too, one that is peculiar to the species, the art of scrimshaw.

The material for this was ready to hand. 'I went up on deck this afternoon,' wrote Annie Ricketson on the *Pedro Varela* in July 1882, 'and they were cutting out the teeth [from a sperm whale jaw]. They cut them right off with a strip of meat on them and in two or three days you can pull them right out.' Once the teeth were clean, the men etched thumbnail sketches on them, which they then stained with lamp black. Flat parts of the jawbone formed the ground for more such pictures, and other men used jack knives and lathes to turn the thicker pieces into small artifacts, which were often very pretty. Fred Smith was particularly keen on this hobby: Sallie recorded in January 1878 that 'Fred has made me some nice Crochet needles today,'

---

## Sallie Smith

Fred Smith was an artistic kind of fellow who was not just an enthusiastic scrimshander but also embellished his log with pictures of boisterous can-can dancers in dubious saloons. In view of this, it is perhaps surprising that he took his wife Sallie on voyage, but, judging by the poetry he also wrote in his journal on bark *Petrel* of New Bedford, 1871-74, he was certainly very fond of her.

Is 'The same dear face, the same old home —
'All the same as it used to be' — he pondered on voyage.

Sallie, for her part, seemed happy enough to sail. However, once she 'started life on the Ocean', on the *Ohio* on 6 July 1875, she found sea-life not only uncomfortable but also fiendishly boring. 'The men seem to find plenty of work,' she sighed in August 1876, 'but it is scarce with me.' The years dragged interminably: 'Oh for something to write about,' she penned in July 1877; 'I have nothing to do nor nothing to read which makes rather a lonesome life for me...' and two days later, 'Oh dear Oh dear what shall I do, everyone finds enough to do but me.'

Not surprisingly, when the familiar outlines of Buzzard's Bay were raised, on October 17, Sallie stopped up all night packing. Never had a woman left a ship so eagerly. Nevertheless, she opted for another 'trial in Whalein', on the *John P. West*, in 1882 — and was just as bored and aimless, with not nearly enough work to do. 'The same thing over & over,' she complained in November, 'sailing along south seeing nothing it is very monotoneous I have done a little of everything I have cut carpet rags and braided some I have made a pair of pants this week what shall I get into next' — and then, three days later, 'I finished the last braid for a mat shall sew it on another day I have to piece out my work if I don't it won't hold out for three years,' she wrote. If any woman failed to learn from experience, that person was Sallie Smith.

and then added, rather engagingly, 'and he has been learning how to use them.'

Other occupations were somewhat more eccentric. Fred Cole, on the *Vigilant* in February 1860, blew soap bubbles for recreation. 'If we don't get whales again soon,' wrote Sarah, 'I don't know what he will do with himself.' When life got boring on the *Catawba*, in May 1854, Obed Swain made a wooden weather vane in the shape of a man — for luck, hoped his wife, Harriet; 'It quite shines up,' she commented; 'he thinks he has done great things, grows rather childish in his old age.' Obed was so pleased with the result that he kept on making them. 'We are now well off for vanes,' Harriet dryly remarked a week later. Other men set about the accommodations, changing them about so drastically that some owners must have found it difficult to recognise their own property when the vessel at last arrived home.

On the *Vigilant* in 1861 Fred Cole turned the bed into a swinging one, and Nelson Waldron on the *Bowditch* in 1853 turned two rooms into one. 'Father has carpeted the floor and painted the table and so we have to eat off of the trunks,' penned Asenath Taber, the captain's daughter on the *Alice Frazier*, in January 1855. In October 1857 Almira Gibbs recorded that 'today we are having a clear-up day painting the staterooms and making some alteration in the Steward's pantry'. Then, two days later, 'Capt and myself painting our sleeping room today and putting it in a little order. We cannot make it look very nice,' she confessed, 'still a little paint improves it very much.'

Hammond, the detestable second mate of the bark *E. Corning*, developed an obsession with painting things and prowled about the ship with a brush in his hand. In May 1861 the stairs became 'stone colour', and in steady succession Elizabeth's washtubs became red, the water closet bright umber and the gangway brilliant blue. Many of the wives weren't above taking part in such games: they sewed curtains, flags, tablecloths and tidies. In October 1876 Sallie Smith made 'Spatterwork to Beautify & Adorn our Cabin. I guess it's beautiful now,' she hoped, 'only our Cellar leaks pretty bad.'

As time went by and the whales stayed out of sight the devices for amusement became almost desperate. 'The Capt employed in shaving the dog,' wrote Dan Lincoln, the steward of ship *Coral* on 26 October 1847, and then, on 19 November, 'The Capt got up the ships muskets and tried to shoot a Bird but to no purpose, the second mate shot one and the Capt shot a dead fish.' The officers on the *E. Corning* forgot to quarrel with Elizabeth Stetson for a little while, and instead they read her their letters. Describing dreams was common — and on all the ships, at some time or other, a preoccupation with weighing took place.

They weighed fish and they weighed potatoes, they weighed the hogs and dogs and they weighed each other. On the *Louisa* in April 1866, 'Wms weighed me...' Lucy Ann Crapo recorded; '127 lbs which is more than I ever weighed before.' Then he weighed the officers, and found that their aggregate weight was 900 pounds. 'Charlie weighed me,' recorded Carrie Turner on the *Napoleon* in February 1879. 'I weighed 155 pounds and he weighed 159, then he weighed the mate and then all the men so we had quite a weighing time.'

Harriet Swain weighed 95 pounds on the *Catawba* in March 1853. Emma McInnes on the *Josephine* weighed 89 pounds: 'Quite heavy for a sailor.' Lack of exercise tended to make them fat. 'Fred weighed me today,' wrote Sarah Cole on the *Vigilant* in January 1860. She weighed 121 pounds and he weighed 151, while when they sailed 'my weight was 105, and Fred's 148.' After four months on the *Phoenix* Betsy Morey weighed 142 pounds – 'Oh! what A buster,' she penned. 'I would like to see sister Maria now and hear her Exclaim O how fat you have grown.'

Lottie Church, who kept the official log on the *Andrew Hicks* in 1908, wrote about herself in the third person. 'Caught one flying fish and one Dauphin,' she wrote 19 May; 'Mrs Church ate all the flying fish and a large portion of Dauphin' – and then followed this up twelve days later with the dry comment that, 'Mrs Church weighs 2 lb more than Mr Gibbons [the mate].'

'I was wayed yesterday,' wrote Elizabeth Marble on the *Awashonks* in April 1860, 'and I wayed One hundred and twelve pounds, George [her son] wayed just fifty and my dog Wash forty five.' This weighing was certainly something to write about, but the preoccupation was always whaling. When Charlotte Dehart's baby son Alexander was weighed at the age of three months his weight, as she proudly recorded, was 'twenty barrels' exactly.

'I hope we will see Sperm Whales soon,' a seaman once wrote. 'If we don't, I don't know but what I shall go off the handle.' The boredom and ineffectuality, however, were most taxing for the wives. Women of that time expected to be busy; it was part of the Puritan work ethic. Their work at home might be arduous and repetitive, but at least it made them feel important. On board ship they were not important at all, because their presence was superfluous – and, perhaps even more mortifying than that, they had no set jobs to do, and this in a time when a popular proverb was *Satan makes work for idle hands*. Satan had scope indeed, for a four years' voyage stretched interminably ahead of them, with a steward to (technically) do the cleaning and a cook to prepare the meals and, more often than not, a boy to wait at the table.

'Myself lonesome enough employed in knitting hardly know what to do with myself,' wrote Almira Gibbs in October 1855 – and she'd only been out from home four months. 'Oh for something to write about,' sighed Sallie Smith in July 1877; 'I have nothing to do nor nothing to read which makes rather a lonesome life for me.' Elizabeth Stetson took more than a hundred books on board and exchanged them as she went along; she was a romantic, and her favourite author was the love-story writer Grace Aquilar. 'If I could not read I don't know what I should do,' wrote Almira Gibbs.

Just like the men, the women were forced to entertain themselves with handiwork. Tatting, lacemaking and crocheting were popular, and the women exchanged patterns eagerly when gamming with each other. Annie Ricketson spent a large part of her 1881 voyage on the *Pedro Varela* in making a 'Job's trouble quilt'. Knitting was more difficult. 'I wore out my dress and my elbows are sore from hanging on so that I might knit,' wrote Lucy Ann Crapo to her sister on 15 January 1878, and then added on a passionate note,

## Lottie Church

'This day sighted Norfolk Island,' runs the entry for 8 March 1907 in the official logbook of the bark *Andrew Hicks*; 'at 9 a.m. Capt Church and wife went on shore in the whaleboat' – and if the reader did not know better, it would be impossible to tell that this entry was written by the captain's wife herself.

The ship's logbook was a precise and formal affair, a requirement of the law and correspondingly boring. The first officer (the 'mate') was the fellow who usually landed the tedious job of keeping it up to date. Occasionally, however, perhaps because the mate could not read and write, the captain took over the job of keeping the book...or handed it over to his wife. 'Harry Green off duty,' wrote Charlotte ('Lottie') Church in May 1907. 'He cut his foot while rendering blubber. Captain Church put two stiches in it and dressed the wound.'

By describing this incident in such emotionless style, Lottie Church conformed most dutifully to the accepted form of logbook keeping. The logkeeper was instructed to keep his comments to the four basics: weather, wind, sails and whales. The sea-log day began at noon and ended at noon, and was divided into three parts: 'First Part', noon to eight in the evening, 'Second Part', eight to four in the morning, and 'Latter Part', four to noon the next day. The weather and any incidents were noted under those three headings, and the entries were brief and terse, so that storms, reefs, ferocious whales and belligerent natives were treated alike, as mere small incidents in a working day.

It is impossible to guess how many wives were landed with this boring task. If it were not for the fact that Sarah Jane Slocum and Maria Clark wrote their names in their books, it would be impossible to guess that the accounts had not been kept by men – simply because, like Lottie Church, if they mentioned themselves at all, they did it in the third person.

And yet, somehow, Lottie Church's personality diffused into the books she kept, along with more than a hint of a boisterous sense of humour. 'Capt – Mr Gibbons & Mr Enos and Mrs Church made a keg of beer today,' she wrote on 24 June 1908, conveying an impression of a right merry set indeed. Lottie was the daughter of a San Francisco Bay pilot, so had the sea in her veins. 'Caught three small fish,' she dryly recorded July 13; 'Mrs Church eat them all – Cat eat up remains.'

On 2 August 'Major Cat passed away – This a.m. prepared Major for burial,' she penned – but, unlike the cat, and despite severe asthma, Lottie Church kept on going: she went on several whaling voyages with her husband, each time signing on as assistant navigator. She was one of the select group of *Charles W. Morgan* wives, sailing on that historic vessel – where this family photograph with daughter Dorothy was taken – from 1909 to 1913.

'I began to think seriously of some place where I might find rest, in fact came nigh to the conclusion that I had been whaling enough, and thought I would write to you and every one of my friends that was liable to a trial, to never, never undertake it.'

The easiest and most popular female activity was sewing, and so much time was consumed by this that some of the female journals (such as Mary Stickney's on the *Cicero*) are little more than lists of sewing accomplished. Their biggest problem was not having enough material. 'I finished the last braid for a mat,' Sallie Smith wrote in November 1882; 'shall sew it on another day I have to piece out my work if I don't it won't hold out for three years...I have more time than work,' she sighed a month later, and finally became so desperate that she 'ripped up' her wedding dress for something to sew.

There were a few other amusements: Mary Brewster and her husband, William, took turns to read aloud to each other, John and Emma McInnes played dominoes and 'fox and geese'; Charlie and Carrie Turner sang so sweetly on the deck of the *Napoleon* in the evenings that the crew used to creep aft to hear them. But all the time the drear months dragged, and as the whales stayed out of sight the boredom became unendurable and tempers became frayed.

Lucy Ann Crapo noted on the *Louisa* in January 1867 that they were 'Still cruising for whales but do not find them. Countenances grow long, and wrinkles accumulate,' she recorded. Next month, 'the "blue disease" begins to manifest itself in some of our number,' she wrote, 'hope it will not prove serious.' Not taking whales could prove more serious than her joking tone indicates: the ships set out from home with only about four gallons of oil to keep the lamps going until the first whale was taken, and often those whales were not raised in time.

This happened in December 1854, on the *Cape Horn Pigeon*. Almira Almy recorded that her husband William was forced to go on board the *Mary Wilder* to beg a few gallons. 'Rather discouraging,' she wrote, 'six months out and so poor as to be obliged to go to the neighbours to get some oil to burn.' When Eleanor Baker was on the *Gazelle* they caught a shark and boiled its liver for oil for the lamps, and the men on the *Louisa* took a turtle for the same reason.

'Very little oil I don't know what the owners will say we cannot help it...' wrote Almira Gibbs in November 1857; 'it was whales we came for not for the pleasure of living on the water four or five years.' As the aimless months went by the cruelty, danger and filth of whaling were all forgotten, in the overriding desire to fill up the ship with oil and get back home. 'I want to see the Oil coming along that this long dreary voyage may be ended,' wrote Eliza Brock on the *Lexington* in April 1855, and in that one short sentence she spoke for them all.

'No whales yet,' wrote Elizabeth Waldron, 'Nelson and Ambrose [the cooper, his brother] are sitting on the sofa with faces as long as your arm, they breathe a long breath every two minutes and speak about once in ten minutes. I hope they will have something to cheer them up soon.' The *Bowditch* was nine months from home at this date of May 1853, with nary a gallon taken.

It was a common complaint. By legend Captain Hayden of the *Roscoe* shaved his head and declared he would keep it bald until he took one hundred barrels. A more practical way of trying to improve luck, however, was to put up a bounty.

'Copy
'This Is a duplicate of a notice that Capt Hamblin wrote &
tacked up. A bounty. It ran thus
'Notice
'Look sharp
'I will pay to the men who will raise the first Sperm Whale
($15) fifteen dollars If he makes one hundred bbls ($20)
twenty dollars.
'Payable In Gold when the Whale comes alongside the Ship
'C.O. Hamblin.' – Abram Briggs, on the *Eliza Adams*, 1872.

The idea was to encourage the men to keep a sharp lookout. On the *Cape Horn Pigeon* a bounty of 1,000 cigars was set, and when that was won, 'Another bounty up for the next whale,' Almira Almy recorded, 'consisting of clothes, shoes, cigars, tobacco, pipes &c.' When the Nantucketer Nancy Grant first sailed, on the *Potomac* in 1849, her husband Charles set up a bounty of one gold dollar — and Nancy won it when she raised the first whale while hanging out her washing on the line. She bored a hole in the coin and wore it on a chain always after that, for luck.

On Sunday 11 September 1853, Charlotte Wyer wrote, 'At breakfast Samuel asked the question if we thought it a sin, to put up a Bounty on Sunday, my reply was, I thought it no more so, than to kill a whale, so he put up half an Ounce, and about 11 o'clock Mr Brown raised sperm whales.' They took one, too, and it made eighty barrels. On the *Bowditch* in May 1853 Nelson Waldron and his brother Ambrose put up a bounty of $5 and a bottle of grog, but his luck — unlike Sam Wyer's — did not improve. Even worse than having no oil, perhaps, was the humiliation: 'Near ten months out and no oil,' Elizabeth Waldron wrote on Sunday 5 June, 'he can hardly credit it, he is glad our friends at home don't know about it.'

'It seems as if dame fortune had set her face against us,' Elizabeth sighed next day. 'I hope she will deign to smile before the season is up.' Those smiles were a long time a-coming. 'Nelson was in hopes to find whales here and I sincerely hope he will,' wrote Elizabeth on the 17th, 'for he is getting quite down hearted, every ship we have spoken has taken one or more whales.'

Sunday 3 July came, and still the whales 'have eluded our hooks and lines with praiseworthy expertness, hope we shall come across some that are taking a *see-esta* pretty soon. I want to see the ship full and the old tryworks knocked overboard, then it will look like going home.' But still good luck evaded them: 'no whales yet,' she wrote on Sunday 11th; 'it is too bad, too bad, when will this luck give place to better? Nelson and the cooper are almost teapots, they groan and sigh, sigh and groan, and then laugh and think they won't worry about it any more.'

And then at last, on 17 July 1853, the *Bowditch* took their first fat whale. That day was a Sunday as well — but nobody was complaining.

# 5
# About the Cape of Good Hope

'...it is of no use for me to Describe my feelings Previous to my Leaving My Dear friends on that Dear Isle of Sea: Where I had spent Twenty three Years of my life, and my Dear friends Can better immagin than what I can write We left that Dear Spot in July the 19 1853 Wendsday Morning I went up on Deck and took My last view for the present of that Dear Spot and my husband and the Pilot stood by My side and observed there is the Old sand heap take one More look and I did...' — Betsy Morey, reminiscing about her feelings when departing from Nantucket, 2 September 1853.

THE first reports of great schools of whales in the Indian and Pacific Oceans had come from the East Indiamen, so it was logical that the first English whalers should sail into those seas via the Cape of Good Hope. That, then, was the route sailed by such women as Mary Hayden Russell on the *Emily* in 1823, and Eliza Underwood on the *Kingsdown* about 1829. Many of the American whalers steered the same course, so that women like Abby Jane Morrell, Betsy Morey, Eliza Brock, Annie Ricketson, Elizabeth Marble and Mary-Ann Sherman experienced the variable calms, winds and gales of the Cape of Good Hope passage to the South Seas Fishery.

The ships stocked up with provisions at various Atlantic islands before tackling the Cape. The Azores — called 'the Western Islands' then — were extremely popular for this, partly because good extra men could be obtained there, as the Portuguese Azoreans were natural whalemen. There were both English and American consuls on Flores and Fayal, so all the visitors could be sure of a hospitable welcome.

For the wives, Fayal was often the first exotic place they saw. The poverty and the number of beggars horrified them, as did the trappings of the Roman Catholic religion, but on the whole they enjoyed themselves. 'Made the island of Fayal at 10 o'clock,' wrote Sarah Taber in August 1848. She took a donkey ride, and employed much time 'in cruising about the town partaking of the excellent frute, received many presents of baskets filled with frute and a large bunch of flowers.'

Other captains took on fresh provisions and topped up their crew lists at the Cape Verde Islands further south, as Captain Abner D. Sherman did on 11 July 1845. 'Saw St Jago and went a shore we gut sum 2 hogs and bananas and sum turkeys ther was 2 manuwar [men-of-war] laing there,' recorded a semi-literate and anonymous journal-keeper in what is, unfortunately, the only surviving shipboard document of Mary-Ann's voyage. Captain John Marble dropped anchor in the Cape Verdes in October 1860. 'I have stayed all night [at Bravo] & slept on the ground with a straw mat and a sheet under me and a chare turned down for a pillow,' Elizabeth recorded. 'John's pillow was a log of wood.'

Lucy Smith's husband, Captain George Smith, recruited for provisions at the island of Pagalu – then called 'Annabon' – on the equatorial west coast of Africa. Lucy became acquainted with the place on 15 September 1870. 'While we were several miles from the island,' as she reminisced later, canoe-loads of natives arrived and boarded the ship. 'We went on deck,' she recorded, 'and were greeted with the screams of all – *be my chummie* repeated many times. Each native had many strings of little shells, black eyed susans or something else hanging around their necks and on the left arm. If they

## Annie Ricketson

Annie Holmes Ricketson was born in Fall River, Massachusetts, on 14 July 1841 and married Daniel Ricketson when she was only sixteen. Daniel's first command was the bark *Stafford*, in 1867. There is no hard evidence that Annie sailed with him then, but she most probably did so. She certainly sailed with him on the bark *A.R. Tucker* in 1871, and on the schooner *Pedro Varela* for four voyages after that. She did not enjoy her whaling life, though she tried to keep a brave face on it.

'What is the use of repining
Where there's a will there's a way
Tomorrow the sun may be shining
Altho' it is cloudy today –'

– she wrote, but her journals often tell a tale of shocking health, of endurance, privation and tragedy.

In Fayal in August 1871, she and Daniel landed on shore so that she could have her baby. 'I felt very proud and happy this morning when I awoke and see our baby lying on my arm,' she wrote on the 30th, and then, next morning, 'I woke as happy as ever, little thinking that before night I should be in sorrow.' The baby – 'such a tiney little thing, only weighed three pounds' – was sick and failing. 'It would cry out with pain all day,' she wrote, 'and towards night I noticed that Its cry was weaker.' When she lifted the blanket 'I see its hands looked very white'. Then Daniel came in, and 'I shall never forget how he looked up

at me'. The baby was dead, and they never had another.

In 1882 she wrote, 'It is New Year's eve and I am homesick and low spirited, have cryed all the evening. I have got tired of this going down to the sea in ships. I suppose it is all for the best,' she added, in a sentiment that many of her whaling sisters echoed, 'or I should not be here.' Thirty months later, in April 1885, she could throw one around your neck – they claimed you as their chummie.'

A whole crowd gathered about Lucy, all anxious that 'Queenie' should become their 'chummie', but Lucy informed them rather primly that she was a married woman and married women did not have chummies. Lucy's sense of propriety was further offended that day: she discovered to her disgust that previous skippers with perverted senses of humour had given some of the natives rude English names, 'both vulgar and profane. . .and they did not know enough of the English language to know it was wrong'.

Lucy was much happier when the *Nautilus* dropped anchor at St Helena in the following month, October. That island was extremely popular with the women, for they considered Napoleon's last resting place romantic. Lucy Smith, in a typical excursion, took a ride up Ladder Hill and looked at the splendid view, 'went over the house where Napoleon lived and died, stood beside the spot where he breathed his last and gazed on a marble bust that

---

was still at sea; it was Daniel's forty-eighth birthday and he was very sick. 'I feel *very* much worried about him,' she confessed to her journal – and she certainly had reason for worry.

Daniel had a very high fever and a gathering in his groin. She soaked his feet in mustard water; the men caught rainwater to give him to drink; the hands took turns to fan him both day and night, but still he did not improve. . .and all the time the schooner was battling headwinds to get to Barbados and a doctor. Each entry in Annie's diary counts off the miles to the island and then, on 24 May, she 'found one of his testicles had come to a sore and bursted and running badly'. Two days later, the schooner finally made port. Captain Ricketson was carried to the hotel in a litter, and Annie sent out for a doctor.

Two doctors responded, and for a while he seemed to improve. Then in June he became sleepy and sluggish. 'I do not like the way he acts at all,' she worried. The doctors examined him, and decided to operate on his groin and clean out the half-healed abscess. 'I do dread it so,' Annie confessed, but she allowed them to do it. . .they gave him ether and performed the operation, and Captain Ricketson went insane.

They had overdone the ether, no doubt. The doctors 'treated' the brain fever with 'a blister plaster to be put on the back of his neck, had to cut quite a lot of his hair off', Annie wrote. 'I never felt so bad in my life as I did when I cut that hair off', she confessed, and even today that page of her journal is

unmistakeably stained with tears.

'Daniel is very sick,' she wrote on 23 June; 'he is real crazy.' Most of the time he seemed stupefied, but at other times he went purple in the face and limbs and was terrifyingly violent. Annie was afraid for her life, and visiting captains and other hotel guests helped her restrain him: when he was bad it took four strong men to hold him down. He was wracked with spells of weeping at other times, and, Annie mourned, 'It seems sometimes as though my heart would break to think he is this way.'

In July she took him back on board the schooner, and he slowly seemed to improve. By the time they got home, in August 1885, he could walk and talk – so, five weeks later, they set out on voyage again.

This voyage proved to be the last for both of them. Twelve months after setting out, the crew of the *Pedro Varela* picked up a boat off Annabon, West Africa. The boat, it seems, had been set adrift with three sick men inside it, two of whom soon died. The disease quickly spread through the schooner. Annie fell ill, but recovered; then Daniel became sick, and was extremely ill by the time the schooner at last made St Michael's in the Azores, on 16 September 1886.

Annie sent ashore for a doctor, but instead the authorities put the schooner under strict quarantine. Likewise, the request to put Captain Ricketson on a home-bound American vessel was refused. On 8 October Annie gave up, and they set course for home, and two days later Daniel Ricketson died.

is placed on the spot,' took a snail shell as a memento and 'several slips of Geranium from inside the Tomb that I have planted and hope they will live.'

Lucy Smith's husband George hunted humpbacks off the western coast of Africa, but other whalemen specialised in hunting sperm whales in the equatorial Indian Ocean, steering north after doubling the Cape of Good Hope, hunting in the Mahé Grounds about the Seychelles and reprovisioning at variously exotic places. In January 1869, 'Delagoa Bay!' wrote Harriet Allen of the *Merlin*, in her usual lively style. '...The land, as far as we can see, is a succession of sandhills partly covered with green. The general scenery is very pretty, the red cliffs beautiful.'

Despite its prettiness Delagoa proved a 'bad place for fever' and provisions were hard to obtain. 'There is a *war* in progress with the "Caffirs". Everything

## Maria Corvelho

As the years went by and whaling was no longer the romantic way to travel the seven seas, the berths on whalers became almost entirely filled with Azoreans and men from the Cape Verde Islands, many of whom were black. In fact it came about that a white face was a novelty in the forecastle, so much so that one fellow who wanted to go a-whaling but had to stow away because his family was so set against the idea, coloured his features with lamp black so he'd have a decent chance of getting away with it.

This lad was an Azorean, Joseph R. Gomes, and the whaler was the *Pedro Varela*, the year 1910. Joe was found out, of course, which put the skipper in quite a quandary – for that skipper was Antonio Corvelho, and he was engaged to be married to Joe's sister, Maria.

It wasn't the only problem Corvelho had to face, for this was the famous voyage of the 'bloodless mutiny'. The crew threw all the whaling gear plus the windlass and a few pots and pans over the side, and so, of course, the voyage had to be abandoned. Joe Gomes went on to become a whaling master himself, and Antonio married Maria and took her to sea on the *Greyhound*, leaving port first in 1913. Maria left the vessel in 1915 to have a baby girl, Floripes. Then – as this historic Packard glass plate photograph testifies – she and Floripes returned to the ship...to face another mutiny, which was not bloodless at all.

It happened while the ship was cruising off the coast of Brazil in 1919. Three boats were down, so that only nine men were left aboard, and Captain Corvelho was aloft, directing the chase. Two of the shipkeepers seized their chance, attacking the cook with a hammer and throttling the steward. The man at the helm was assaulted as well and chased from his station. The steward escaped and locked himself in a cabin, and the mutineers attacked the door with a sledge-hammer, making such a noise that Corvelho's attention was drawn. As resourceful as any whaling master, he descended the mast and quelled the riot with boots and fists. Then he clapped the mutineers in irons and took them to Barbados.

It was an eventful voyage altogether. When the *Greyhound* finally made New Bedford on 22 August 1919, the old bark was falling apart, eaten to a shell by shipworms. Corvelho – resourceful to the end – had kept her going by wrapping fluke chains about her, dropping them over one side and then hooking them up the other side and securing both ends, thus tying her hull together. It was also Maria's last voyage, for Corvelho died just a few months later: the sea could not beat him, but influenza did.

in consequence is very high,' she wrote on 25 January. However, her husband David managed to buy a tiger skin (for $2.50) before the *Merlin* set sail.

A more favoured port was Johanna in the Comoros, where the *Merlin* dropped anchor in May of that same year of 1869. There, Harriet's daughter Nellie Allen met the Sultan. 'I liked the king very much,' she wrote in the essay she penned about six years later, 'although he teased me frequently, trying to make me say I would remain on the island, marry the little prince and be the future Queen. I took it quite seriously and was troubled.' Then the whole family received an invitation to a banquet, and, as Nellie recorded, 'Mother and I were objects of great interest, especially to the women, who were most curious about our clothes and general appearance.'

There was much to amaze Nellie as well: 'The furniture was covered in

## Go forth and preach

James Henry Sherman was one of the later breed of wife-carrying masters, and his wife Phebe was one of the most unusual voyaging wives. It was not unusual, perhaps, that he should be known as a 'fiery and outspoken' man, or that she was remarkably gentle and pious – but it was certainly remarkable that she should be the first female preacher from the whaling fleet.

Phebe went to sea first in 1883, with two small sons, after ten years of marriage. There was no need to beg permission from the owners for this, for James Henry was the owner of the whaler, *Mermaid*. When he bid Phebe pack her trunks and her sons he gave her no choice: the ship 'stood us in $45,000 – ship and outfit – before we ever set a sail on her,' he recorded, so 'the *Mermaid* was to be our home as well as our business.'

The preaching happened in St Helena. The Sherman family went to the Baptist Church for morning service, but, while there was a good congregation, augmented by crews from the ships in port, the minister failed to turn up. In the end the young and harassed Sunday School superintendant asked for volunteers – and James Henry volunteered his wife. He didn't give her any choice in that, either. From the time she was twelve 'her father kept her out of school to study the Bible', and so he reckoned she could do it better than anyone else in the church. The Baptists didn't believe in women speaking in public, but that didn't put him off, though Phebe must have felt a few qualms. It is little wonder, perhaps, that James Henry outlived her by 28 years.

crimson silk, and the costumes of the men were long flowing robes of rich colors elaborately embroidered with gold thread. They also wore brilliant coloured sashes and various decorations, carried gold and silver mounted swords, and on their heads wore white or coloured turbans.' After dinner, according to Harriet's journal, she and Nellie were taken to the harem to visit the Sultana. However, that lady was not satisfied with seeing one Yankee woman and one little girl. She wanted to view Harriet's husband, Captain David Allen, as well. She was more than usually curious about his appearance, having heard strange things concerning this particular skipper. As Harriet described it:

> 'She had heard that D[avid] had artificial *teeth* and expressed a wish that she might see him. The King sent for him. After the usual salutations I saw her looking at him closely and told him to take them out. She did not understand me and was filled with astonishment when he did so, as were the other women who were present. . .She examined the teeth very attentively, enquired all about the process of extracting and making the new ones and did not rest until she understood all he could tell her.'

The *Merlin* dropped anchor in Johanna again in August, and found an English bark-of-war, *Nympha*, in port. Captain Mara of that vessel was 'a "wild Irishman" — or so he styled himself, as Harriet wrote rather tartly. Her husband David went on board 'and nothing more was seen of him. . .until a very late hour'. Then, on the 16th, the whole Allen family was invited on board to a party.

> 'Capt. Mara sent his boat. He met us as we stepped on board and took us into his cabin. The officers soon joined us and we had a merry time. They have two fine music boxes (they play ten airs) with drum and bell accompaniment. At six we had dinner in the wardroom. . .A very good dinner, with plenty of wine &c &c. The sailing master toasted us and D made a neat reply. After dinner we had coffee in the Captain's cabin, music and conversation and finally the men who were having a jubilee among themselves, with nearly all our men as guests, were called aft and we went upon the poop to witness their performance — Music, dancing and recitals from Shakespeare.'

Then, next day, the *Nympha* departed, and that was turned into a convivial occasion, too. Captain Allen and his first officer were invited on board for a hearty breakfast, and then the *Nympha* 'got up steam and started at half past nine. We lowered our flag three times, they returned the compliment. They went out some little distance, fired at a target, turned round, steamed in and out, fired a volley of musketry and finally gave us a parting cheer and kept on their way.

'They are a jolly set,' Harriet penned. However she fancied that the officers of the steam-bark might have preferred 'a more dignified commander'. It didn't seem right that showing the British flag in foreign parts should be so hilarious.

In February 1870, at the island of Diego Garcia in the Chagos Archipelago, Harriet played the bountiful hostess herself, inviting the local inhabitants on board for a meal. 'There was an awning over the deck,' she wrote. 'The breakfast was excellent. Salt meat nicely *sliced*, pork ditto, some very nice fried Irish potatoes…and some oyster fritters…We had *wine* on the table…The only thing that troubled me,' she confessed, 'was the *dancing*. I had *no idea* they would dance on board. I gave them the choice of a day and they selected Sunday.'

Harriet Allen was well ahead of her time. She was a Women's Rightist who read Amelia Bloomer's paper *The Lily*, and, in an age when religion was every proper woman's comfort, she was not by any means pious. She made no pretence of being devoted to her husband – 'I do wish he was different in *some* respects,' she wrote once, and added with characteristic candour, 'Perhaps he wishes the same about me' – and yet she longed to accompany him on voyage. 'D will go to sea, very likely this *Fall*,' she scrawled in her shore journal, 28 May 1864. 'He thinks *now* that he will not go without his *family* but he *will*. He will not find ship owners willing to allow us all to go and he will go for three years and probably *longer* – and I shall remain at home *just* as I *did* this last voyage.' Then, when he did go, on the *Sea Fox* exactly one year later, she was right. Harriet and the children had to stop at home, presumably because he had not found owners who would allow them to sail.

That shore journal gives eloquent evidence of Harriet's real reason for wanting to go on the voyage. In that age when women were supposed to be unquestioningly domestic, Harriet Allen loathed domestic responsibilities, particularly the management of money. 'It's of no use trying to be honorable with people unless you are content to suffer imposition. If you are not *sharp* everyone is ready to infringe upon your rights and you are laughed at for being a *sheep*,' she wrote, and, 'I have been arranging to settle my accounts and calculating expenses. It always makes me *sick*.'

'I shall do the best I can,' she penned furiously the day after David left, when adding up the money he'd given her: $3,668, for two or more years' maintenance of house and extended family – a very extended family, for the instant he was gone all his freeloading relatives moved in. On 10 December 1870, on board the *Merlin*, she wrote, 'What a *bother* clothes *are*, either to make or take care of! Without the fuss of them how much time there would be for reading, study and thought.' This was a truly amazing statement from a woman of her place and time. In many ways Harriet was the ideal whaling wife – and yet this little matter of dancing on the sabbath troubled her greatly; in this she conformed.

Lydia Beebe, who was another woman who sailed the whaling grounds of the Indian Ocean and the East Indies, would have felt more than merely troubled about guests who drank *wine* – let alone *danced* – on a Sunday. Lydia would have been shocked.

Mrs Beebe's declared reason for sailing on her husband John's bark *Brewster* in 1864 was devotion. 'I believe this is where I ought to be with my husband, in the six years of our married life we lived together about six months and I trust now we shall never be separated again till death parts us,' she wrote in January – but her most remarkable diary reveals a very different motive. Lydia Beebe was religious to an extreme. She sailed determined to convert not only her husband John (a tough proposition), but every other man on board his ship.

'I had quite a talk with John about Salvation and my prayer is that he may feel sincerely the need of a Saviour's love and take his yoke upon him,' she recorded on 13 December 1863. Nor were the officers exempt. On 14 February 1864 she wrote, 'This morning I had quite a talk with Mr Keith on the subject of religion he thinks it is about impossible for a man to live his religion at sea but I cannot agree with him for nothing is impossible with God. . .This afternoon I talked a while with Mr Weeks about swearing,' she went on. 'It makes me feel bad to hear the men taking the name of God in vain.'

'I want my husband and all these men to love and fear God,' she added the following Sabbath, and she did her most earnest best to achieve that aim. It was an uphill task and an eventful voyage. The ship fell in with great schools of whales off the north coast of New Guinea. All the casks were filled with oil and the whales kept on a-coming. So John, no doubt with the value of oil firmly in mind – for it was fetching $2.65 a gallon in the New Bedford market, because of the Civil War – ordered the provisions thrown overboard to make room for still more of the 'black stuff'.

The emotions that the men (not to mention Lydia) must have felt to see the grub discarded so blithely can only be imagined. John, however, seemed quite serene about it. 'The biscuits would not float one on top of another, and the contents of each cask would cover nearly an acre in area. It was a novel sight to look upon,' he mused later. 'The molasses went down to sweeten the home of the squid and the octopus, while the salt beef and pork, flour etc., became food for sharks.'

Fresh water went the same way, dumped to make room for the oil taken from yet another huge whale, and then at last John turned for home. He was immediately given cause to regret the wilful loss of his provisions (though he didn't admit it). The ship firstly had a close shave with the Confederate privateer *Shenandoah* (escaping only because of a providential fog), and then they struck a reef in the Java Sea.

The bow was jammed and the stern was free. It was a wonder the ship did not snap in half. Any other man in such circumstances would have thrown the oil overboard to lighten the vessel – but not John Beebe. Instead the casks were shifted aft and the *Brewster* was levered off the reef by means of a spar, a kedge anchor and the windlass. Against all odds they succeeded, leaving 'a couple of tons of material on the reef' and John, undeterred, resumed their course to Surabaja on the east end of Java.

It was by no means the last of their trials: at that port some men came back from liberty ill, and the rest proceeded to go down like flies with 'Asiatic cholera'. 'The next day our situation became truly appalling,' he remembered, 'with thirteen men prostrate with the most alarming symptoms of the disease. We were now sailing west through the Java Sea toward the Straits of Sunda. The sea was smooth, the wind light; the sun was hot and fiery. We had been so long in those eastern seas that our ship was filled with vermin.'

More people fell ill (including Lydia); four men died and were hastily buried in the sea. The crew became panic-stricken, and 'only harsh authority kept them to their duty'. Then the ship began to fall apart in a storm on the home-bound passage. They rounded the Cape of Good Hope, 'pumping night and day', and somehow, by hazing the crew into gargantuan efforts, John guided the ship into St Helena...and there he left the *Brewster* and took his wife on a pleasure jaunt — to Napoleon's Tomb, of course.

Not surprisingly, John Beebe arrived back on board to find a full-scale mutiny in progress. Indefatigable to the last, he put down the uprising with argument, fists and pistol. The *Brewster* finally arrived home, 'on Nov. 28, 1865, almost ready to sink'...and Lydia sailed again, on the bark *Xantho* in 1866. Her reasons were clear enough still. Her missionary fervour was undiminished: on 9 January 1867 she 'learned the boy how to steer; he is a good boy and is trying to live a Christian life and I pray God to help him,' she wrote.

Obviously, some women were better suited to the exigencies of the whaling business than others. One who was rather better adapted than Lydia Beebe was an Englishwoman, Hannah Fawkes, who accompanied her husband on an English Southern Whale Fishing operation about the same time that Harriet Allen sailed. Hannah's husband died in a whaling accident, but she

## Desire Fisher

When Jared Fisher of Edgartown was in command of the *Omega* of Fairhaven on the 1850 voyage, he adorned an otherwise businesslike log with poetry penned to his wife, Desire. For instance, in the entry for April 15 1851, he wrote, 'Strong trades and squaly from NNE steering N middle & latter parts the same. Latt obs 15:14 Long chr 141:25 TO MY WIFE

'She who sleeps upon my heart
was the first to win it
She who dreams upon my breast
ever reigns within it

She who kisses oft my lips
makes their warmest blessing
She who rests within my arms
feels their closest pressing — Jed & Dez.'

Inside the cover of the log are written three 'receipts' for the treatment of dysentery (one of them being, 'tincture camphore, rheubarb, laudanum      Equal parts for a dose 3 times a day') and yet another ditty, which begins:

'Love thee, dearest, love thee
Yes, by yonder star I swear...'

Considering this preoccupation with his lovely wife, it seems little wonder that 'Jed'

carried 'Dez' along with him on the 1858 Indian Ocean voyage of the Edgartown ship *Navigator*. As an experiment in wife-carrying, however, it did not turn out well. Desire was appallingly seasick — so sick, in fact, that Jed had to turn back into the Atlantic after only six months of the voyage.

He left Desire on shore at St Helena. She took passage home and he returned to the Indian Ocean, doubtless to compose much poetry again. Jed and Dez were not reunited until 27 July 1862, and after that he never went whaling again.

not only married another whaleman – George Cook of Russell, New Zealand – but accompanied him on his voyages as well. 'Talk about iron men and wooden ships,' her son (another George) reminisced; 'my mother was an iron woman.' Hannah looked after the ship while the boats were off chasing whales, with no more help than that given by two old men and a boy.

It is hard to imagine a woman like Hannah feeling shocked about drinking and dancing on the sabbath; it's much more likely that she dealt out a ration of grog when whales were taken, whatever day of the week it happened to be. Such adaptability was not confined to Englishwomen, either: in February 1859, Karl Scherzer of the Austrian man-of-war *Novara*, met a most remarkable female, Mrs Joseph B. Chase of the New Bedford whaleship *Emily Morgan*. She, according to his account, was a spirited and energetic soul, 'who on occasions could take her trick at the helm, or even direct the ship's manoeuvres. So completely had she fallen into the ways on board ship,' he added, 'that even in ordinary conversation she frequently let slip a few sea-phrases, and recounted, with much pride, how, when the boats had been away in pursuit, she had kept her watch like a regular officer.'

Others did not cope at all – and the wife least adapted to the dissensions of a voyage to the Indian Ocean and beyond must, without doubt, have been one of the earliest, Eliza Underwood.

Eliza sailed with her husband on the London whaleship *Kingsdown* in the late 1820s and early 1830s. Like Lydia Beebe, she declared that she sailed for love, and this, in her case, was most certainly the truth. Eliza was obsessively devoted to her 'Mr U', and, 'in undertaking this voyage' she had hoped to stir 'an interest in my husband's breast'. Instead she found that her husband, who had seemed civilised enough when at home in England, was in reality a drunk with a violent temper.

It was a most disillusioning voyage. None of the officers was over the age of twenty, and seemed as helpless as Eliza was to control their captain's illogical rages. Underwood was often ill, with gout as well as some rheumatic complaint. 'Mr U is now mending,' Eliza noted after one attack, on 16 June 1831, 'and will then be violent with all who oppose him, I never judge him so safe as when he is ill.' She lived in dread that they would speak a man-of-war when he was in one of his 'passions', because she believed he might be charged and arrested, or perhaps even certified insane.

When they did speak other ships – which they did often, for Underwood sold liquor to other skippers to supplement his whaling profits – he abused her before the visiting captains. This was mortifying enough, though on the whole she felt nothing but contempt for the other masters, calling one who sold them provisions (on 7 July 1831) more of a 'greengrocer' than the commander of a ship.

However, Underwood insulted her in front of his own officers, too. On 4 June 1831 the first mate, Mr Milling, was struck off the crew list for the 'crime' of talking to Eliza during an off-duty hour. 'Another day of dissention...far from a day of peace and Christian exercise,' she wrote on the 5th, which was the sabbath. Young Mr Milling was more resilient: on

4 July it was observed that he was weaving straw hats and sewing cloth trousers and selling them to the men. Even more gallingly, perhaps, he probably made more money by this than he would have in his proper duties as the ship's first officer.

Even more bizarre, however, was the episode 'in the month of Feby 1830' when Captain Underwood courtmartialed his wife, for 'certain Crimes and Misdemeanors committed in the Ship *Kingsdown* on the High Seas in defience of the authority of his Sovereign Majesty the King'. Eliza's sins were manifold and varied. He first charged her 'with endeavouring to defraud the Revenue of his Majesty by a claim and transfer of certain stores in Grog &c as a right of bounty on the largest whale as first seen by the Prisoner.

> 'Secondly she stood charged with embezelment of his Majesty's stores taking from thence one bottle of beer and four sausage cakes as a supper for the two men who killed the said whale.
>
> 'Thirdly she stood charged with an offence against the dignity of his Majesty the King by telling him she wished he had given a man his grog who had sent for it he having signified that this man who was an invalid should have anything he sent for.'

And so on and on the accounting went, in a list of crimes that included asking the steward to carry cakes to the oven when the decks were slippery, feeding the livestock during cutting in, requesting in a familiar manner if the mate had a paddle in his boat, cooking during cutting in, and 'Indecent conduct in holding up her cloaths while stepping up the companion so as to expose the whole of her ancle to his Majesty. . .we are happy to learn,' she scrawled in wild black inkstrokes at the end of this, '[that] his Majesty has been graciously pleased to spare her life, on condition that she be banished for ever from every part of his Majesty's dominions.'

Like Harriet Allen in the tropical Indian Ocean, Eliza played both guest and hostess with the local 'gentry' of the Celebes Sea. Not surprisingly, in view of her strange relationship with her husband, Eliza's experiences were dramatic. In mid-July 1831 she went on shore at Kwandang Bay (which she called 'Quanton') on the northern peninsula of Celebes Island, to call on the Dutch commandant and his wife. 'As usual I was entertained with the novelty,' she related, 'which began as some would judge rather unpleasantly by our boat grounding [in the mud] when we were near half a mile from the shore.'

It was impossible to haul the boat any further, so they were forced to go the rest of the way by foot. Underwood ordered the ship's surgeon to carry Eliza: 'And we got some distance,' she wrote, 'but Mr U being heavier was not so fortunate.' Hearing him 'utter an exclamation', she looked back, to see both Underwood and the boy who carried him well stuck down in the mud.

This was a less amusing situation than perhaps it appears to be: the previous day the Underwoods had been warned that the water was 'full of Alagators. . .[which] often when pressed by hunger jump up and carry away a man'. However, Mrs Underwood responded nobly to the emergency. 'Pointing to a spot which looked rather firmer,' she recounted, 'I asked doctor to set me down there and go himself to Mr U [which] he did, but he as well as both boys stuck fast while I stood sinking slowly.'

Then, in the nick of time, a horse arrived — which was promptly commandeered by Underwood. 'As it was beginning to rain I let the boy take me on rather than wait for another horse,' Eliza remembered. She made it safely to the beach and then looked back — to see her husband 'still in

---

## John and Maria Hamblin

The Hamblin captains of West Falmouth, Massachusetts (Josiah, John, Caleb, Joseph, Otis) were confirmed wife-carrying masters and frequent visitors to south-western New Holland. On 25 July 1871 Maria Hamblin sailed with her husband John from New Bedford on a whaling and trading voyage to Australia, taking two of their six children along with her. It was by no means her first voyage: her daughter Alice had been born in Australia and her son Harry had arrived on Norfolk Island. Four more had been born at home in West Falmouth, Massachusetts, in the intervening years, and the two youngest of these — Bertha, aged five, and two-and-a-half-year-old Ben — were taken along on the *Islander*.

Despite sentimental tradition, many seamen did not like children 'that ought to be home at school' on board ship, 'to learn nothing but deviltry' and make a nuisance of themselves — and Maria Hamblin's two children certainly seemed to have a lot of fun on the bark. Bertha rode about on the back of the ship's Galápagos tortoise, and young Ben swung about the rigging. Bertha, in a memoir of her childhood on the bark, written in her 96th year,

remembered that Ben swung out too far on a rope one day and found himself dangling above the deep blue sea. He hung on and the lee pitch swung him back over deck, so at least the sailors weren't put to the trouble of rescuing the little lad.

On 30 August 1872, in the Indian Ocean, the log-keeper laconically noted, 'This day Captain's wife gave birth to a strong healthy male child.' The boy was named Ernest and Australia was the first land he touched. In future years the boys at home teased him by saying he could never be president of the United States, for he had not been born on American soil.

In March 1873 John decided to give up whaling and steered for Tasmania, where the family lodged with a missionary, Mrs Tassell, before catching a steamer to London. The first officer, Hiram E. Swift, took over the command of the *Islander*. One of his first decisions was to send for his wife and their daughter Amy Louise — so perhaps having a family on board had not been really quite so bad.

the same hole, the horse having sunk'. She sent him another horse, but it proved unnecessary, for 'I saw him coming carried between two [boys] with another holding an umbrella over him'. At length they arrived at the Dutch commandant's house, wet, muddy, bedraggled and out of temper. A good dinner was served, but Eliza could only eat an egg, 'as I find leaving the Sea I usually am as I call it landsick'. Then, when she found out that the 'black looking steak' they were served was horseflesh, she was pleased she'd had no appetite.

This series of disasters proved trivial, however, compared to their troubles next day, when the Dutch commandant and his wife and the local rajah's daughter were expected to dinner on the *Kingsdown*. At dawn Underwood got out of bed to find the ship just about deserted, for half the crew had made off in the night, along with the doctor, who seems to have been as incorrigible as the rest of the men. The missing hands made their appearance about ten in the morning, 'very drunk. . .' expostulated Eliza; 'several were obliged to be hauled up. Mr U ordered them all to their work [except for] two men cripled by fighting and two others senseless from liquor.' However, no one followed orders, for within a startlingly short time there was not a single sober hand about decks: 'They had drunk or made off with as much as three case bottles of arrack as much as six quarts a man [and] they were cunning enough to convey some on board to their messmates [and so] we soon found those on board not much better than those who had liberty.'

At this unpropitious moment the guests arrived. 'The dinner was well done and he [Underwood] seemed kind through the day,' Eliza wrote, 'but I had a dreadful lecture when they [the guests] left [the dinner table] for the first time. We quarrelled at table as my spirit was quite roused.' Underwood, it seems, was as drunk as his men. 'I am likely always to suffer from Mr U being in company in these climates,' she mourned, 'as only one water glass or two [of arrack or wine] inflames the blood almost to a brain fever.'

Other wives managed better. Mary Hayden Russell, the prim and proper Nantucket wife of the captain of the English whaler *Emily*, was entertained by East Indies notables even earlier in the century, in 1823, and coped with unruffled dignity. In July, in Kupang, Timor, she was invited to dine by no less a person than the Governor.

'Our dinner was served in the greatest style and did credit to our kind entertainers,' she recorded. 'There were three women, two men and two boys that waited at table. The house slaves are neatly dressed, the women in check cotton *kines* and blue cotton short gowns, the men and boys in long, loose gowns made of India print. The women's hair comb'd up and formed into a Knot fasten'd on the top with a long silver pin. . .Tea, coffee and sweetmeats were brought in directly after dinner. We then were invited to walk in the pleasure grounds which are very tastefully laid out. . .A band of music formed entirely of the governor's own slaves were placed in the gardens. I was greatly delighted with their performance. . .little boys with tamborines, and one little fellow with a drum was so small that he lay down on the grass to play, several playing the violin apparently not more than seven years old. The master musician, an old man, seemed quite delighted with the praise I bestowed on his pupils.'

Mrs Russell was such a popular guest that she was invited on shore each day as long as the ship lay in the harbour. In fact, it seems she created quite a pleasurable stir in the little place, right from the moment she first arrived. 'Crowds of people had assembled on the beach,' she penned with perceptible complacency, 'to witness the uncommon spectacle, the sight of an English woman. As it is a place where the whale ships touch for refreshments, a white man was no novelty, but a female created a wonderful commotion.'

She was by no means the last to create a 'commotion' in some exotic Indonesian port. Another was Lydia Beebe, who was persuaded by her hardheaded husband John to try her hand at trading at the island of Kepulauan Banda. John had carried along five dozen hoop-skirt frames as part of his private cargo of trade goods. They were going rusty, so he wished to get rid of them, and Lydia was ordered to model the hoops to help the sales pitch along. She was far too modest to strip down to stays and shift, so she simply dropped the hoops over her dress. All five dozen were snapped up eagerly by awestruck locals — and so (according to the legend) a fashion for wearing hoop-frames over sarongs was born.

In March 1872 Captain Daniel Ricketson of the bark *A.R. Tucker* took his wife Annie on shore at the island of Salebabu, and she was a source of similar fuss. Annie visited 'the King and his wife and the King's father and Mother'. Conversation was limited, but they 'brought out there beetle nut and they eat there nut and daniel had a smoke. They broke a Coconut for me.' Then, 'one of the Kings and his wife came off to see me. . .I played on the Organ for them and it was amusing to see them stare at it to see where the sound come from. Then I showed them my Stereoscope views which was a greater wonder to them than the organ.'

Two days later Annie was invited to a concert — and perhaps was the first American woman to attempt to describe an Indonesian pot-gong band:

'They got their music and danced for us. I hardly know how to describe their instruments that they make music with. They take a large round pillow and lay [it] on the floor and on this pillow they put three things made of iron. They are round but open at the bottom. They sit this open part on the pillow and then take two bamboo sticks and knock on them playing a regular tune. . .It is their Custome to take a hankerchief in one hand and a fan in the other when dancing and when they get through dancing put the hankerchief in some ones lap and that one is expected to dance so one of them put it in my lap so I got up and did the best I could We had a very amuseing time.'

Elizabeth Marble was perhaps the first Yankee woman to set foot in Bali, when the bark *Kathleen* dropped anchor there in June 1858. She enjoyed her jaunt too, despite the fact that the men were armed to the teeth with what Annie Ricketson later called 'creases'. The women she thought somewhat under-dressed. 'There onely clothing is a piece of clorth around the hips. . .[though] some of the big bugs wore a long piece a crost one shoulder as a sorte of mantle,' she added. And the people, highborn or lowly, were one and all astounded at the sight of this American woman.

'They followed us in droves, ev'ry step we went,' she wrote, in a letter to her mother dated 28 June. 'They would take hold of [son] George, and feal of him and rub hands on his face and feal of his years.' Elizabeth's 'year rings' got the same attention, but the detail that amazed them the most was her corseted waist. One man put his hands on her midriff and said, 'Too small, too small.' Another tried to exchange George for one of his sons, but Elizabeth turned the bargain down.

Elizabeth Marble was one of the few American wives who visited the

## Ellen Scott Howland

The sere scenery of the colony of south-western New Holland even provided romance, of a kind, for several of the Yankee whaling captains found wives in the small, farflung ports. One was Captain John Stackpole of the whaling brig *Harvest*, who arrived at Fremantle in May 1838, feeling ill and downhearted. He had tried all kinds of remedies: 'The captain says he has left off swearing and has took the Bible,' the log-keeper once noted, but that, apparently, did no good, for a month later, in February, he recorded, 'All hands well except the Capt and he has got so he swears as bad as ever.' So Stackpole went on shore, to see if that would work the trick and make him feel better. Then, in September, two men arrived at the ship in a boat, with the news 'that the Capt was married & to get the ship under weigh'. The bride was a girl from the island of Rottnest.

Another swain was Captain John Prentis Hempstead, who in December 1852 was wed to 'Miss Harriet Layman of W. Australia, N. Holland' by the Reverend Samuel Damon in Honolulu. John Hempstead, a widower, was one of five brothers, all whaling masters from New London who habitually cruised the waters off New Holland, and Harriet was the young daughter of a man who was murdered by an aborigine, Gayware, in 1841. Apparently the marriage was very successful. John died within ten years, in May 1862 at Honolulu, but in the meantime he and Harriet were constant visitors to south-western Australia, her homeland.

The tradition of finding a wife in south-western Australia continued as late as 1886, when Captain George Lyman Howland of the bark *Canton* met Ellen Scott, the daughter of a farmer, and married her shortly afterwards, on 21 April. Twenty-five days later he carried her off to spend a miserably seasick honeymoon on a four-month passage from her home, Albany, to his home, New Bedford.

Once in New Bedford, this Australian girl took up the strange detached marriage existence that so many New England wives endured, for Ellen Scott Howland never set up residence on a whaler again. In the following June Captain Howland sailed off on a 41-month voyage, leaving Ellen alone with a small baby son to cope with life in a bustling city half a world away from the tiny port that had been her home, and 'relatives' with whom she was barely acquainted.

Captain Howland returned in November 1880. Six months later he was off again: when their second son was born he was cruising the coast of Africa, and by the time he returned the boy was two years old. Ellen died before the century was out, of complications following 'simple surgery'; she was only 39 years old, a bride of 13 years who had lived with her husband for less than half of that time.

small and farflung ports of south-western Australia. She first set foot in Geographe Bay in 1858, and returned there on the 1860 voyage of the *Awashonks*. Like most of her compatriots, she was not impressed. 'Well at last I am at Vass and it is nothing very charming eather. . .it is nothing but sand with a few huts called houses,' she decided at the time of that first visit — and yet she found another whaling wife living on shore there. This was Mrs Gerardus Harrison of the New Bedford whaler *Mars*, who 'has ben

## Desolation Island

Taking on oil was a bloody business at best, and whalemen were hard by necessity. However the hardiest of all, without doubt, were the Connecticut captains who whaled along the latitude of fifty south during the southern hemisphere winters, and who spent long 'summer' months at Desolation (now called Kerguelen) and her sister sub-antarctic islands, to direct the killing and flensing of great herds of elephant-seals.

One of these tough customers was the New London whaleman Franklin Smith. In the 1855 season at Heard Island, in the icy deep south of the Indian Ocean, he oversaw the slaughter of more than 500 sea-elephants, a huge and brutal task that yielded 3,000 barrels of oil. The labour involved was enormous: each and every barrel had to be rolled three miles over rocks to the beach and then towed to the ship, in indescribably awful conditions. Even the

tenacious local vegetation crouched close to rocks and precipices to avoid the constant bitter wind — and yet Captain Franklin Smith took his wife Mary Caroline along on his voyages to those icy regions.

The logbook of one of these expeditions, on the New London ship *Chelsea*, which sailed from Connecticut in June 1837, survives. It is a vast affair, bound in huge sheets of canvas; it is full of terse misspelled descriptions of icy gales and savage seas. . .but no entries in that log are more telling than those for August 1840.

On the 17th the notation reads, '. . .we have had an addisshion to Capt Smiths Family In the Course of this 24 hours of a Daughter and I Call her Chelsea Smith So Ends well.' The day after that, 'All this day strong breezes with thick rain,' the scrawling script records. 'At 9 AM the schooner *Amizon* left for the Bluff [New Zealand] to sell her Capt Smith Being on Board thinks It will be Best for All the Consern as the Master and Mate are Both

dead      At 7 PM Cooled the tryworks down the weather being Bad.'

The schooner *Amazon* had worked as a tender for the whaleship, and the day before little Chelsea Smith was born Captain Jeremiah Beebe of the schooner had drowned, along with five of his men, when their boat tipped over in the icy surf. It was an old maritime tradition to call a baby after the ship, but surely few infants have been born into such a bleak scene.

Another wife to voyage to these harsh latitudes was Mrs William Brown of the *Peruvian*, who spent the 1851 sea-elephanting season at Desolation Island. Just as the ship was readying for home, with 1,300 bbls oil on board, two more New London ships arrived, and both of these, too, were petticoat whalers. One was the *Corinthian*, with Mrs Henry Williams on board, and the other was the *Julius Caesar*, commanded by Captain Ebenezer 'Rattler' Morgan, who carried his wife Elizabeth.

The surgeon of the *Julius Caesar*, Nathaniel Taylor, wrote an account of his three seasons at Desolation Island, and recorded that he was fascinated by the domestic scene he found on the *Peruvian* when he first arrived. 'A spacious house is erected upon the after part of the deck, and there. . .' he described, 'Captain William R. Brown, his wife, Miss Mary with her piano, and Master Johnny with his playthings pass the time as pleasantly as if at home.'

The *Peruvian* sailed shortly after this, but over the next three years Mrs Morgan and Mrs Williams managed to establish the same cosy scene on board their ships. Like Mrs Brown, Mrs Morgan had a room on deck, that held a cooking stove, a table, sofa and chairs, and on pleasant afternoons she and Mrs Williams paid calls on each other.

In fact – or so Dr Taylor claimed – Mrs Morgan passed her time 'much as the sex do on shore'. She washed and ironed, read books and sewed, and did not forget, 'as a dutiful and tidy wife to give sufficient time to her husband's stockings and her own address.' The *Julius Caesar* carried a little two-oared 'dinkey' for gamming, and the ship's carpenter made a flight of steps from the deck down to the water so that the women could go up and down with ease (though Taylor also recorded that the men were glad of the steps as well). Mrs Williams embellished the homely scene still further: she

presented 'Captain Williams with a fine ten pound boy, a Christmas gift from his wife.'

The American success in sea-elephanting encouraged a Hobart owner, Dr Crowther, to send a vessel to Heard Island, and so, in 1858, an Australian whaling wife accompanied her husband there, to take up the same strange existence as her American predecessors. This was Mrs Robinson. The expedition proved outstandingly unsuccessful. Crowther sent along two tenders but neither arrived, for in both cases the crewmen refused to steer towards such guaranteed misery, and sailed off somewhere else instead. Captain Robinson did find an American schooner – the *Mary Powell* – at Heard Island when he got there, however, and the skipper agreed to act as tender instead. However, no sooner had the killing and flensing got well under way, than the schooner was holed by an iceberg and lost, along with one man and her deck-load of blubber.

Captain J.W. Robinson was resourceful enough: among other feats, he amputated the frostbitten fingers of one of his men with an axe. However, even he could not turn a profit from such terrible luck. On 11 January 1860 the *Offley* finally arrived back in Hobart, reporting a loss of £5,000 and with a live sealion (some say a sea-elephant) on deck. The animal was put on exhibition and the money raised was given to the man who had lost his fingers to Captain Robinson's hatchet – but that was not enough to prevent the court action (citing ill-usage and misery) that the crew brought against Crowther at a subsequent date.

Later, in a letter written in 1898, Captain Robinson admitted that he might have been unkind when he concluded to take his wife and family along to such a godforsaken place.

'It was a wrong thing perhaps to do, to take my wife with me and two young children, but she begged to go and brought home two boys and one girl instead of a boy and a girl. I have been at all kinds of trades in my time, Merchant Service, Whaling, Guano trade, etc. etc., but the sea-elephant voyage to Heard Island capped all.'

That son Mrs Robinson bore him on that awful voyage was known afterwards as 'Kerguelen Jim': many years later he perished of thirst in the Australian desert.

on shore boarding one year'. Somewhat understandably, Mrs Harrison was looking out anxiously for the return of her husband, 'and she will go the next Cruse…she is very well and has a fine boy,'. Elizabeth added.

In March 1873 another Yankee petticoat whaler, the *Eliza Adams*, with Mrs Emily Hamblin on board, came to anchor 'at the entrance of the Harbor of Albany, at the head of [King George] Sound. Of all the places this Is the worst place I ever had my foot In,' third mate Abram Briggs wrote with evident passion. 'It was the last place God made & It was Sat. night & he never finished It. the people are so stuck up & from nothing to they think a seafaring man Is beneath there notice except a Capt or officers all the rest Is below par.'

However, Briggs' acrimony was mostly reserved for Mrs Hamblin and her naughty little boys: he heartily wished them out of the ship, and seemingly the rest of the crew did too. 'If he could meet his Cousin In the Bk *Islander* who was going home,' he grumbled, 'he would send her home with him. God knows we all wish he had meet him here, & when she went took the children with her (Oh what a loud breath of satisfaction we could have drawn to see them all go, everything would then go on with peace & quietness) but now trouble & misery.'

The colonial administrators might have agreed with Briggs heartily, if they'd known his views, and extended the sentiment to Captain Caleb Hamblin and his crew as well, for the official attitude was that the colony benefited little from the seasonal influx of whalemen. According to William Whitecar, a whaleman who visited Australia on the 1855 voyage of the New Bedford whaler *Pacific*, the biggest business that the Americans brought was tobacco, and very little of that yielded taxes, for most of it was smuggled.

'Every whaleship that comes into this vicinity brings tons of tobacco in her outfit,' he claimed; it was easy, he said, to get up to 30 pounds ashore at a time. However the skippers — and their wives — did go in for some legal trade, as items such as clocks and junk jewellery found an eager market in the luxury-deprived ports. Elizabeth Marble was a dab hand at the business, as her husband John related to her mother, in a letter written at Vasse in April, 1861:

> 'We took our trade ashore to A privet House that an Elderly Lady ocipide we found [supplied] the provisions and the old woman dun the cooking and we went to trading and we sold $800 woth and if we had ben in sooner we should dun much better     you would laft to see Lizza tending store she is what I call A Srude little Body Gest think hoop skirts that cost 62 cents she had the face to take two Dollars and Brest pin that Cost 25c. She would have $1.50 for and them that Cost 50c she would have $2.00 for and so she went on in spite of all I could do…'

The stuff might have been the most frivolous kind of frippery, and the official attitude might have been sniffish, but nonetheless the skippers — and, most particularly, their wives — were certain of a welcome. Even Mrs Emily Hamblin and her small rascals of sons found some citizen who was pleased to give them hospitality, while Emily waited on shore to have yet another baby boy. The settlements of south-western Australia were so small

# David and Eleanor Gifford

On 19 April 1875 the ship *Strathmore*, with 50 passengers on board, left Gravesend on her maiden voyage, bound for New Zealand. One of the passengers was a Scottish widow, Mrs Wordsworth, who travelled with her son Charles. The commander of the ship was Captain Charles MacDonald, a master mariner with a fine reputation.

The *Strathmore* took the Cape of Good Hope route, sailing south into the Indian Ocean without incident. Then, near the Crozet Islands off the Antarctic shelf, the ship was overtaken by fog. Captain MacDonald saw no reason for alarm; he kept his course, ordering only that a sharp lookout be kept. At four in the morning on 1 July the ship struck — and panic reigned.

There had been no lifeboat drills, and two of the boats were found to be jammed and useless. Only the port lifeboat was freed and it was lowered with 19 people, including Mrs Wordsworth. The rest were forced to take to the rigging as the ship foundered. Many drowned, including the captain and first officer. When day dawned a head count proved that only 49 crew and passengers had survived, and only one of those, Mrs Wordsworth, was a woman. In the nightmare day that followed she

and the men struggled ashore on Grande Isle, one of the Crozets.

Uninhabited and precipitous, lashed with icy winds, it was an appalling place to be marooned. Tents were rigged out of the ship's canvas to make a temporary shelter until stone huts could be made. Many of the survivors developed frostbite, and the others killed albatrosses and wrapped the warm and dripping skins about the sufferers' feet. This was a measure that set the pattern for the eight desperate months that followed, for the *Strathmore* castaways survived by making use of the birds that flocked on the bleak and inhospitable cliffs.

The men dug up muttonbird nests and killed the petrels for food; they collected mollymawk eggs, to eat and to beat up into a kind of soap. They hunted penguins, which satisfied different needs. Fat oily penguins made good fuel for their fires, while the skins of thin penguins made a kind of fabric, graded according to whether it was soft for clothes or strong for mocassins. The castaways were very aware that the birds had migratory patterns, and lived in constant apprehension that this only source of food and fuel would fly away. The thrifty men laid down stores of eggs and dried meat, and the improvident stole them. Keeping order was impossible, for the second mate — who was only 23 and no natural leader — was incompetent.

Men died, others were crippled with scurvy and frostbite. Worst of all, perhaps, was the fact that at least two ships — the *Helen Denny* and the *White Eagle* — passed Grande Isle without acknowledging the castaways' signals. In New Zealand Colonel Henry Brett petitioned the Legislative Council, but nothing was done about setting up a search for the missing ship or any survivors.

Back on the island, as the weeks dragged by and the squabbling for food and space became obsessive, men began to go mad. To break the tension, the castaways made a habit of telling each other their dreams — 'served up to breakfast like the newspaper', as described by one of the passengers, Robert Wilson, in his journal. Most of the dreams were about rescue: 'Many and varied were the yarns of safe arrival home, happy greetings and all that sort of thing,' Wilson wrote. However, every now and then 'a vision more marvellous than ordinary' was related. One of the survivors, for instance, dreamed about Mrs Wordsworth's daughter at home and was able to describe her with weird accuracy, despite the fact that Mrs Wordsworth had never given him any idea of what her daughter was like in manner or appearance.

Mrs Wordsworth had an uncanny dream of her own, in which she saw what she called a 'white lady', a young woman whom she described in detail, down to separate items of dress. Then, on 21 January 1876, a sail was raised. . .and that ship did respond to their signals. The vessel was a whaler, the *Young Phoenix* of New Bedford, skippered by David L. Gifford, his wife Eleanor with him.

Their cruise had been extremely unlucky thus far, and Captain Gifford already had 30 men he had rescued from a derelict ship on board, but nevertheless boats were lowered for the *Strathmore* castaways. Later, for this act of charity, the New Zealand Government presented him with a gold watch. Mrs Wordsworth was one of the first to be taken on board — and when she arrived on deck she came face to face with a tall, slender woman, with lambent eyes, Eleanor Gifford, the 'white lady' of her dream.

and isolated that the social opportunities offered by the whalemen and their wives were valued greatly.

'Since my last, we have all been on an excursion to Cape Naturaliste, Castle Bay and Rock,' wrote Georgiana Molloy in January 1841.

'We spent a week there. We sailed to Castle Rock in the *Napoleon*, Captn. Plaskett, in company with the *Mon[t]pelier*, found the *Hibernia* there, and in the evening — a lovely, beauteous Sabbath evening — two other American ships came to anchor, the *Izette* of Salem and the *Uncas* of Falmouth. . .we pitched a Tent and remained two days and returned to "Fair Lawn", being one week absent. A most delightful trip, this is the clime for such excursions, no apprehension of insecure weather or danger of taking cold.'

Like her whaling sisters, Elizabeth Marble made friends and became both guest (of 'Curnal Maloy' among others) and hostess. She described entertaining shore visitors on board the anchored ship, in a letter written in April 1861. 'There was eight ladies,' she wrote; 'we had a very pleasant time although some of them was seasick.' She had other fun, too: she and John and some of the captains hired horses and went on long rides, passing the time until the *Awashonks* sailed away, bound north through the Coast of New Holland ground, cruising for sperm whales on the way to the South China Sea.

And so over the decades families like the Harrisons, the Marbles and the Hamblins became part of the social fabric of places like Albany, Augusta and Vasse. . .just as other petticoat whaler families did in the farflung port of Russell in the Bay of Islands.

# 6
# Steering in for the Bay of Islands

'...it was A Delightful Morning and the [sun] never shone Brighter than it appeared to now as we wer approaching the Cottage I stopt for A moment and took survey of the Sea and our Good Ship and then at land around me and it appear'd to me that the whole Heavens wer smileing upon us for I found myself not among Heathens but among Christians.' – Betsy Morey, at the Chatham Islands, 19 January 1854.

THE exploratory schooner *Antarctic*, with Abby Jane Morrell on board, made Cape Brett on 19 January 1830, after surveying the east coast of New Zealand for new grounds. It would not be surprising if Abby Jane felt a little nervous about this part of her adventure. One week previously the schooner had been visited by a war canoe, 'which contained about fifty men', as she recorded.

Two of the complement of fifty were chiefs, who were 'whimsically tattooed; their ears marked, and their bodies stained with red or blue. From all that we could learn,' she went on, 'their chief occupation is war. They carry about them a greater variety of offensive and defensive weapons than most other savages. Their looks are bold and fierce, and they have no small share of martial dignity. Like other savages they delight in the war-song, and carry their phrensy and fury to the greatest excess. They have been, as near as I could learn, cannibals, and now, when prisoners are taken, they frequently cut from them while alive pieces of flesh and masticate it, to show their fury and fiendish joy at their success. Their dexterity in the use of their war-clubs, spears &c,' she mused, 'is said to be surprising' – but not as surprising as the calm tone of this journal entry. 'I have had much to do with cannibals...' her husband declared; 'I have been present when the New-Zealanders have celebrated their victories on the field of battle, and witnessed their disgusting banquet' – and it is highly unlikely that he would have spared her any of the ghastly details.

In the event, however, the Bay turned out to be as pleasantly rural as her home village of Stonington, Connecticut. There were no more than about twenty permanent white settlers in the village of Kororareka, two of them sea-captains, the rest tradesmen discharged from the ships, all of them, it seems, reasonably respectable. The Maoris, too, were cooperative and friendly and not the least cannibalistic in appearance.

It was all most reassuring. 'A few years ago not a ship's crew could land [here] without arms and a guard,' Abby Jane wrote, 'and, perchance, some of them were massacred in attempting to get a little wood or water; but now they may travel anywhere. . .and eat and sleep in security, without guard or arms, or without fear.' She knew exactly where the credit belonged: the missionaries at Paihia, on the further side of the bay, had brought about this most commendable alteration. 'When I thought of these changes. . .' she wrote, 'I wondered how any one could doubt the truth and efficacy of the Christian religion.'

Benjamin Morrell was equally appreciative. 'Go on, ye messengers of Divine mercy;' he enthused, 'pursue the good work, until all the isles of the ocean shall rejoice; "until the knowledge of Jehovah covers the earth as the waters cover the sea".' Not only could he recommend the Bay to his brother whalemen as a safe place to anchor now, for the 'wild and ferocious cannibals' had been transformed by the missionaries into folk who were 'civilized, friendly, hospitable, and anxious to do good to others', but the agriculture that the mission had introduced to the Bay had brought a bountiful and *bargain-priced* harvest.

'The common kitchen-garden vegetables are excellent, and in fine variety; some apples may be had, and the small meats and poultry are supplied in abundance,' Abby Jane noted. 'Refreshments may be obtained here in any quantities, on very moderate terms,' confirmed her husband. 'Hogs are sold at the rate of half a dollar a hundred weight, and potatoes at six cents a bushel; and they are the best to keep of any I ever saw' – and this paragraph, too, was well calculated to encourage Yankee whalemen to steer for the Bay of Islands.

Abby Jane Morrell went to pay her respects to the missionary establishment on 23 January 1830. It appears to have been an emotional experience. 'Oh! there is religion in the world,' she exclaimed in her journal. She was overcome with admiration. 'Their labours were incessant,' she wrote, 'for they did not allow themselves more than eight hours out of the twenty-four for repose and meals. All the rest were devoted to civilizing and Christianizing the natives. The male missionaries work many hours in the field, clothed in duck frocks and trousers. . .The wives and daughters of these pious labourers are engaged in teaching the females to sew and to read.'

While this part of the Reverend Henry Williams' journal is missing, it seems likely that Mrs Morrell's visit should have given him much food for thought. For a start, she was a woman, probably the first American sea-wife to visit the bay. Secondly, her husband was preparing a report for his brother whalemen, one that could very well bring them to Kororareka in even greater numbers than had afflicted the Bay of Islands before, and pastor Williams had always considered the whalemen a corrupting factor in his battle for the souls of the heathen. Despite this, however, Abby Jane was warmly welcomed at the Paihia mission. Williams may well have felt that her presence on board the *Antarctic* would surely do no harm to the moral

# McNab letter

The Reverend Henry Williams was certainly not the only missionary to wish that the whaleships would stay away from his little flock of converts: his brethren all about the Pacific harboured very similar feelings. Conflict between the missions and the whalemen was inevitable, given the very clear cut ambitions of each faction. The sailors wanted an open port, with all the blandishments that the Pacific paradises promised, and, quite logically, they blamed the missionaries when the grog and the girls were not available.

The missionaries, with equally good logic, blamed the whalemen when the girls ran away from their catechism classes and flocked out to the ships. In Williams' case, however, his stance was more than a trifle ungrateful, for the mission in the Bay of Islands was so dependent on the whalers for trade, provisions, news and letters – as this letter bag listing from the *New Bedford Daily Mercury* of 20 July 1835 illustrates.

The whaleship *Samuel Robertson*, with Captain Daniel McKenzie in command, was carrying a letter bag for 'South Atlantic Ocean and New Zealand', departing 5 August – and, as the letter from the eminent New Zealand historian, Robert McNab, certifies, this is the earliest known record of an official mail delivery to New Zealand. It reads:

G.H. Tripp Esq
Librarian
New Bedford
Sept 11, 1909

Dear Sir,

Referring to the photo of advertised list of Letter Bags contained in the New Bedford Daily Mercury of 20th July 1835 I cannot remember whether I told you that that is the earliest known intimation of a mail leaving for New Zealand from any port in the World. That statement I am able to make on the authority of the Secretary of the NZ Postal Department given to me some short time ago.

    Yours faithfully
    Robert McNab
Gore, New Zealand.

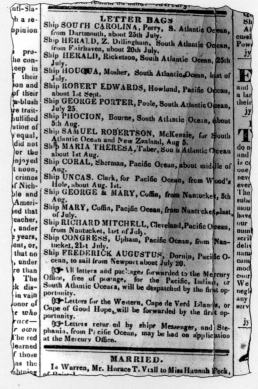

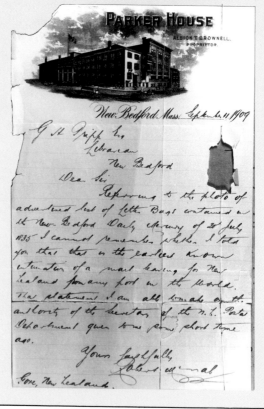

state of the crew, and might even do a bit of good.

It is even more tempting to consider how the mission women felt about the visit. Surely they were pleased, perhaps even flattered. Abby Jane called them those 'accomplished females who had left all the comforts of society and the charms of friendship in England, to come to these shores of heathenish ignorance and ferocity, for the sake of extending the Redeemer's kingdom' – and it seems very likely that they did not hear such effusive praise very often.

What Abby Jane said was true, as well. Mission women all over the Pacific gave up a great deal when they agreed to try the foreign field. When Williams' wife Marianne arrived in Paihia in September 1823 she was faced with the challenge of making a home in a thatched 'raupo hut, which had, except in shape, the appearance of a bee-hive'; she had three small children when she arrived in New Zealand, and she bore eight more in short order. In 1829 she wrote, 'My work will be much lightened when we get a house large enough for all purposes under one roof. Now on a rainy day. . .the getting of seven children across from the nursery [in one raupo hut] to the kitchen for meals [in another] is a work of difficulty.'

No doubt, however, she was ready for all that. What she and her mission sisters were not prepared for was to find that the female sacrifice was so seldom recognised; their work was taken for granted, being domestic and therefore 'ordinary'. Even today, in more enlightened times, history books don't often mention the missionary wives. The accomplishments of the male missionaries were, by contrast, dramatic. Like Williams and his fellows, men in missions all over the Pacific built roads and bridges and introduced agriculture to a restless people; they translated strange languages and printed books and played politics with chieftains and colonial administrators. Even if the number of converts was still small (as was then the case in the Bay of Islands) these accomplishments were a tangible reward in themselves.

Undoubtedly the missionary wives longed for such achievements of their own, but they didn't have the time or the energy to do anything out of the 'ordinary'. Those precious commodities were almost totally used up with pregnancies, nursing, raising children and trying to teach the native girls as well. The services provided by the missionary wives were essential to family comfort, but knowing that did not give them much satisfaction. Their husbands might have tried to reassure them, by saying that the domestic example they provided was part of the battle against prostitution. The mission wives must, however, have felt at times as if the real battle was to get through each day.

Consequently, the admiring interest of a sympathetic female stranger was extremely soothing, surely, for only another woman could understand exactly how hard the daily battles had been. Abby Jane stayed overnight at the insistence of Marianne Williams, and would have stayed longer if she could, 'but inflexible duty would not suffer my husband to linger here on my account', she wrote. When Benjamin firmly escorted her off the mission, the women 'prayed for my temporal and eternal happiness. . .' she recorded, 'and then sang a hymn that went to my soul, and waked up all its sympathies.

They all accompanied me to the beach, and with tears, embraces, and kisses, I and my female friends parted.'

The *Antarctic* did not leave as expected, however. The wind changed, and Captain and Mrs Morrell spent the next day on shore, as guests of 'KIPPY-KIPPY, the king' and his queen.

This 'Kippy-Kippy' was most probably Kiwikiwi of the Ngati-Manu tribe — more usually called 'Kivee Kivee' by the sailors — and the 'queen', his wife Uru Mihi. 'Her appearance,' wrote Abby Jane, 'was affable and kind.

'After our greeting was passed, she waved a fan she held in her left hand, and at this signal more than seven thousand of her train, of both sexes, broke out into a song of joyous welcome. . .I was carried on a sort of stage or chair, by six of their principal warriors, who proceeded with great state and solemnity. . .The women all bore a green branch in their hands, and the heads of the men were ornamented with branches and feathers. When we came within fifty yards of the king's palace, the pathway was strewed with beautiful wild flowers, quite to the door, where we found elegant mats spread for at least ten yards square. The king now spread before us a superb banquet of the choicest fruits of his clime, and the young women entertained us with many songs, of no ordinary melody; after which the warriors gave us a war-dance for our amusement. There were at least two hundred of them.'

This, too, was an extremely successful visit. The queen was as reluctant as the mission wives and daughters had been to see Mrs Morrell go: 'she clasped me in her arms, and kissed me several times', and then gave Abby Jane 'many presents of elegant mats and delicate shells'. When the Morrells reached the schooner they 'found many canoes alongside, loaded with potatoes and hogs in abundance, presents from the king and queen'.

As it happens, these provisions (unlike the mats and shells) were probably not gifts at all, but part of the highly satisfactory trade Morrell had conducted with Kiwikiwi, for Benjamin Morrell's account tersely refers to having 'taken on board a large supply of hogs and potatoes'. However, Mrs Morrell's delusion was a comfortable one, and flattering, too: 'I did not consider that these honours were paid to me as an individual,' she modestly recorded, 'but to all females of my own country and to those of the English nation.'

And then at last the *Antarctic* sailed away, steering for uncharted seas and unknown shores, but that visit to the Bay of Islands was never forgotten. Not only was Abby Jane greatly impressed with 'the great work of mental improvement and religious advancement' accomplished by the missionaries and their wives, but the possibilities the land offered were unmistakable: 'I hope to live to see the islands in this ocean inhabited by my countrymen,' she wrote, and, 'Settlements might be made. . .with every prospect of securing the commerce of those seas, or at least with sharing it with other nations.'

These stirring phrases, once published (in 1833), proved a sure recommendation for Americans to turn their speculative attentions to New Zealand. Back in the Bay of Islands, however, the tranquillity of the scene was rapidly falling into disarray: no sooner had the *Antarctic* cleared the horizon than Kiwikiwi and Uru Mihi got themselves embroiled in an ugly little conflict, over which girls were to have the 'privilege' of going on board the visiting ships. It led to some slaughter, but the competitive Americans, once a profitable opportunity was scented, were not likely to be put off by a little native bloodshed. The ships arrived in the Bay in ever-growing numbers; trade grew apace along with the grogshops; Kororareka was filled with a commotion of sex-hungry whalemen – and the Reverend Henry Williams' worst fears came true.

'The Missionaries hate the Ships to come into the Bay,' wrote Edward Markham, a visitor to the Bay of Islands in 1834; 'the Reason is this:

> 'Thirty to five and Thirty sail of Whalers come in for three weeks to the Bay and 400 to 500 Sailors require as many Women, and they have been out one year. I saw some that had been out Thirty two Months and of course the Ladies were in great request, and even the Relations of those who are living as Servants with the Missionaries go. . .[to the mission] and bring them away, in spite of all their prayer lessons. These young ladies go off to the Ships, and three weeks on board are spent much to their satisfaction as they get from the Sailors a Fowling piece for the Father or Brother, Blankets, Gowns & as much as they would from the Missionary in a year.'

In April 1838 the *Samuel Robertson* of New Bedford dropped anchor, and Daniel MacKenzie jr. (the son of the captain) noted that the ship was immediately surrounded 'with natives and canoes Loaded with potatoes, peaches, melons, grapes, fish, hogs &c &c for traffic also women'. As it happened, Captain MacKenzie sent the women away, but this was not often the case with the whalemen, and, anyway, the liberty men could find plenty of women on shore, along with all other kinds of hell-raising. Young Dan MacKenzie related that he spent his day off in strolling about the countryside with the cooper, and 'happily by so doing kept out of all quarrels and difficulties to which we might have been exposed by joining with the larger company who jest at night got into an affray with a passel of beachcombers'.

And so it seems that even the character of the permanent citizenry had gone all to perdition, and Kororareka's fast-growing reputation as 'the whorehouse of the Pacific' was well-merited. There were two villages, or so Dan described – one the old Kororareka that Abby Jane had viewed, and another, 'the Parr', where there were 'several grog shops kept by Englishmen. . .The white residents are mostly refugees and emancipated convicts from Sidney and deserters from whaling vessels and it may readily be infered,' he added, 'what influence the society and example of such characters will naturally have over the uncultivated sons of nature.'

The trade might be good and the Bay might be bustling; the profits might be pouring in, but the few respectable residents were not about to tolerate this torrid state of affairs much longer. And so it came about that the British Government was petitioned to take the country over, which feat they did accomplish in February 1840. The blessing immediately proved to be a mixed one. British duties and taxes arrived along with the Union Jack, and Kororareka, along with all the other ports of New Zealand, was no longer free.

Lieutenant Wilkes, of the U.S. exploring ship *Vincennes*, visited the Bay of Islands in March 1840, just a few weeks after Hobson signed the Treaty of Waitangi with the Maori chiefs, and predicted that Yankee skippers would turn to other ports for refreshment; they would do that, he declared, because the taxes were weighted heavily in favour of British nationals, and discriminated against 'foreigners' such as Americans. His prediction was perfectly correct. Within a few short years the major part of the American whaling fleet was recruiting in the Hawaiian Islands, and American whalemen like William Mayhew, who in the meantime had invested heavily in the country, faced financial ruin.

## Caroline Mayhew

In 1831 Captain William Mayhew of Martha's Vineyard, Massachusetts, set off on a whaling voyage to New Zealand on the *Warren*, of the port of Warren, Rhode Island. He returned on 12 June 1834 with a most gratifying cargo, and married a distant relative and near neighbour, Caroline (also Mayhew) the daughter and grand-daughter of doctors, in August. He sailed again in September, and she sailed with him. This voyage was lucky, too, and the opportunities offered by the new country seemed so appealing that after they arrived home in 1837, Caroline and William decided to go out to New Zealand again, this time to settle.

Their luck, however, had run out, and their speculative ventures ended in ruin. The British moved into New Zealand, and Caroline and William were eventually forced out of business. They returned home to Martha's Vineyard and William went back to his old career of whaling. In February 1846 he took command of the ship *Powhattan*, and he and Caroline set off again, heading — as in times gone past — for a voyage a-whaling, south to New Zealand.

Times gone past were times gone for ever; even their whaling luck had deserted them. In all respects, Caroline's 1846 voyage to New Zealand and the Bay of Islands was appalling. Three days out from home the ship ran into a hurricane, 'a very severe gale of wind [which] lasted without cessation for 25 days'. Then, on 12 April, the *Powhattan* limped into St Jago in the Cape Verde Islands, 'in quarantine having 8 men down with small pox'. Being in quarantine, a port doctor would not come off, so the captain and his wife were left to care for the patients as best they could. However, perhaps because of the expertise Caroline had learned from her father, none of the men died.

The ship lay in port 20 days before sailing away, still with smallpox on board. William fell ill, 'and had it quite bad, but got through it', perhaps (again) because of his wife's skill in nursing. According to the legend, Caroline navigated while he was ill and kept the ship safely on course.

On 4 January 1848 William wrote to the owners from the Bay of Islands, saying, 'I have at last arrived in this place in rather a bad state. I have had a deal of misfortune,' he confessed; he had 'cruised all over creation' but hadn't seen a single chance at a whale. 'Hard luck makes everybody dissatisfied,' he declared.

The general shipboard temper had no chance to improve, for their luck stayed awful. Eventually the *Powhattan* arrived home on 9 March 1849 with a miserable report of 360 bbls of oil.

If all the legends are true, then Caroline was most surely a memorable character. She was given a pet wallaby in her New Zealand years, and was famous for taking it everywhere with her. She also had a stirring turn of phrase. Once, off Cape Horn, she wrote, 'We made twenty knots, ten straight ahead and ten up and down.' She lived to be eighty and kept one room in her house as a kind of museum to hold her huge collection of New Zealand and Pacific 'curiosities'. Unlike Abby Jane Morrell, however, she was no advertisement at all for taking one's wife to the Bay of Islands — or anywhere else in New Zealand.

William and Caroline Mayhew, of the island of Martha's Vineyard, Massachusetts, had made the decision to settle in New Zealand in 1838. William didn't do things by halves: he purchased Tahoramaurea Island near Cook Strait, and outfitted it as a whaling station; he was one of the eight original directors of the New Zealand Banking Company, which commenced operations on 4 September 1840 with its head office in Kororareka; he took on the lease of a large Bay of Islands property as a going concern.

Then, on 20 April 1841, Acting United States Consul Clendon appointed Mayhew to the position of vice-consul, writing to Daniel Webster, Secretary of State, that he was well-fitted for such a responsibility, being 'a citizen of the U.S., a reputable merchant, and a gentleman qualified – in every respect – to fulfil the duties' of his position. Everything should have looked rosy, but did not, for the British administration had moved in, along with all those discriminatory policies. On 21 February 1842 Mayhew sent a letter to the Secretary of State, saying,

> '. . . many of our countrymen are expensively engaged in general mercantile pursuits, some in the valuable Timber Trade of the Country and others in that very important branch of our Commerce the Whale Fishery, for carrying on each of which lands have been purchased from the Chiefs and establishments erected at a great outlay of capital, but H.B.M.'s Government here have passed laws which they decl' to be now in force by which they assume to the Queen of Great Britain all lands purchased of Native chiefs prior to the Treaty with the Natives and during the acknowledged Independence of the Islands of New Zealand. . . whereas it is too well known that the foresight taken and industry of our citizens have given the sale value as far as it regards the natives to the Lands they may have purchased And which the chiefs to the present time are willing and anxious to confirm declaring that their signatures were obtained without their understanding the purpose of the Treaty.'

To put it broadly, Mayhew and his fellow speculators were being forced to hand over to the Crown any land they had bought from the Maori chiefs. 'The destructive effect of many of the laws on our commerce is too general to detail,' he wrote. '[But] our whaling interests are deeply affected by the loss of rights and privileges.' Then, to add insult to injury, Mayhew was accused of fomenting unrest among the Bay of Islands Maoris and supplying arms to help the cause along. The chief Hone Heke flew the Stars and Stripes at the head of his canoe, certainly, but there was no evidence at all that Mayhew had incited rebellion. He and Caroline abandoned their investments and eventually, broke and disappointed, made their way home. The seasonal flow of American whaler-trade in the Bay of Islands had been reduced to a dribble, and American speculation in Kororareka had ended.

Then, in March 1845, scandalous Kororareka suddenly ceased to exist: in that month Captain Jabez Howland and his wife, of the whaleship *London Packet*, called at the Bay of Islands to find 'that the natives of New Zealand had risen upon the English inhabitants of the Bay of Islands and completely overpowered them. The English,' their report continued, 'fled to the vessels in port, leaving the town in possession of the natives, who soon reduced it to ashes.' It was the end of one era and the beginning of another. A pretty little village called Russell became the premier place in the Bay of Islands.

A few grogshops still supplied the occasional whalers as they came into port, and canoes still surrounded the ships as they drifted to anchor, but an appearance of tranquillity had returned to the Bay.

The Nantucket whaler *Lexington* dropped anchor off Russell on 12 February 1855, and found four other ships in port: the *Planter* and the *Ganges* of Nantucket, and the *Swift* and *Enterprise* of New Bedford. There were more than 500 ships recruiting in Honolulu that year, but for Russell five ships all at once made a bustle. On the 13th, 'the decks thronged with natives,' wrote Eliza Brock. The Maoris sold peaches, pears and honey, which they brought to the ship in canoes: Eliza saw 'One large Canoe Paddled by eight ladies, they seem to manage them as easily as our sailors do their boats, it is a matter of wonder to me how they do it.'

On 14 February she went on shore, 'stopping at the Russell hotel', and found friends from her home island of Nantucket in town. Nancy Grant (of the *Mohawk*, which had gone out on a cruise) and Mrs Nickerson (of the *Ganges*) were staying with Dr Ford and the doctor's wife Martha, and Mrs Nickerson had an infant, delivered six weeks before. Eliza called and 'took Tea, found Mrs Grant well and in good spirits. Stayed until two o'clock, heard some sweet music, a German teacher Played and Sung to the Pianoforte, he is the most delightful singer I ever heard'.

Unlike Kororareka earlier, Russell was very quiet, disturbed 'only now and then [by] a Fracas with the Sailors'. By then Benjamin Morrell's bargain-priced recruits were expensive: 'Everything here is very dear. Eggs 50 cents per dozen Onion $6 per bbl. Board for three, $4 per day.' However, it seems, despite high prices and taxes and duties, a few whalemen kept on calling at Russell, and at least part of the reason for that was that the Bay of Islands was a very fine place to bring their wives.

One of the junior residents of Russell in the late part of the century was a little girl, Lulu Mair, who reminisced (under her married name, Louisa Worsfold) that the seasons were marked by the comings and goings of the whalers.

> 'Among Mrs Johnson's lodgers, at some times of the year, Spring and Autumn, were the Captains and their wives off the American whaleships – The ships called into the Bay on the way North to the whaling grounds and again south in the season. The American women were very dear people – sweet New England women we used to read about in their stories – American children's books were the first I had to read...

'The ships stocked up with books when they left New Bedford,' Louisa was told. The books were exchanged as the ships gammed or came into the Bay, and 'Russell was [the] headquarters for the accumulation of mail'. The ships straggled in and 'stayed some weeks – cleaning up and re-fitting, taking in water and fire-wood...When the time was approaching for the ships to come to port it was quite exciting to get up one morning to find a ship at anchor...or we might hear the flapping of sails during the night; then the morning could not come quickly enough to see which one it was.'

'Steering in for Bay of Islands,' wrote one of the wives, Rachel Beckerman, on 18 May 1870; 'at 11 AM came to anchor.' Her husband's vessel *Live Oak*

## Louisa Worsfold

Louisa Worsfold, born Louise ("Lulu") Blanche Norwood Mair in 1872, had the rare distinction (though perhaps not so rare in those days) of losing her father to a cannibal feast.

Lulu's grandfather was Gilbert Mair, a Peterhead Scot who went to sea at a very young age. Gilbert became a ship's carpenter, making several voyages in English whalers to the South Seas Fishery. During a visit to the Bay of Islands in 1824 he decided to make the raw new colony his home — perhaps because he had fallen in love with Elizabeth Puckey, the daughter of missionaries at Paihia. He was the earliest shipbuilder in New Zealand, launching a schooner, *Herald*, in 1826, amid a scene of confusion: the Maoris had gathered in great numbers to witness the event, anticipating much largesse for hauling the craft down into the sea. To their loud chagrin, however, when Gilbert knocked away the chocks the schooner slid into the water of her own accord.

Gilbert Mair worked at the mission station until 1830, when he purchased a large block of land at Te Wahapu (near Kororareka) from the Maoris, paying them in muskets, powder, shot, spades, hoes, tobacco and scissors. He set up a trading station there, providing the Maoris with European goods and supplying the whalers as the fleets came in. The business flourished, but Gilbert Mair was canny enough to guess what would happen when British administration arrived. He bailed out in 1840, leasing the property to Captain William Mayhew for the sum of £7,000. Mayhew's affairs were in such a parlous state, however, that Gilbert received only £900. The rest was paid in promissory bills, most of which were never honoured. However, Mair had made enough to set up again in Whangarei.

Gilbert and Elizabeth had a large family, all solid citizens except for their second son, Henry Abbott. The best word to describe Henry was 'adventurer', for his life reads like something out of Robert Louis Stevenson. At the age of 20 Henry was trying his luck in the Australian goldfields; his thirtieth year found him back in New Zealand, ambushing Ngatitama Hauhau warriors in the forests of the Bay of Plenty. In 1869 he was in Auckland, fighting a lawsuit and marrying Jane Norwood Greenway of the Bay of Islands. Marriage did

not settle him down: despite the fact that she bore him two daughters — Lulu and then Jessie (born in 1875) — Jane saw very little of her husband, for he was off about the Pacific on various voyages.

The South Pacific was a free-for-all paradise still, and Henry fell in with two compatibly free-booting souls, Handley Sterndale and his wife, and the trio established some mysterious enterprise on a Cook Islands atoll, Suwarrow. They called the business a 'trading station', a highly suspect claim, for — apart from a coconut-planting gang the three entrepreneurs imported — the island was (and is) uninhabited. The British administration was certainly suspicious, for in 1876 a government vessel, the *Kriemhilda*, was sent from Auckland to investigate. Henry was away, but the Sterndales, resenting this unseemly interference, fired on the ship from the wooden fort they'd made.

Then, in the middle of the fuss, Henry Mair arrived, as supercargo on the trader *Ryno*. Once he understood the situation, the captain of the trader refused to let Henry land. Henry Abbott Mair was not the sort to let mere sea-captains stand in his way: that night he stripped naked, rubbed himself all over with coconut oil (which he fondly regarded as a shark repellent), dived overboard and swam to shore. He almost didn't make it. When he did, he lay prone and exhausted on the sand, listening with little interest to the turtles which at that season were digging out holes to lay their eggs. Then, dimly, he heard the scrape of flippers on metal.

Somehow Henry found the strength to drag himself over to the hole to investigate. . . and there he found treasure, a heap of gold doubloons, and an iron box heaped with precious stones.

This presented quite a dilemma – for Henry Mair, remember, had nowhere about his person to hide such a trove. Also, apparently, he did not trust his friends the Sterndales, for he dug up all the treasure and buried it elsewhere.

The hoard was never rediscovered. The Sterndales were driven out of their fort in spite of Henry's help, and he spent the few years left of his life in roving the Pacific and trying to get back to Suwarrow. In 1877 he was supercargo on the schooner *Canterbury* and in 1878 he was first mate on the brig *Heather Bell*. By 1881 he was an agent on board the Fiji schooner *Isabella*, involved, it seems, in 'recruiting' labour for the sugar plantations – the so-called 'blackbirding' business.

Blackbirding killed Henry Mair. When the *Isabella* called at the island of Espiritu Santo in the New Hebrides on 12 November 1881, Henry Mair was clubbed to death on the beach.

When the news reached Auckland his daughters Lulu and Jessie were sent to live in Russell in the Bay of Islands, in a house which was owned by their maternal uncle Hamlyn Greenway, then called 'Greenways', and now known as Pompallier House. . . and so a ten-year-old girl made the acquaintance of many New England whaling skippers, and several of their pretty wives.

In 1894 Lulu married Richard Kelly, and they had a little boy: 'His name is Dick, after his Daddy,' wrote Lulu to Parnell Fisher (of the whaling bark *Alaska*) in February 1905. Later, the lad was known affectionately to the family as 'Kelly'. His father had died six years before the date of the letter, 'of consumption, but with this life & work [Dick] ought to escape,' the anxious mother added. Lulu had an elderly mother and an aunt – 'Aunt Greenway' – to care for, as well as a farm and a household: 'It

Dick Kelly

is somewhat hard to get on without a man,' she confessed. However, in 1905 she remarried. Her second husband was Frank Worsfold, and life became even busier. Lulu – now known as 'Louisa' – raised a large family, taught at 'native' school and corresponded with family and friends (including those in New England) as well as with scholars of New Zealand history and women's issues.

Life was hectic, but the childhood years in Russell were not forgotten. The poet A.R.D. Fairburn encouraged Louisa to record what 'Lulu' remembered, and thus a manuscript was written.

joined eight other whalers in the anchorage, and Rachel found three female friends on shore: Sarah Luce of the *Cleone*, Charity Norton of the *Ionia* and Mrs Charles E. Allen of the *Sea Ranger*. 'It looks very green and pretty on shore,' Sarah Luce remarked when she first arrived. They all boarded at the Cricketer's Hotel, which was kept by a Mrs Williams, and Sarah recorded that there were fourteen Americans at table.

Fourteen was not many, perhaps, but Russell boasted only about 150 citizens, so fourteen was enough to create some excitement. 'When the men first came ashore the Captains would walk up and down talking – all dressed

## Hervey and Sarah Luce

Hervey Luce's whaling career began in 1845 when he shipped as cooper and boatsteerer on the *Champion*, and then, after several voyages, he became first mate of the *Morning Light* in 1856. His skipper was John Oliver Norton, one of the toughest old salts around, but this, apparently, failed to sour Hervey's nature, for he was known as a practical joker, an excellent singer and – as Carrie Turner put it once – 'good company and very droll'.

Elizabeth Stetson met him in Tombez, Peru, on 6 September 1864, when he was skipper of the *Cleone*, and recorded that 'He has been married twice; his first wife lived a fortnight' – so it seems little wonder, then, that he carried his second wife Sarah and their small son on

the *Morning Star* in 1862, and that despite the fact that the Southern Confederate privateers *Alabama* and *Shenandoah* were hunting down Yankee whalers and burning most, along with their valuable cargoes. That was an Atlantic voyage (which they survived unmolested) but the following two voyages, on the *Cleone*, Hervey steered for New Zealand and the South Pacific.

And so Sarah Luce became one of the wives who went on shore to socialise at Russell and Norfolk Island, and to visit such curiosities as the 'Flower Pot' on Pitt Island, which had been built from the wreck of the whaler *Franklin*. 'Capt. and Mrs Luce, and Son, took dinner on board today,' wrote Rachel Beckerman of the *Live Oak* on 23 October 1871, at the tropical island of Tongataboo (Tongatapu); 'at daylight hove short, at 7 am took our anchor and went to sea.'

in their best broad-cloth — navy blue, "Square-cut" the style was called,' Louisa Worsfold remembered. 'The clothes smelt of camphor, quite strong — much more pleasant than our moth-balls — and the other smell was currie-powder, and they smoked lovely cigars — we loved all this.'

The women were busy the first few days in port, 'writing letters to catch the 'Frisco mail, which left Auckland once in three weeks'. After that they 'gave themselves up to receiving visitors and paying calls, with each other as well as with all of us residents — We had lots of parties'. For best the women wore black silk, Louisa remembered: 'Gowns, they called them, even if they were well fitting...

'They had a good allowance of clothes for the four years' voyage, but said that when they got home they...would not appear in public, in clothes four years out of fashion, until they had a re-fit — they would take a cab and go home by back ways — then dress-makers would be called in, and an orgie of sewing would be mixed with a torrent of talk — friends would call and much excitement, you may imagine. They told us that they never bought material in the rash way we do here — the pattern desired was taken to the shop, and laid on the material on the counter, and bought accordingly.'

'The wives of these Captains were such pretty women,' Lulu mused in another part of her memoir, and then added (somewhat engagingly), 'The way of it was, that only the nice women 'were allowed, by the shipping authorities in New Bedford, to accompany their husbands on these long voyages.'

While these *nice* captains' wives went about their social rounds the crews were at work on the ships, readying for yet another whaling season. 'Remained at the Bay of Islands until June 16 [1870] had rainy squally weather most of the time,' Rachel Beckerman noted in her journal. 'Employed shipping oil, getting wood, water, Recruits, Painting Ship &c &c.' Then the *Live Oak* sailed north-east to the Equator, steering as far east as 'Hope Island' in Kiribati, and then slowly returning south-west to the whaling grounds north and east of New Zealand.

This was a typical cruise for a South Seas whaler, and the *Live Oak* was seldom alone. The whalers hunted in groups, cruising the South Pacific in a great seasonal ellipse, speaking and gamming with the other ships often. They reprovisioned at certain islands in a seasonal pattern too; Norfolk Island, for instance, was visited in October. When Rachel Beckerman went on shore there she 'landed at the Cascade, it being too rough to land at the town'. This was common enough; the Norfolk Island people used to set a blue flag to warn incoming ships of a rugged landing. 'The Town is about three miles from the Cascade, we got a horse and a two-wheeled cart to take us to the town...' she wrote. 'I had the good fortune to find two lady friends of mine on shore, Mrs Norton and Mrs Baker [of the *Tamerlane* and the *Northern Light*], their husbands having gone out for a short cruise and left them on shore.'

It was quite common for the wives to be left on shore for a few weeks, and Norfolk Island, having a mission, was popular for this. A young Martha's Vineyard wife, Parnell ('Nellie') Fisher, of the *Alaska*, was left at Norfolk

## Coopers

Coopering and whaling were synonymous, for, while the tried out oil was eventually pumped into casks that were kept permanently down in the hold, everything else, from newly tried out oil to fresh water and sails, was kept in some kind of barrel. Consequently, whenever a whaler was some days in port, some coopering was bound to be done, for fresh water had to be collected in new, unpolluted casks and provisions had to be packed away as they were brought on board.

The barrel staves were carried from home in bundles, then were knocked into shape and bound with hoops. Finally the cracks between the staves were caulked with pitch and some kind of fibre. It was a musical job. 'At break of day the work would begin...[and] over the water came the sound of singing...' wrote Louisa Worsfold, who spent part of her childhood in Russell.

'The Coopers were at work,' she elaborated, 'tapping, tapping, making up new casks...When a number of new casks were ready, they were roped together, end to end, a long line of them floating high on the water, and towed ashore, and stood under a small

waterfall that ran over a rocky ledge onto a beach...

'A [boat's] crew stayed by to attend to the filling and prepare them for the return tow to the ship in the evening — By this time the casks were heavy and only a bit of them could be seen above the sea — we could hear the gear taking them aboard and the 'heave ho' at the work. The staves were brought from America and the caulking for the heads — Sometimes raupo was used for this purpose...it was the tapping of putting on the hoops we used to hear — I loved the sound, and would recognise it now.'

# Charles and Parnell Fisher

'Captain Charles William Fisher of the *Alaska* used to tell us stories about his own home in New England,' reminisced Louisa Worsfold of Russell; 'he came from the state of Martha's Vineyard – his people had a farm.' When the citizens of the Bay of Islands first became acquainted with Fisher, he was a widower with an adult son – 'but after he got home he married again – he sent us a paper with the announcement in it, so that we should know when he came next time – Her name was given thus, to "Parnell S. Pease of Edgartown – Mass.".'

The year was 1885, and Parnell was 29 while Charles was in his fifties. No doubt the people of Russell awaited the next arrival of the *Alaska* with some lively curiosity. 'She was a very pretty woman and became a great friend of ours,' wrote Louisa; 'he called her "Nellie",' she added – and it was probably little wonder that he carried pretty Nellie on voyage.

As an experiment in wife-carrying, however, it did not work out. When the Fishers got back to Edgartown in Martha's Vineyard Charles built a fine house with a view of the sea, but Nellie refused to move into it – she preferred her old house, she said, because she couldn't see the water from there, and she'd seen enough of the sea.

Fisher's son, Charles junior, was somewhat of a rascal, in the family mould. He and Prescott Jernegan, the son of another whaling master, claimed to be able to extract gold from seawater, and set up a scam called 'The Electrolytic Marine Salts Company', which separated a number of gullible folks from their money. A week before the confidence trick was exposed Charles jr fled the country with a suitcase of money, heading for New Zealand. 'Lulu Kelly' (Louisa Worsfold) wrote a letter to Parnell Fisher from Kerikeri, dated February 1905, and saying, 'Tell your good Captain to remember that I was the last girl in New Zealand to sit on his knee!' Then she added wryly, 'Alas! I was a girl then, I am over thirty now.'

She also wrote, 'Your boy Charlie – always called Fisher – is on one of the Union Company steamers going to Australia – he is working his way up, he says – he is expected home soon for his holiday – he's a dear boy.' Charlie Fisher might well have been a 'dear boy', but his father made no attempt to follow up this news of his whereabouts. Instead, in true obstinate New Englander style, he put up a gravestone and declared his son dead.

'I corresponded with them for years, until Captain Fisher died in 1906,' Louisa Worsfold continued in her memoir. 'He had been Arctic whaling on the Pacific side, and Mrs Fisher came across America to meet him, and he had died coming into port, San Francisco – I did not know if she took his remains back East. She wrote a few times after that – she went to live with her sister, Christine Pease – then the letters stopped.'

in September 1886. She had been on shore at Russell only four weeks before: her husband Charles Fisher made a habit of dropping her in all kinds of likely and unlikely places, for Nellie had a habit of being thoroughly seasick.

'My husband just left. It was so hard to say goodbye,' she wrote on the 12th, but nonetheless she enjoyed a remarkably good time. Parnell taught sewing and embroidery at the mission, and went to parties and dances, one great occasion being a ball for Lord Dudley, a future Governor General of Australia. No sooner had Charles Fisher come to fetch her than he changed his mind and left her again, to enjoy Christmas on shore while he took the *Alaska* to the Solander ground south of Stewart Island.

'Capt. Chase of the *Niger* is here and his wife,' wrote Nellie. 'Also Capt Potter & wife. It makes it pleasant for me. I have been out with them to the mission at Cascade. . .We had a grand dinner. Lots of laughter & I took wine in a great silver cup which was passed all around the table.' She got letters from home and no doubt answered, for she had so much to relate. 'I am indulging in quite a lot of social life here,' she confessed in her journal. 'Only wish I could hear from Capt.'

However, June arrived before Charles Fisher did, and when Nellie did get back on board the ship it was to find that the *Alaska* was unsettlingly leaky: the bark had lost her caulking on both sides, the full length of the hull. The mate wrote, 'First, last, and greatest evil, pumping ship. She seems to leak more as we carry sail looking for whales' — but Captain Fisher carried on as blithely as ever, setting the men to pumping night and day as he optimistically cruised the gale-tossed waters of the 'Chatham' ground to the east of New Zealand. When he finally arrived in Russell the ship was in such an unseaworthy condition that he had to take her to Auckland, to have her hove down and re-caulked.

The Chatham Islands and the seas about them made up an important part of the seasonal hunt, for right whales could be taken there from January to March, and sperm whales congregated there from November to June. The ground was popular with all the whalemen, and not just those who kept to the South Pacific. Israel Morey of the *Phoenix* arrived in the Pacific in January 1854, after crossing the Indian Ocean, and made for the Chatham ground to 'fish' there for a while before heading north for the North Pacific whaling season in the middle of the year.

His wife Betsy went on shore at Pitt Island (Rangiauria) on 17 January 1854, and was greeted by Mr Hunt 'and four little Girls and two Dogs he appeared verry Glad to see us', she recorded, 'and Esscorted [us] up A short Steep Hill to the Little Cottage and Met with the Lady of the house at the Door to receive us and here we met with A verry pleasant Reception I can Assure you I was verry much pleased with the manners of the Lady'. Betsy, who was incurably naïve, felt surprised that the English Mrs Hunt 'could speak verry good English' — but then it must be remembered that the last place she had touched (St Paul's) had been French. 'My husband was verry well acquainted with her,' she continued, 'and observed to her this is the first American Woman that you have ever seen here. She replied yes. And I supose,' Betsy mused, 'that I was as much of A curiosity to them as they was to me.' However Betsy Morey was by no means the last of the species that Mrs Hunt received.

Fred Hunt wrote in his biography, 'Occasionally a captain would arrive, bringing his wife with him. We have been favored with the society of ladies for months at a time.' The usual reason for this was seasickness: the weather was inarguably awful, for some reason worse than it is today. One of those

## Whaler 'hove down' for repair

When the whalemen ventured into oceanic waters, they encountered the problem of teredo, the so-called 'shipworms'. These long, wormlike clams bore into wood below the waterline and reduce a plank to a fragile honeycomb in a shockingly short time: Starbuck, the great whaling historian, recorded that the whaleship *Niphon* of Nantucket sank on her maiden voyage, scuttled by the depredations of shipworms.

To counter this, the hull was sheathed with thin sheets of copper – which worked very well, just as long as the copper was not scraped off. Interestingly enough, the New Zealand wood totara (*Podocarpus totara*) is naturally impervious to shipworms, so the loss of an unknown number of ships could have been avoided by sheathing the vessels with that timber. As it was, the slightest nudge against a coral outcrop could tear off a few square centimetres of copper and allow the teredo to move in. If captain and crew were lucky, the leaks caused by the worms were noticed in time to get to port for repair, before the honeycombed planks gave way and the vessel sank with all hands.

Once safely in harbour, the ship was 'hove down'. The cargo was offloaded, and then the ship was winched over so that one side of the hull was exposed for inspection and repair. Once that side was finished, the ship was hove down in the other direction, and the business of recaulking and replacement of damaged copper was completed.

laid low by motion sickness was Emma Thomas, who first arrived on Pitt Island on 4 February 1873. It was the beginning of a routine: she stopped with the Hunts each time her husband's bark *Merlin* cruised about the Chathams. At the end of 1873 she was left there for almost three months, and enjoyed an English-style Christmas dinner of 'geese, ducks, chicken pies, boiled ham pies, and plum pudding', for which the women 'dressed up as though they lived in a City!' – or so she wrote in a letter to her stepmother.

Fourteen years later, on 22 January 1886, Charles Fisher left young and determinedly seasick Nellie on the largest island of the group, Chatham (Wharekauri): it was the beginning of his tradition of dropping her off in variously civilised and godforsaken places all about the South Pacific. 'I am

## Emma Thomas

Emma Thomas, seen here (standing at the right) with two of Fred Hunt's daughters (Ann Hunt Langdale, seated left, and Elizabeth Hunt Gregory, seated centre) and two unidentified women, made five visits in all to Pitt Island in the Chathams, and stayed there several months. Her reason for stopping there was seasickness: 'Mrs Thomas very sick,' the log of the *Merlin* recorded on 7 July 1872, five days after departure, and throughout the voyage Emma never improved.

'I expect I shall be real seasick,' Emma wrote to her stepmother in January 1874, after a ten-week spell on Pitt Island (her third visit there), 'for I have been on shore for so long but Albert will take good care of me and I shall get up after a while. Oh if I could only get over being seasick I should like it.'

She did not get over it, and would not learn to like her life at sea – and the effect on her naturally short temper was disastrous. Emma had needed some persuasion from her husband before she agreed to sail in 1872, and over the next four years Captain Albert Thomas was given much cause to regret that she'd ever said yes. It had seemed such a good idea, too. Emma was only twenty-six years old when she sailed (though with a five-year-old son) and seemed even more lovely than the nineteen-year-old bride he'd left behind at the start of his previous voyage. Also his new command – the same bark *Merlin* that John Deblois had taken on her maiden voyage, along with his wife Henrietta – was more comfortable than most. However, in every respect this venture in wife-carrying proved a spectacular failure.

Three weeks after that January 1874 letter

Emma was back on the island, and she stopped there till May, while Albert grappled with whales, a difficult crew and loneliness on the Chatham ground. Then, when she finally rejoined the ship, it was for the last thirteen months of the voyage. When the lighthouse at the entrance of Buzzard's Bay was finally raised, 'Emma was flooded by waves of relief and happiness. A great peace came over her,' her granddaughter, Sylvia Thomas, related much later. 'Never again would she have to be tossed by the tumultuous sea.' Albert retired from whaling and bought an orange grove in Florida, but the strain that the voyage had put on the marriage proved to be beyond repair: Emma neglected to leave New Bedford and join him.

to be left here 2 or 3 months to get well,' she sighed in her journal. Charles had bought her a horse named Dickens, and she boarded with an English family named Ritchie. 'Mr Ritchie,' she wrote, 'is a perfect gentleman.' That is, when he was not overtaken with liquor. 'Then, thank the Lord, he lives in a separate house and we are safe from his awful ways. It is so shocking! I hope the Capt. returns soon,' she added.

Charles, however, took fourteen weeks to return, and within three weeks she found herself on shore again. 'Here I am at Pitt's Island at Mr Hunt's place,' she wrote 30 April 1886. 'The sea was so bad the boat almost upset at the landing. This is a very rich place. Mr Hunt has ten thousand sheep.' Then at last her husband collected her, to carry her to Russell in the Bay of Islands — but troubles arrived even then.

Charles Fisher, it must be confessed, was a bit of a rogue. 'There is more trouble with the whalers,' reported the *New Zealand Herald* in unmistakeably weary tones on 29 July 1886. Rumours 'were afloat that dutiable goods had been landed from the *Alaska* at the Chatham Islands, and that the matter must be inquired into'. The 'goods' that had been smuggled ashore were 'two cases rum and six boxes tobacco' — which could not have been good for Mr Ritchie's sobriety.

Being caught out didn't do Captain Fisher's pocket any good, either. Louisa Worsfold recorded that he 'was fined £100 — he had to go to Auckland and delay sailing, with the wind right too — I know I was aghast at the mention of the fine. . .Fancy what £100 would have meant to an inhabitant of Russell, and have it taken that way!'

> 'This is a small place but very pretty and after my six weeks on ship I enjoyed it very much. Capt. Potter's wife is here. Had a child born here the 3rd. I enjoy her very much tho we shall not stop long. Lots of letters from home up to June. We have had so many storms since we left Chatham, I am thankful for our safety. — Parnell Fisher, in Russell, 11 July 1886.

Charles Fisher, it seems, had a knack of arriving at the Bay of Islands in circumstances that were less than ideal. However, the *Alaska* was by no means the first or last whaler to do so. Another was the *California*, commanded by Captain Brightman, whose wife Elizabeth Douglass Brightman accompanied him on all three voyages when he was master of the vessel — 1876, 1881 and 1886. Elizabeth Brightman was a remarkable woman, who learned navigation so that she could help out if needed. This attribute came in useful when Brightman was stricken with typhoid at Norfolk Island during the first of those voyages; she took over the helm (so to speak) and navigated the ship to Russell.

Louisa Worsfold remembered Captain Brightman as 'a large square-built man, used to dress like those pictures of George Washington — in square felt hat and wide-tailed coat'. Elizabeth Brightman was 'a beautiful woman, always so perfectly dressed. . .

> 'She told us one experience they had coming down to the Bay of Islands — They left Norfolk Island, thinking to get here before the storm — they knew it was coming and there was no shelter at Norfolk Island — it struck them off the New Zealand coast north of Mangonui — she said she had sailed with

George all the seas of the world and had never been in such a storm – George came down to our cabin, and I knew by his face how things were – I just had to say, "Wa-al, George, how's things?" and he answered, "Wa-al, Lizzie, they're pretty bad" – I had never heard George speak like that before – so I hied me to my cabin to look for a suitable costume to be cast away in...When they got to port, she said, George broke down with the long strain – he addressed the crew, but could only say, "Boys, you've been splendid."'

The *Live Oak* was another petticoat whaler to arrive in Russell in a battered state. Back in the southern summer of 1870 she cruised the Chatham Islands ground according to the timeworn pattern, and then, on 25 March 1871, 'experienced a severe cyclone, at 11 PM shipped a very heavy sea, lost two Boats with everything belonging to them Davitts and cranes also broke Rudder head off close to the water's edge'. The bark limped into the Bay on 30 March 1871, and remained in port until 30 April, 'repairing damages sustained in the gale'. During that time five of Rachel's friends arrived: Mrs Allen of the *Sea Ranger*, Mrs William D. Gifford, Eleanor Baker of the *Northern Light*, Mrs William Fuller of the *Napoleon*, and, lastly, Nancy Grant of the *Niger*.

Like so many of her whaling sisters, the Nantucketer Nancy Grant was something of a legend. Her husband Charles Grant spent 56 years at sea, and Nancy accompanied him for 32 of them. She married him in 1839 at the age of sixteen (her father went along on their honeymoon), and then Charles made two voyages without her, the second as captain of the *Walter Scott*.

According to the tale as it is told in Nantucket, not long after he got back home from that one, Nancy heard a knock on the door. She turned to Charles, set her fists on her hips, and pronounced very firmly, 'If that be Mr Macy after you to go a-whalin', then you can jest ship me too.' She was duly shipped and in August 1849 sailed on the *Potomac*.

In the following December she had a son, born at Pitcairn. The *Potomac* called to collect her on 13 February 1851: '...at 4½ AM Capt went on shore found a young Heir so ends,' noted the logbook keeper. On Nancy's next voyage, *Mohawk* 1854, a daughter was born in Dr Ford's house in Russell (not long after Eliza Brock's visit). Two years later a second son, George, was born at Upolu, in the house of the British consul in Samoa.

Next voyage, *Japan* 1859, Charles sailed off without her, so Nancy left the two older children in the care of friends and family, carried young George on the steamer *Belle of the West* from Boston to Melbourne, and travelled from there to New Zealand again, where she caught up with her husband in Russell. Again, in 1865, Charles sailed alone, and Nancy and George took the overland route across the isthmus of Panama and a steamer from thence to the Bay of Islands. Somewhat unsurprisingly, Nancy Grant and young George were familiar personalities in Russell, as well-known, in fact, as citizens who lived there all year.

With such a lengthy shipboard career behind her, it is also not amazing that Nancy picked up a few sea-phrases. Louisa Worsfold testified that she 'spoke broad Yankee, [and] said, "I like to have one gown that is only 'bent'

on the sabbath" − "bent",' explained Louisa, 'was the term used for setting
out new sails!' However it is surprising − considering her husband Charles
Grant's long experience of sailing into the Bay of Islands − that on that
date of 29 April 1871, when the couple joined the little fleet at Russell, 'he
came near putting ashore on Brampton, would, I think,' that journal-keeper
on the *Napoleon* (the third mate) meditated, 'if a Steamer had not come along
[and] towed him out of A bad scrape'.

The *Napoleon* was itself in a doubtful state of seaworthiness, for the
mainmast was rotten. Mrs Fuller, who preferred not to board on shore,
stopped on the ship while her husband took a boat up the river 'looking
for A stick for main mast'. He found one tree that was right for the job
− just one. On 19 May he arrived back in Russell, 'had cut down the tree
for the mast but in falling it broke off about two feet too short'.

Whaling captains were resourceful by nature, however. Leaving ship, wife,
son and crew in Russell, Fuller went to Auckland in the steamer, and on
the 27th, 'the steamer arrived from Auckland she had A spar in tow for
us to make A main mast of, we towed it ashore and rooled it up where the
Carpenters could work on it'. They didn't finish the re-rigging until 17 June
− but in the meantime there had been a Queen's Birthday to celebrate, on
24 May. The Americans were surely not Victoria's subjects, but nevertheless
the crews participated wholeheartedly, 'Colors set ashore and on board of
all the vessels in harbor, we went gamming and boat-sailing &c'.

And so, in far-off New Zealand, a floating American community became
part of the social fabric of the small but pretty port of Russell, Bay of Islands.
On 16 May 1874 the *Eliza Adams* came into the Bay, with Captain Caleb
Hamblin in command and his wife Emily and their three naughty little
boys on board. 'The whole tribe went on shore,' the ill-natured third mate,
Abram Briggs, reported:

> 'the Capt must have a Flag on shore to hoist up when he wants the boat, or
> anything, he wants to act the part of Comodore next the Steerage boy must
> go on shore every morning to look out for the calf. . .they say to the Hotel
> she is the first one to the table, and the last one to get up, she has gone the
> most of the night to a Ball, and left the child abed to cry or sleep. Their children
> are spoken of on shore as the worst behaved children they ever saw, setting
> the dogs on to people's geese trying to break other children's fingers, and calling
> each other names which i debar from writing.'

Emily Hamblin also visited Akaroa, as another wife, Mary Lawrence of
the *Addison*, did in February 1860. The *Addison* called at the South Island
port for the purpose of taking on fresh provisions ready for the passage home,
and Mrs Lawrence was the guest of both Mr Greaves the Harbour-master,
and Mr White, 'the merchant of the place, where we were very pleasantly
received by Mrs White. His is "the house" of the place,' Mary elaborated,
'adorned with lawns, walks, arbors, waterfalls, brooks, caves, etc.' She also
saw an orchard, 'which consists of four hundred peach trees all borne down
with fruit. Such a sight I never saw before. It looked wicked to see them
lying upon the ground. We were feasted with peaches, currants, raspberries,
and strawberries.'

Emily Hamblin arrived in Akaroa on 25 November 1874, for a different purpose altogether. 'Could not leave her in Hobart Town but must come away from the cruising ground,' grumbled young Briggs, 'and come to this insignificant place, to stop on shore, where everything is as dear as it is in Hobart Town, the idea is they want to be in a place where no one knows them, for where they are known, there room is better than there company. . .

'But one thing sertain,' he added with obvious satisfaction, 'we will have a little peace now, and thank God for small favors' – and the ship sailed off on a cruise, without the hated 'cow' and 'calves' on board. Then in April 1875 the *Eliza Adams* arrived back to collect the captain's wife and family. . .but, once dropped, the anchor was slow to get weighed again.

'It is now 5 weeks next day after tomorrow since we came in here,' grizzled young Briggs on 23 May, 'and for the last 3 weeks, we have been ready for sea.' Instead of sailing they were all waiting about – 'Waiting, waiting for what?' Briggs asked rhetorically. He knew the answer, even if 'the Capt thinks we don't': Captain Hamblin was 'keeping the ship waiting here for the Cow to calf'. The 'cow' was slow to oblige, however; evidently someone's arithmetic left much to be desired.

The *Eliza Adams* did, in fact, make sail the day after that, but went only a very short distance, just out into the bay. To the surprise of everyone they actually took a whale there, a humpback, on the 25th:

> '. . .with our boats & the volunteered assistence of the Steamer that came down to see the whale we towed him to the Ship at 3 PM quite a number of visitors come on board to see the whale, next day took the whale on the beach at high water & at low water went & took the blubber off of him & gave the carcass to parties on shore for the Christchurch museum.'

The crew otherwise filled in time by smuggling. Briggs noted that he 'Smuggled on shore at different times (mostly in the night) 2½ boxes Tobacco (20 pound boxes)', and then added (somewhat mysteriously) that he also sneaked in 'the skins of 8 Sheep'. Then, at last, on 14 June 1875, 'the news came off that the Capt's cow had another calf (a Bull)' which was a pity, according to Briggs. Captain Hamblin's aim was 'to be the father of a girl, as it is now his underlip hang down, nothing go right, everything goes wrong, no one to blame but himself'. Providence could be blamed as well, however. Once upon a time Caleb and Emily Hamblin had had a daughter. She was born in February 1871 and they named her Gertrude. Then the little girl had died, aged four months and sixteen days.

The 'calf' was by no means the first or last American infant to be born on or off New Zealand. Ever since Mary Caroline Smith of the *Chelsea* had brought her baby daughter on shore at Russell in January 1841, the babies (like the ships) had kept on a-coming. At times it almost seemed that Dr Ford was bringing more Yankees into the world than were born back in Nantucket. It was a natural consequence of sharing the captain's stateroom, one that perhaps the skippers had not considered.

The management of a confinement was not written up in *The Sea-Captain's Medical Guide* and it is little wonder if the onset of labour pains was the signal to square the yards and run. The tricky bit, however, was to raise a port before matters reached a crisis. Some ships arrived in New Zealand in a fearful hurry. One such skipper in a rush was Thomas Wilson, who carried his wife Rhoda on the whaleship *James Arnold* of New Bedford, on her 1874 voyage to New Zealand.

They arrived at the Bay of Islands before things got out of hand, but dropped anchor to find no doctor in town. So a boat was sent off up the Kawakawa River with hasty directions to find one. The boat's crew laboured mightily, pulling a full 14 miles; they found their doctor and rowed all the way back – and when they got to the quay Captain Wilson was there and waiting. 'It's a girl,' he sheepishly announced.

This was a situation to be avoided if humanly possible. However, a head wind was a contrary wind, no matter how urgent the errand, and every captain had to face the possibility that he might be in charge when the baby was born. Some, like Charles Robbins of the *Thomas Pope* in 1862, managed with commendable insouciance: 'Looking for whales,' recorded the logkeeper in April. 'Reduced sail to double reef topsails at 9 PM Mrs Robbins gave birth of a Daughter and doing nicely latter part fresh breezes and squally at 11 AM took in the mainsail...'

Others, however, were unashamedly apprehensive, and that with good reason. The possible complications of a confinement were well-known. John States was a seaman on board the *Nantasket* of New London, Captain Parker Hempstead Smith, when Mrs Smith went into labour. 'Last night we had an addition to our ships company,' he recorded on 18 February 1846, 'for at nine PM Mrs Smith was safely delivered of a fine boy whose weight is eight lbs this is quite a rare thing at sea but fortunately no accident happened had any thing occurred there would have been no remedy and we should have had to deplore the loss of a fine good hearted woman...

'Success to him may he live to be a good whaleman though that would make him a great rascal,' States added dryly, but the atmosphere, it seems, was generally one of relief.

When Captain Charles Nicholls first carried his wife to the New Zealand ground, on the 1853 voyage of the *Sea Gull*, he was faced with much the same problem. According to a story that is told in Nantucket, when he gammed with Captain Peter G. Smith of the *Young Hector*, he asked for advice. ''Tis easy,' Smith reportedly declared. There was only one rule to be remembered. The expectant husband had to devote all of his attention to his wife, and the easy way to make sure of that was to have the first mate at the ready in the cabin, all prepared to take over the baby the moment the infant was born.

And so, when the time came, a nervous first officer waited at the stateroom door. Matters progressed, the door popped open, Captain Nicholls passed out a squalling bundle, and the first mate commenced his well-schooled juggling. Then, to that fellow's horror, the door flew open again. 'My God!' cried Nicholls. 'Get the second mate, fast!' Sure enough, a second infant was handed out, and, 'By heaven, we need the third officer too!' However – as things turned out – the third mate was not needed.

Many skippers, like Captain Caleb Hamblin, avoided the problem by making port in good season. On 21 January 1861 Captain Dehart of the *Roman* dropped anchor in Mangonui, a small port north of Russell. His wife, Charlotte, somewhat coyly, gave a good excuse for their arrival there: 'we were so clost in to the Land and was in want of potatoes very much [so] the Capt thought best to get them now...it looks very pleasant on shore,' she meditated. 'All the boys are seen to be enjoying it much...and all are quite well excepting I do not feel very well.' Then, on the 23rd, the real reason for the visit was confessed: 'our darling little boy was borned we took also 212 bbls of sperm oil from Ship *Navy*.'

Charlotte had been to Mangonui previously, in February 1858, but her husband had not timed it so well on that occasion, for when she arrived in port her first baby boy was two weeks old, having been born on the Tasman Sea on 23 January 1858. Providentially another petticoat whaler, the *Aladdin* of Hobart with Captain John McArthur in command, had been sighted just in time for Mrs McArthur to come on board and deliver the child. 'We had not seen a ship for a number of weeks,' Charlotte recorded; '[but] that day two came into sight, spoke one, ther was a Lady on board. She come to our Ship and spent two days with me [and] thankful enough was we,' she added, and it is easy enough to believe her.

However, on that first occasion the village had proved a capital place for convalescence. Mrs Butler, the wife of William Butler (who styled himself the 'Custom House and Commission Agent'), called to see Mrs Dehart each day, and three other whaling wives were there — Mrs Childs of the *William Thompson*, Mrs Palmer of the *Kingfisher*, and Mrs Weeks of the *Scotland*.

Eliza Williams arrived in Mangonui on 17 January 1859, also with a new baby that had chosen, inconveniently, to be born at sea. She wrote of 'Captain Butler, the Harbor Master', and Mrs Butler, who 'came every day and washed and dressed the Baby'. There were eight other ships in the harbour. 'One of the Captains — Capt. Charry, of the Ship *Harvest* — had his wife with him,' wrote Eliza. 'She had been stopping with Capt. Butler's family ten months. She came to see me with Mrs Butler. She had a fine boy born at their house.' Other visits, however, did not have so happy an outcome. In August 1864 Mrs Willard, 'wife of Capt W. of bk *Washington* NB, died in Monganui'. She left one child, an infant. There is no record of what happened to the baby.

It was a lonely place to give birth and die. When the *Abraham Barker*, with Mrs Alden T. Potter on board, arrived on 29 December 1872, a logkeeper called it, 'the "Far Famed City" of Monganui [sic] New Zealand. There is about 3 houses here,' he stated, 'two of them are behind the other so one only is visible.' However, Mangonui was quite popular for recruiting, partly because the potatoes were famous, and partly — as an agent, C.B. Waetford, advertised in 1852 — 'at this port there are no [port] charges or dues upon whaleships. Pilots are always ready but unless their services are availed of no charge is made.' In February 1856 Captain Charles Evans of the *Arctic* married Sarah Gorsell, the daughter of one of those ever-ready pilots. Eight months later, on 28 October, he fell overboard while beating up to a whale,

## The Earle family

Any family that has heard the click of a camera shutter at precisely the wrong instant will know how the Earle family felt at the moment this picture was taken. As the little boy, Jamie, remembered it, his mother had ('shall I say') *cautioned* him to stop up on deck. 'Well,' he said, 'I heard what she said' — but his father was down in the hold, so Jamie didn't see why he should not be down there, too. 'I came up when he did and I got warned for being down there. About the time that mother got through with that process, Tripp came along and wanted to take a picture. My father kind of stands there, rather nonchalant; well, what could he do? My mother was still quite upset and I was more than upset! I didn't like it at all.'

Despite her early reluctance to take up a life at sea, the New Zealander Honor Matthews Earle adjusted very well to the routine of whaling. She certainly navigated, and Jamie's recollection was that she kept the logbooks as well — but, as that was not official, there is no hard evidence that she did so. Like other wives, she took to the swinging bed during storms, and, as Jamie remembered, she was adept at freeing the bed when it swung so far that it stuck: she 'put her foot out and pried it loose so that the bed righted as the ship came up.

Course the water came down the stairways,' he added, but that did not seem to bother her.

Jamie's father got up each morning at change of watch, eight bells, four in the morning, and he and Honor had doughnuts and coffee and then the family had breakfast at seven. The meals were all substantial. 'My father...' he said, 'had pretty much the pick of the best men because he fed well. Pretty much what they ate at his table, they ate right through, whether it was the petty officers or the fellows before the mast.' Salt meat was carried, and live animals as well, and there were eggs if there were chickens and they'd laid any. And then there were the bugs.

Bugs? 'Glory be!' said he. The crackers were bought in metal tins with soldered seams. Jamie took one once, and put it in a tub of water, and when it did not leak he took it out and opened it — and, 'The bugs were there!'

And did the presence of a wife and family improve the morale of a ship? Well, said Jamie, he had only ever come across one fellow who'd had that strange idea; he 'must have been quite a young fellow when he went on the *Morgan* 'cause he said my mother rather mothered him a little bit and perhaps as a young fellow he appreciated it.'

The others didn't seem to think that it made any difference at all.

and was killed when his ship sailed over him. 'It was proposed to bury him at St Paul's Island, but the weather was so bad that it was found impossible,' the *New Bedford Whalemen's Shipping List* for 2 June 1857 reported.

'His body was therefore put in a coffin which was enclosed in a much larger one and the space between the two coffins filled with lime and sand and he was brought to this port (Mangonui) and buried on an island at the east end of the harbor.

'At the time of the accident his wife (whom he had married from this place 8 months before) was on board and she had the melancholy satisfaction of seeing him interred within a few yards of her father's house. The funeral took place on Friday the 23rd January and was attended by all the masters and most of

# Marion Smith

'WOMEN RIVALS NAVIGATE HIGH LINE WHALERS,' ran a headline in the *Boston Globe* for 23 June 1907. These remarkable women were the New Zealander Honor Matthews Earle of the *Charles W. Morgan*, and Marion, Mrs Horace Smith, of the *Josephine*. 'Both women are the wives of the captains and their husbands are captains of the ships,' the report elaborated, 'but they are considered the equals of their husbands as navigators.'

Marion Smith had been sailing with her husband for more than a decade, and her reputation was famous. 'Mrs Smith could, if anything should happen to her husband, navigate the *Josephine* to any part of the globe,' the item continued. 'At least one captain out of New Bedford has Mrs Smith to thank for her knowledge, and this is Captain Rose of the bark *Canton*, the oldest whaler in the world. Rose, a Cape Verde Portuguese, was for several years on the *Josephine*. Mrs Smith took a liking to the big, good-natured whaleman and she taught him navigation, so that he rose from the humble position of boatsteerer to mate, and this year the Messrs. Wing, owners of the largest fleet of whalers in the world, put him in as master of their pet vessel, and he owes it all to Mrs Smith.'

The ground the two petticoat whalers were cruising that season was the sub-Antarctic Indian Ocean, about the Crozet Islands. That part of the sea had been neglected for many years, as it had the reputation of being 'fished out', but Horace Smith had tried it again two seasons previously and had made an excellent voyage, despite the notorious climate.

'Only the staunchest of ships can make the

voyage to the Crozettes,' the reporter related, 'for there is likely to be a gale every 24 hours once a whaler gets on the grounds, and foggy weather is a common occurrence.' Legend had it that one old captain once stated baldly that he would rather die in the Ochotsk Sea off Russia than whale off the Crozets – and yet Marion Smith and Honor Earle sailed there so matter-of-factly that they competed with each other in traditional whaling style, to see whose voyage would turn out to be the most successful.

The banner went to Marion Smith: the *Josephine* arrived home on 13 July with a catch that was worth over $100,000 in the New Bedford market.

the officers of the whaleships in harbor and the principal inhabitants of the place. The procession of whaleboats extended over half a mile — and the funeral service was performed by WB White Esq Resident Magistrate.'

Sarah Gorsell Evans was then sent 'home' to New Hampshire on the ship *Jireh Swift*, to live with 'relatives' she had never met. There is no record of what happened to her after that, either.

Romances with happier endings took place in Russell. 'Miss Hickton, Martha, married Captain Frederick Barker, who was in command of an American whale-ship, and sailed out of New Bedford...', Louisa Worsfold related.

'Capt. Barker sailed the Pacific, even to Arctic whaling — On one occasion he was not heard of for two years, yet Mrs Barker, who lived next [door to] our home at the time, never wavered in her belief that he would be heard of soon. She had sailed with him, with the family, and was sure he was alright, somewhere. Then there were rumours going among the shipping through the Pacific, that a ship's crew had been found in the Arctic, living among Esquimos — She was sure that was Fred. She had walked up to the flagstaff hill, the lookout station behind Russell, at the north end, almost every day of the time in between, for sign of a sail — She ceased when she heard this rumour. Then in time she got a cable from San Francisco from her husband. She placed her children, four of them, among relatives and friends and took passage to San Francisco.'

Another American skipper, James Earle, met Honor Matthews, a mathematics teacher, in Russell in 1891. He proposed marriage almost at once, but Honor was reluctant to adopt a life at sea. She 'wanted something to do', as she told an interviewer from the *Boston Globe* several years later, 'and a whaler, you know, is not the place to have the liveliest time in the world'. However, once she found she could be signed on as 'assistant navigator' the proposition became a lot more exciting. 'Navigation came very easy to me,'. she admitted. 'Figures didn't bother me in the least.' Honor travelled by steamer to Honolulu to meet James; they sailed immediately after the wedding, and spent their honeymoon whaling in the Ochotsk Sea.

And so it was that a girl from New Zealand sailed several voyages under the American flag, on the *Charles W. Morgan*, the last and most famous of the windjammer whaleships.

'So was the "Stars and Stripes" the first flag I ever saw — so I still like it and hope to always — how it "dipped" in good-bye, as it left port, and the ship in full sail — they waited for the right wind to take them away like that.' — Louisa Worsfold.

# 7
# *Uncharted seas, unknown shores*

'The *Juno*, Banks, R. Jones Esq., has been wrecked on one of the Feegee Islands and all the crew have been brutally massacred by the cannibals. The Captain's wife and children have been kept by the natives in the hope they will be able to exchange them for goods.' – *Sydney Morning Herald*, 6 December 1839.

**B**ENJAMIN Morrell, when he quit New Zealand in January 1830, decided to sail to the Fiji Islands, despite their fearful reputation. He planned to chart the reefs and 'fish' for *bêche de mer*, or seaslugs, which when cured and dried were greatly valued by elderly Chinese gentlemen as a rejuvenating soup. He sailed to Manila first, and left Abby Jane there when he sailed away on 12 April. However, he soon returned, on 26 June, with a bloodcurdling story to tell.

Instead of steering for Fiji the *Antarctic* had sailed to the Bismarck Archipelago north of New Guinea, and he had set a boat's crew ashore to build a *bêche de mer* curing house. The natives seemed friendly 'although it was evident that they had never seen a white man before', as Abby Jane recounted later, 'and the islands bore no traces of ever having been visited by civilized men'.

Then, on 28 May, according to Benjamin Morrell's record, 'my ears were startled by a sound that sent the life-blood curdling to my heart. It was the warhoop of the savages on shore.' A desperate fight took place on the beach; 'for every white man that fell, half a dozen black cannibals bit the dust', but the outcome was inevitable. Morrell and the men on board were forced to witness 'the heart-rending spectacle of...shipmates lying mangled on the beach, while some of their ruthless butchers were cutting and carving them with their own cutlasses! Others again were churning their spears into the writhing bodies of those who yet had life...

'Fires were kindled on the beach...' Morrell morbidly continued, 'among the dead bodies of my unfortunate crew, from which those hell-hounds were cutting the flesh, and roasting it in the fire; and then, with savage ferocity, tearing it to pieces with their teeth, while from the half-cooked fragments the fresh blood was running down their ebony chins!'

'I grew pale over the narrative,' Abby Jane confessed, which is not amazing. What is surprising is that when Benjamin announced his intention to return to the islands and exact revenge, Abby Jane resolved to go with him. 'I was with my husband,' wrote she; 'he was not afraid, why should I be?' Even more astoundingly, Morrell blithely agreed to take her along.

On 14 September, according to his record, the schooner came to anchor 'within a quarter of a mile of the beach of that island which had drunk the blood of fourteen as gallant tars as ever sailed under the star-spangled banner'. According to Abby Jane, no sooner had the *Antarctic* made an appearance 'than we were attacked by about three hundred warriors.

'We opened a brisk fire upon them, and they immediately retreated. This was the first battle I ever saw where men in anger met men in earnest,'. she penned. The outcome of the skirmish was swift and inevitable: the natives retired to lick their wounds and re-think their tactics.

Morrell had a garrison built on shore, while the war canoes assembled from the surrounding islands. Then a violent battle commenced, again with an inevitable outcome. The warriors were mown down in short order and the village was destroyed with cannon. Despite her feminine frailty (and the fact that she was popularly supposed to be a moderating, peaceable influence on board) Mrs Morrell, it seems, was an eager spectator. 'I saw all this without any sensation of fear,' she wrote, 'so easy is it for a woman to catch the spirit of those near her.

> 'If I had, a few months before this time, read of such a battle, I should have trembled at the detail of the incidents; but seeing all the animation and courage which were displayed, and noticing, at the same time, how coolly all was done, every particle of fear left me, and I stood quite as collected as any heroine of former days.'

Then, after striking up 'Yankee Doodle' and 'Rule, Britannia' in celebration, the crew collected and cured their *bêche de mer* and sailed away, leaving a beaten and smarting populace behind them — who, surely, were as anxious for revenge as Morrell and his men had been earlier. One ship looked much the same as another to unsophisticated eyes, particularly if of similar rig, and the next captain, however peaceable and well-meaning, could well fall foul of this ominous state of affairs. No one on the schooner, however, seems to have put much thought to that possibility.

'A fearful outrage has occurred in the Port of Buckatoo in the island of Isabella, in the Southern Pacific, 'ran an item in the Boston *Daily Evening Traveller* of 31 December 1860. On the '7th of June last' almost the whole of the crew of the South Seas whaler *Henrietta*, Captain Brown, had been massacred.

> '...the ship was suddenly boarded by a number of natives, who attempted to take forcible possession...[Captain Brown] had his wife and two children on board. The natives first endeavoured to secure him and throw him overboard; but he managed to break away from them, and rushed to his cabin for firearms.
> 'They next attacked his wife, who also succeeded in escaping their vengeance, and sought refuge with her husband in the cabin, where they kept up a constant firing on the natives, who...jumped into their canoes and made off, carrying

with them one of the children, a fine little boy about five years old...[Captain Brown] pursued some of the canoes in the hope of recovering his child, but failed to do so.'

It is very interesting that the 'Port of Buckatoo', in 'lat 9'03'S lon 159'E', is in the Bismarck Archipelago, the very same island group where Morrell wreaked his bloody revenge thirty years before – and it is very tempting to wonder if, in the eyes of the natives, this attack on the *Henrietta* was just another battle in a war that had started three decades earlier.

The explorers were not the only ones to work up the natives; men-of-war intent on retribution left similarly dangerous legacies behind. A few whaler skippers as well as their merchant and naval brethren had the charming habit of taking on provisions and then neglecting to pay for them, sailing off and 'paying with the foretops'l' instead. Logically, the next captain who came along would find a very suspicious and perhaps dishonest market, for the natives couldn't be blamed for learning well from the previous lesson. For all they knew, cheating was admired behaviour back in the homelands of those Europeans and Yankees.

## Alice Henrietta Handy

In December 1844 Captain Ichabod Handy of New Bedford took the whaling bark *Belle* to New Zealand and the South Pacific, on one of the longest voyages on record. He was 43 years old and had been married (to Mary Warren of New Bedford) for 22 of them, but had had no children – any of which circumstances might have explained why he did not return home for almost eight years.

Handy's voyaging, in fact, was the stuff of fable and legend: he led the kind of existence that belongs in story books, cruising about uncharted seas and visiting tropical islands where no European had landed before, leaving men on shore to trade for coconut oil, whaling when he had sufficient crew, and taking on Pacific Islanders to work their passage from one island to another when he didn't.

It is part of the popular tradition, too, that such men should form liaisons with the native girls, and Ichabod Handy conformed in this as well, when he took a beautiful Maori girl as a 'season wife' in the Bay of Islands, New Zealand, about 1846. As was the custom, he left her when he sailed – but, as we shall see, that Maori wife was not forgotten.

Handy finally arrived back in New Bedford on 10 September 1852, and left again swiftly, departing on 7 January 1853, in command of the same vessel. Around the Cape of Good Hope he steered, and then he made those familiar islands with their warm lagoons, and things went on as if he'd never gone, in trading for coconut oil and in occasional whaling.

Then, in May 1855, Handy made port in the Hawaiian Islands, for he was sick and needed a doctor. By coincidence Dr George Pierson and his wife, a missionary couple from the American Board of Foreign Missions, were

Other captains deliberately terrified the islanders. When the *Nauticon* was in the Society Islands, 26-27 March 1850, Susan Veeder recorded that two of their men deserted. Her husband 'told the natives he should return in a few days and if they had not caught them he should take away their pigs and burn their houses'. The runaways were swiftly found and returned but it was perhaps only natural that, in future encounters with whalemen, the natives should make sure that they wouldn't be intimidated again.

Then there was the strange habit, common in the early years of the century, of kidnapping one or a few of the savages, and carrying them off as 'curiosities'. The *Antarctic* captured a man in the Caroline Islands, 'for the purpose of educating him, by giving him the opportunity of seeing civilisation' – or so Abby Jane explained. Two more men were taken from an island near New Britain, and named 'Sunday' and 'Monday'. Monday, according to her description, was 'rather sullen in his temper', which seems not surprising. 'Perhaps the thoughts of being a prisoner preyed on his mind,' she admitted. 'At times this savage would sit and look steadfastly upon the ocean towards, as he probably thought, the point from whence he came.'

---

in Honolulu at the same time, looking for a skipper who would take them to 'Strong's Island' in the Caroline Islands, where they wished to establish a mission. According to Pierson's account, he found Handy and asked him if he was going there, but Handy said no, and turned to leave.

Then, all at once, as Pierson remembered it, Handy turned back 'and looked at me very closely and asked, "In what capacity do you go?" I replied, "As a missionary." He looked at me very seriously for a minute or more, without saying a word; after which he said, "I have a mind to take you...for I love the missionary work. I want missionaries to be placed on every island in the ocean...Whalers have been a curse to these islands long enough."'

Handy was as good as his word. The *Belle* left Honolulu on the 24th and cruised along the Equator through the Kingsmill and Marshall Islands (modern Kiribati), on a voyage which finally ended in October, at Kusrae in the Caroline Islands, where the mission party was landed. It was an eventful five months. On several occasions Handy had to intercede between the missionaries and bloodthirsty chieftains: at Ebon, for instance, he managed to extract a promise from the chiefs 'that they would not cut off any more ships, or put any more foreigners to death who might chance to be cast upon their shore'.

It seems only logical then, considering Handy's pious character, that when the *Belle* recruited at the Bay of Islands for home, in February 1857, he should try to seek out his Maori wife of eleven years before. The young woman, however, was gone from the Bay...but she had had a daughter, now living with an aunt who had married an English settler. Handy perceived that the ten-year-old girl was his, and – as one of his sisters in Boston wrote to his granddaughter Alice 33 years later – 'he Professed to be a Christian Man and it was his duty to take [her] home with him'.

And that Handy did. He named her Alice Henrietta Handy, and took her on board his ship...and so a dainty ten-year-old girl sailed across the Pacific on the roaring forties, around Cape Horn and into the alien grey waters of the North Atlantic.

Obviously, however, he could not take her home to his wife. Alice Henrietta was sent to Boston, and cared for by her father's sisters, Mary Himes and Alice Borden, both widows of sea-captains. Like any proper Boston miss she went to school and played the piano, wrote poetry, drew pictures and painted. She was dainty even when grown up, weighing only 86 pounds. When she was twenty she married a carpenter, William A. Vincent. She bore him two children, Alice in 1868, and William, in 1870 – and then she died, at the age of twenty-eight, of consumption.

Benjamin Morrell's stated aim was to turn the natives into 'interpreters and missionaries to open an intercourse with their native isles' and to teach them 'how pleasant it is to attend the worship of the Great Spirit in a Christian temple'. One cannot help but wonder how the natives felt when they were off-loaded in New York, as happened in mid-1831: it gives a whole new dimension to the modern term, 'culture-shock'. Sunday and Monday were by no means alone in their bewilderment, however. The colonisation of Hawaii was drastically affected when a Hawaiian boy, 'Obookiah of Napoopoo', was found crying on the steps of the Yale Chapel in New Haven. Obookiah had been carried to Connecticut by one such souveniring captain, and the pitiful story he told his rescuers led to the beginnings of the Hawaiian mission.

When, in July 1850, the whaleship *Phoenix* 'lowered a boat and went ashore' in the Society Islands, and took 'some few fowls and two men — had some difficulty in keeping them after getting them aboard', the reader feels a harrowing certainty that the logkeeper was talking about the men, not the fowls. However, some natives, particularly Polynesians, seemed to welcome the chance of sailing on a whaler and learning the trade. George Cook of Russell (the man who eventually married Hannah Fawkes) was 'adopted' and taken to England by a whaling captain, and became a skilled whaleman himself.

As the years went by, it became common for Pacific Islanders to ship on the whalers more formally, as greenhands, and, because of the constant problem of desertions in the Pacific, the captains were pleased to take them on. Native seamen could be picked up anywhere, from the Azores and the Cape Verde Islands onwards, but Polynesians (including Hawaiians, Tahitians and Maoris, usually referred to as 'New Zealanders'), were particularly in demand, for they were strong, courageous and instinctively good seamen. The Americans called any Polynesian 'kanaka', which is Hawaiian for 'man', and (to add insult to injury) pronounced it 'ker*nack*'er'.

They also, like Morrell, gave their native recruits fanciful names. When Mrs Alden Potter was on the *Abraham Barker*, 'Shipped one man have nicknamed him Abraham Barker,' noted her husband on 5 December 1871, and then, on the 8th: 'we have shipped four men here. One nicknamed Julius Caesar one Fredrick Douglas one Henry Ward Beecher and the other General Grant all black as ebony.' On the *Nautilus* in 1874 one of the natives was called Jack Knife, and Captain David Briggs of the *Benjamin Cummings* 1859 named his kanakas after rich merchants and owners in New Bedford, and then taught them the ropes with mischievous glee.

The islanders had good reasons for agreeing to sail. There was the adventure, of course, and the opportunity of seeing the world, which appealed to the inquisitive and daring part of the Polynesian nature. It was often a chance to get away from grim conditions on shore. When the *Europa* was at Ocean Island in 1872 Susan McKenzie noted that the natives were starving, for there had been no rain for two years. They shipped two, and could have shipped any number. 'As it was they left one man to drown and James had to turn about and pick him up. So they gave him the name of Moses. The others

# Curiosities

While the early custom of uplifting unwary natives and carrying them off to 'civilisation' might seem eccentric enough, it was just one symptom of a nineteenth century passion for collecting exotica. The fad was started by the early explorers, and nothing – as long as it was foreign enough – was exempt. The New Bedford shipping paper for 15 March 1859 reported that there had been a crisis on board a British man-of-war. The ship was carrying a mixed lot of wild animals, a present to Queen Victoria from the Emperor of Morocco. The lion got loose, and every manjack on board took refuge in the rigging. 'The king of the forest (and pro tem of the ship),' the report went on, attacked a buffalo, which retaliated. Some hardy soul lassooed the cat, and then it was stunned with a marlinspike and order once more reigned.

When Helen Jernegan and her family arrived on one of the Marquesas Islands in 1870, her small son Prescott was presented with a little black pig, which was exciting and noteworthy, too. Shells and native handcrafts, however, were more readily collected, being more manageable. Lucy Smith traded in mats on the coast of Africa, and headed up great numbers in casks to take home. When Betsy Morey was in the Gilbert Islands (Kiribati) in March 1855 her husband 'bought me some nice Mats and A few Shells and one Basket that I prize verry much,' she wrote, and the third mate, Mr Briggs 'Presented me with A Sword made verry Curious of Coconut wood and Sharks Teeth.'

Such presents were, of course, interesting and acceptable, and it is little wonder that many homes in London and New England became crammed with rare and wonderful artifacts – as this photograph, taken in New Bedford, testifies. However, the fashion was worth money as well. Such was the craze for 'curiosities' that museums and private collectors were willing to hand over large sums for anything unusual or rare.

Rare shells were eagerly sought after, and Eliza Underwood specialised in these, with a shrewd eye for the price they would fetch back in London. Men were more likely to collect lacquerwork – such as erotic Chinese screens – preserved heads and weapons. Idols with impressive genitals were also very popular.

It was probably inevitable that the busy trade in curiosities should be augmented by a brisk trade in fakes. James Edward Little of Taunton, Somerset, for instance, was a furniture restorer with a profitable sideline in trading in curiosities. It is hardly surprising that a man of his skills should fall for the temptation to make curiosities of his own, and his fakes are still occasionally found in collections and sales.

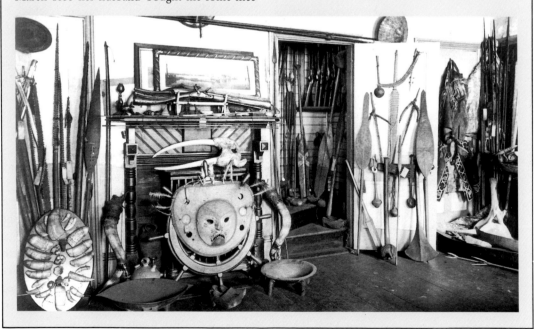

they named Sam Slick and Jim Crow. Not a particle of clothing do they wear.'

Natives who returned home had acquired skills and goods that were valued highly, and could attain high positions as translators, traders or pilots. 'Natives in a canoe came,' noted Asenath Taber, the eleven-year-old daughter of the master of the *Alice Frazier*, at Tongatabu, 2 January 1855. 'One of them argued to show us the anchorage for one hatchet. He is now on board. . . He had no clothes on and he maid me shamed, so Father gave him some pants and Mr Edwards a shirt. I gave him a pipe and Mr Smith some tobacco. And then he was allright.'

Shipping an islander could lead to an improvement in whaleman relationships with his neighbours and kinfolk. Not only had he learned English the way the whalemen spoke it, but he could vouch for the character of many of the captains and men. In February 1855 Betsy Morey visited one of the Society Islands, and when she went on deck 'saw three Natives verry good looking men one informed me his name was Whitfield,' she wrote. 'I observed to him that he had a good name he says Yes sir my Capt named me, I found he had ben to sea, and he could talk verry good English. I asked him if he thought he should ever go to sea again he says No Sir I dont calculate to for I have got married I got a wife and child to      I did like to converse with him,' she confessed, 'he appeared so Bright and Inteligent.'

With trust and liking established on both sides favours could be asked and given. When Mrs Potter was on the *Abraham Barker*, 27 July 1872, her husband quite amiably carried 'the Governor, Family and Suite' from one island in the Society group to another: 'about fifty persons in all. The Governor's daughter is also on board,' the logkeeper noted. 'She is to be married to a prince when we arrive in Haapia, she is sixteen years old and weighs *360* pounds.'

However, this happy situation, obviously, would only develop when the kanaka recruits were well-treated. It was by no means always the outcome, for some whaling skippers treated their native seamen abominably. Captain Solomon Gray 'kicked and pounded John Bull (a Kanaka) at the wheel so that he can scarcely move, and cannot turn himself in his berth,' wrote Nat Morgan, the steerage boy on board ship *Hannibal* in 1849. He continued:

> 'This is not the first man he has pounded at the wheel – and the worst and most profane language I ever heard from mortal lips flows from his – He thinks nothing of calling a man "a d--n w----s ghost" or "wh----s pup" or son of b---h and like elegant expressions are his common address – even in the presence of his wife – His little daughter will accomplish her education young I think, if she is on shipboard with her father.'

'Fine times today – the ship would not work to suit the Capt and he has sworn most blasphemously. . .' Nat Morgan wrote another time. 'His wife begged him not to curse and swear so, and he told her to go below and she would not hear it.' It seems poetic justice, then, when the reader of Nat's journal finds that on 7 June 1850 Captain Gray was 'taken sick in the night, so as to require aid to turn in his bed'. Then, next morning, 'Mrs Gray came on deck and said her husband was dying.' The instant she went back below a kind of party broke out. 'Mahe the Kanaka danced, threw up his hat and kept saying in broken English – good-good-good – and many others,' remarked young Nat, 'expressed a similar feeling.'

Unfortunately the celebration was somewhat premature. The 'dying' captain had taken leave of the first mate, along with many solemn instructions

# Flogging

'The captain whipped the [cabin] boy Sam for calling the Steward a liar,' wrote the steerage boy, Nat Morgan, on the *Hannibal* in 1849. 'The steward first called the boy a damn liar – For my part I think the officers more to blame than the boy – for they allow him to call them damn fools – and the Captain sets such an example and uses such language before him that I consider the boy's chance for a most accomplished education a fine one. The Captain,' he added with evident feeling, 'can curse and swear beyond any think in Webster's Dictionary.'

One cannot help but feel some sympathy for Mrs Gray, surrounded as she was with such unpleasantness. She was a kind soul, who made gruel and sent it to men who were sick, and treated all hands on occasion with 'some nice cakes'. She even loved her awful husband: 'Capt Gray lowered once alone,' Nat recorded, 'and was soon lost to sight in a dense fog – his wife was alarmed and cried till he came aboard again.'

No one was exempt from a 'bucko' captain's rages: Luther Little, who commanded the *Israel* on the 1841 voyage, flogged his own son so savagely that the lad was laid up for three days. Captain Hiram Fisher of the *Meridian* 1829-31 was another such nasty piece of work, and his men were much more upset about his floggings than this etching might indicate: 'We did not ship to be bumbused about,' wrote a seaman, Henry Collins; 'we Shiped to get A voiage but this way we shant     We are dertaminated Not to see Another man Whipped for the voiage if we die by the doing.'

concerning the voyage; the vessel was running 'colors half mast, union down', and Captain Clark of the *Henry Kneeland* came on board. Gray instantly felt better for the company. 'At noon when I went aft to dinner,' Nathaniel Morgan observed, 'he was sitting up in a chair and called Franklin Brown (one of the owners) all the damn sons of bitches that he could think of, and that was by no means a few – I thought then that the prospect of his dying was not so great as some of the crew wished.'

> 'Whaling vessels have been in the habit of visiting this place [Nauru] for many years, and here are shown the effects of a heathen intercourse with white (I can scarcely say civilized) men from civilized lands. It is true that at home this class appear like civilized beings, but it is too often the case that when men visit foreign climes, their conduct shows that they have left their souls at home.' – Mary Wallis.

On 1 September 1842 Captain Norris of the *Sharon* killed one of his native seamen, for no comprehensible reason. He kicked the poor fellow in the 'face head and temples' and then ordered him to fill the salt water tub, flogging him all the while. The seaman began stumbling and falling while the captain followed him 'swearing at him at an Awful rate at the same time pooting

## Gertrude West

Ellsworth Luce West of Martha's Vineyard, Massachusetts, shipped first on the *James Arnold* in 1882 at the age of eighteen. He was a prudent sort of fellow, perhaps because his mother had been widowed when he was just a few months old, and had kept herself and her five children by taking in laundry at $1 per day. Most unusually, he managed to save money on his first voyage, paying for his own outfit and making the immense sum of $25 by selling the scrimshaw he made.

In 1892 he came home from voyage and found a young schoolteacher boarding with his brother Clem. He and this young lady, Gertrude Eager, became engaged, and when he went off again, as the mate of the *California*, they made a pact to read the same chapter of the *Bible* each night, and apparently the pledge was kept. Then, the following year, he was given the command of the ship and the agent, William Lewis, offered to pay all expenses for Ellsworth to go east and get married; he even suggested that he take her on the ship for a honeymoon. West followed this generous advice, but his experiences as a wife-carrying master did not run at all smoothly.

In December 1894 he ignored the owners' strict instructions and took Gertrude with him

when he sailed for the Arctic Ocean. The moment he made port in San Francisco, on 7 November 1895, he lost command of the ship; 18 days later the *California* went out again with Charles Fisher in command, and West was demoted to first mate of the *Belvedere*, Captain Whitesides. It was not a happy experience.

Whitesides was 56 years old and had recently married an eighteen-year-old salesgirl from a New Bedford department store, and Ellsworth West was a testy sort of fellow who was candidly critical of his captains. Within a few the piece of Whaleline Acrost his back with all his mite'. The native fell down for the last time 'by the side of the Triworks on the larboard side there to rise no more'. Norris remarked to the second mate that he did believe 'the nigger was dying', and then the corpse was launched overboard without ceremony.

When the reader of this remarkable journal finds that Captain Norris was attacked and slaughtered most bloodily by natives at Rotumah on 5 November 1845 (his throat was cut with one of his own whaling spades), this event, too, seems like poetic justice. It meant, however, that many of the wives were very nervous about going on shore. When the *Bowditch* recruited at Rotumah on 13 March 1853, Elizabeth Waldron noted that 'there have been lots of kanakers on board all day'.

They seemed friendly enough, though 'nearly naked', and 'appeared to be very much pleased with the baby and was looking down in the cabin through the side lights all day, the first white picaniny I suppose they ever saw'. The natives were evidently trustworthy too, for 'three of them are going in the ship', and the island 'looked delightful and pleasant'. However, Elizabeth did not go on shore — and, when it is remembered that Captain Norris

short weeks West and the girl were corresponding only by notes (presumably passed across the table) and Whitesides (who, it seems, doted on the lass) retaliated by handing over the whole responsibility of the ship to West, so that he could devote his full attention to his wife — much to West's fury and the amusement of the crew and other captains. The outcome was probably inevitable: West was laid off and he and Gertrude filled in the time by taking a course in navigation in San Francisco.

In 1897 he was given the command of the *Horatio*. The vessel was reputed to be unlucky, but nevertheless Gertrude went along with him. She seemed to cope very well; she wore Bloomer costume in practical style, and kept a diary made up of such notelike entries as, 'Jan 4 [1898] Washed gingham dress & apron Lat. 0.28 N Lon 173.51.' Then, in February, the ship was battered by a severe typhoon. 'The captain lashed me to a chair,' she told a reporter in San Francisco later; 'because the fury of the storm made it impossible to stand up anywhere.' Then, when a large amount of the rigging was abruptly ripped away, Ellsworth came down to the cabin and ordered her to put on all the warm clothes she could, ready to abandon ship.

'I was so frightened my fingers were numb,' she related, 'but somehow I managed to put on four dresses over my bloomers. I knew without question that I was preparing for an open boat in that awful sea.' As it happened, the storm moderated and the *Horatio*, 'though badly strained, weathered the gale.'

The whaler's end was not far off, however. When Gertrude boarded the ship again, on 14 December 1898, she was oppressed with a sense of impending disaster. She dreamed about the pets she carried — a yellow canary, a black kitten and a terrier: the ship was 'metamorphosed into the bird, and the cat sat on a rock splashed by the sea. The cat's eyes seemed dilated and steadfast, and I knew that it was charming the bird and luring her to destruction. All at once the dog set up a bark...Then [in the dream] I heard the captain shouting, "Clear away the boats".'

The dream terrified Gertrude so much that she woke her husband and made him go up to deck to check. The ship was sailing serenely then...but on 27 January 1899 the *Horatio* ran onto a reef at Kusaie, in the Caroline Islands. Gertrude was sitting in the transom, reading, when the dog barked wildly and ran up the stairs. Gertrude followed the terrier, and when she was halfway up the companionway the ship struck. An instant later she heard Ellsworth shouting, 'Clear away the boats' — in the exact tone and words of her dream.

was slaughtered at that same place less than eight years before, who can blame her for feeling rather shy?

This made the prospect of shipwreck extremely harrowing. The best one could hope for, perhaps, was that the island where one was wrecked should be uninhabited. According to an old whaleman, Captain Roland F. Coffin, that is exactly what happened to one Nantucket woman. In his youth he was in a whaleboat that was towed off by a whale and then got lost. Twenty-four hours later the ship was still nowhere in sight and the boat's crew were getting short of provisions, so they left the whale, set sail and made a small island.

It appeared deserted when they landed, but there was a very welcome spring of fresh water. The ground about the pool seemed 'alive with some kind of creepin' animal' which ran off when they came, but the men paid little attention to that. Then they sighted a 'native' who appeared very timid, but when they got within hailing distance the figure turned out to be a very tattered and weatherbeaten American female.

This castaway had been the wife of a whaling captain, the only survivor when his ship was wrecked on the reef. In true romantic style she scavenged enough material from the wreck to set herself up and then she settled down to waiting for rescue; she had been waiting, in fact, for five years. Somewhat naturally, she was overcome with relief and delight to see these fellow Yankees. 'It ain't no dream, you are real,' she cried. 'Thank God, I am saved!' Then, when she'd calmed down, she promised to make them a capital stew.

And she did. And they ate it, 'The woman' – as Coffin told it – 'looked on quite delighted for to see us eat, and a-fillin' each chap's dish as fast as it was empty; but after she had helped us all around for the sixth time. . . says she, "I'll bet you don't any of you know what you've been eatin'."'

'"Well, marm," said our skipper' – but had to admit he couldn't guess, for all that it was 'a powerful good stew. . ."Well," says she, "that there was a rat stew."' The ship-rats had also survived the wreck, and she had been living on those rats for all those five years.

Unfortunately the ship took a while to find the lost boat, so the sailors were forced to survive as she had, on 'roast rat, broiled rat, fried rat, rat fricassee, and rat stew'; but then at last the vessel came and took the people away, leaving the rats in full possession of the island.

The whaling habit of poking about in seldom visited corners of the ocean also meant that the whalemen (and, sometimes, their wives) made a large number of discoveries. 'At 10 this morning discovered a small island some 5 miles distant,' noted Mary Brewster 9 February 1849. '. . .as there is no such island laid down in the charts or books I gave it the name of Brewster's Island. The latitude of it was 00.48 miles North Long 176.30 West.' Many a woman had the satisfaction, too, of noting that she was the first 'white', 'English' or 'American' woman to set foot in some exotic place.

It was a mixed delight, however, for the experience was apt to be so suspenseful. Betsy Tower could not have been pleased on 12 May 1848, when her husband 'saw a China [Japanese] Junk in distress, took the crew on board our Ship' and then steered for the misty shores of Japan. That country was shrouded in mystery as well as fog, and had the reputation of treating shipwrecked seamen with barbaric cruelty.

Betsy Tower had only 48 hours of suspense, however, for on 14 May 'at 11 AM saw fishing Boats and run down to them...Found them to be Japanese and put on board those that we took from the Junk then Tacked off shore'.

The doubtful honour of being the first white woman in Japan went to another whaling wife, Abigail Jernegan, in April 1856. She was on board her husband Nathaniel's ship, *Eliza F. Mason*, when they found themselves with a head wind and, according to the logbook, 'the Capt concluded to go into the harbor of Hakodate and stay till the wind came fair'. Luckily for Abigail Jernegan's equanimity, there were 'two British frigates-of-war of over forty guns each' in the harbour. Then, however, Mrs Jernegan received a somewhat disturbing invitation.

'She said a delegation of [Japanese] officers rowed out to the ship and escorted her and Uncle Nat ashore — and through the streets and shops,' reminisced a niece, Louise Winter Nolen Huntsman. According to the ship's log, Mrs Jernegan 'had not been on shore more than two minutes before there were more than a thousand Japanese collected around them'.

> 'But she said they were not allowed to touch anything,' Louise Huntsman continued. 'The next morning there came another boatload of Japanese officers resplendent in scads of gold braid. They boarded the ship — and Uncle Nat and Aunt Abbie were really scared — for they thought that they had committed some offence — But the officers marched up to them — bowed very low — and presented Aunt Abbie with a pin — just a common one. She said she must have dropped it while ashore — and they had never seen a pin.'

'And,' the logbook keeper declared, 'we ascertained after some enquiry that she is the first white woman that has visited this place.'

Mary Brewster broke new ground for her whaling sisters when she accompanied her husband on a bay-whaling cruise to lower California in November 1846. While the whalemen knew that grey whales congregated in the warm shallow lagoons of Baja California during the northern winter, they had left that species alone before. Firstly, grey whales were small and the oil was poor, and, secondly, they were extremely pugnacious. Legend has it that one infuriated specimen broke a boat to splinters and then chased the boat's crew up a tree: it was yarns like this that inspired the whalemen to call grey whales 'devil fish'.

However, as the usual prey of the whalemen became scarce in the grounds, any kind of oil, taken with whatever difficulty, was acceptable. During the Christmas season of 1845-6 two American ships, the *Hibernia* of New London and the *United States* of Stonington, negotiated treacherous channels and mudbanks into Magdalena Bay, anchored there and took 32 whales between them. The second mate of the *United States* had been killed and the first mate badly injured, but nonetheless William Brewster, deliberating as the *Tiger* cruised along the California coast after the nor'west season of 1846, concluded to try the lagoons himself. The ship almost went aground in the uncharted shallows, but then at last they made the bay. The migrating whales had not arrived as yet, but the Brewsters found that two other ships had got in there before them.

These were the *Hibernia* and the *Brooklyn*, both of New London. Captain Smith of the *Hibernia* sent a boat, with word, Mary recorded, 'that it was a very bad place to get in with a ship and said we had better go right out'. As a welcome, this was less than satisfactory. As Mary commented, 'the conclusion is that he does not want any company'. Why not? The whole affair looked definitely shady, and Captain Smith (when he arrived on board the *Tiger*) had an appropriately shifty look, too. He, according to Mrs Brewster, was 'a man somewhere about 50 with nothing prepossessing in his appearance and wears a yellow wig'.

Captain Jeffrey of the *Brooklyn* was no better. 'Capt J– is a very ignorant uneducated man,' Mary decided, 'and I have taken an uncountable dislike to him. Capt Smith talks and he utters the same or swears it is just so.' There was a war going on in the hinterland between the Mexicans and the American forces, to add to the uncertainty of the situation, but nevertheless Brewster decided to stay on and Mary was 'very much pleased'. Like the whaling wives who followed in her wake in future years, she found that the weather was beautiful and the food abundant: 'can get a great variety of fish, clams or what we call cohaug oysters, crawfish and birds.'

And so they filled in the time while waiting for the whales in clamming, fishing, going on picnics — and wondering what the crews of the *Brooklyn* and the *Hibernia* were up to, for they seemed to spend most of their time on Marguerita Island, labouring away at something mysterious. The crew of the *Tiger*, being bored, sent out stealthy parties to investigate. Then, on 3 December, after tracking footsteps hither and about, the fellows from the *Tiger* discovered the chaps from the *Brooklyn* and *Hibernia*, encamped in a gully and digging for gold.

They had anticipated the Californian goldrush by almost exactly one year, but not quite in the right locality. The two ships 'had come up the bay on purpose to dig it,' Mary was told, 'and did not intend anyone should know it. Gold is all the talk here,' she noted; she found it highly amusing. 'The spaniards have told them it is gold and they believe they are making their everlasting fortunes.'

The men from the *Tiger*, by contrast, found the idea of gold beguiling. They got settled down to digging too, and so did the crews of two more ships, the *Cabinet* and the *Trescott*, when they arrived in the bay. 'Capt. Smith says dig oh dig, only don't disturb our place, says the whole Island is full enough to load 30 ships. I,' Mary added, 'have been busily employed in sewing.'

And so the days passed by, as Mary sewed and observed the doings. 'Capt Jeffrey has just left us,' she recorded on 10 December; 'he is really beside himself. It is gold and no mistake, said he took a piece of it over to La Paz and they said it was first rate kind. They have got some 12 casks full [of stone] and are as eager as though it was really solid metal just from the mint. I hear and laugh at some of the sayings which are truly ridiculous.' Four days later she went on shore to inspect the diggings for herself.

'Here we found the different companies to work. . .we walked to the place where the tents were pitched. . .I entered one tent and such a looking place blankets pillows and dishes kettles pots chests provisions pumkins potatoes all mixed up together and dirt and grease in profusion. Whilst here we heard Capt. Bottum's gang had found some of the mineral some quarter of a mile up the gully and we concluded we would walk up and look at them. They had just blasted a rock and were breaking it up in small pieces, the scene was truly laughable. . .A woolen mitten was kept, to put and keep this choice stuff in and was constantly passed round for all the small particles. I set up on the ridge which commanded a view of the whole proceedings, no poor mortals ever worked with half the evident satisfaction as they did.'

'Oh what calculations what riches and what talk,' she commented next day when Captain Jeffrey came on board. 'It is as good as the Park theater,' she decided, and went back to her sewing. On 22 December she received a call from 'A spanish lady and her husband', who had ridden 30 miles 'to see an American woman and in her wish was gratified in seeing my dear self. She could not speak a word of english nor I spanish,' Mary commented, 'so the interview was something like a quaker meeting.' Nevertheless she was pleased with her visitor. 'She appeared well, was dressed in a light calico dress made with short sleeves, short plain waist, a small shall round her neck, a long shawl of worsted trimmed with lace. Both sexes smoke,' Mary added, obviously intrigued. 'The tobaco is cut up very fine and put into small strips of white paper, when folded make a neat cigar.'

She received more visitors, who brought trade and presents of produce, including cheese which was 'made in small cakes and patted out with the hand and laid on sticks and dryed'. All this was merely an interlude, however, in the overriding preoccupation with gold. Then, on 7 January 1847, just one week after the whales began to come in, the bubble burst. 'The supposed gold is proved to be dross which shews us that it is not all gold that glitters. . .' Mary ruminated. 'I laugh when I think of the mining work and Capt J-- and S-- are truly disappointed, they had each 20 casks full of the stone, probably blubber will do for ballast now.'

Mary was also the first American woman in the western Arctic, and while she might have relished the glamour of this later on, at the time she did not enjoy the experience. On the night of 26 June 1849 she and her husband William 'had just got to sleep when the fourth officer came and said the indians was coming. . .

'. . .[as] a former visitor to these regions had given them a hard name our officers and crew was far from being pleased with the sound when Mr Cook went below and gave the alarm — *The bloody indians are coming.*" Neither was I pleased       I had in a measure got use to the ice. . .but the indians was a new subject & very unexpected — I asked husband what he should do, [he] said he should not allow them to come on board till he could see something of them [by daylight] — a few spades was got down — four old muskets loaded neither of them though would go off — or not more than one.'

As it happened, the natives were even more surprised than the people on board the *Tiger* (particularly when they laid eyes on Mary), and rather hurt at receiving such a suspicious reception, but nonetheless it was quite a fright — and it was certainly not the first time that she'd been alarmed. 'We are now in the neighborhood of a number of small low islands. . .' Mary wrote in the Tuamotu Archipelago on 10 October 1847. 'It is said they are inhabited by cannibals. I feel anxious till we get clear of them.'

Mary Brewster had an opportunity to show that she was made of sterner stuff when she went ashore at Tutuila in the Navigator Islands (Samoa) on 26 January 1849. As she and her husband returned to the boat from a visit to the mission, they encountered 'some two hundred of natives all marching with their war implements singing and acting out the numerous parts of their battles'. One would think that the sight of massed warriors in war paint would set up a shudder in any whaling wife's breast — but not our Mary. 'They kept excellent time,' she merely observed, 'and made a manly appearance.'

Much of her calmness, however, was not due to her courage, but to the fact that the mission there was so well established. Mary Wallis stated once that 'civilization does not follow intercourse with civilized people, unless accompanied with the gospel', and the state of affairs in Tutuila then was certainly an illustration of this. The missionary in charge, Archibald Wright Murray, had excellent rapport with the chiefs, with the result that Tutuila was one of the most peaceful and orderly of the South Seas islands.

Wilkes, who surveyed and explored Tutuila in 1839, remarked on the 'beneficial effects of the labors of the missionaries'. The whaling wives agreed with him heartily, and so did Benjamin Morrell. 'Thanks to the missionaries, and the blessing of Heaven which has attended their pious and humane exertions,' he wrote while in New Zealand, 'ships may now anchor in safety in many of those very harbours where the greatest danger was once to be apprehended.' A mission — obviously — made all the difference.

A place with a mission was not only safer, but a mission was a fit place to take a decent woman to call. Tough old salts, with uneasy memories of groggeries and naked maidens, must have been glad of that when their wives insisted on shipping. A woman, most surely, had no place in the usual kind of Pacific paradise (or on a whaleship, for that matter) but the gruffest of rough diamonds found the notion of his wife visiting some mission quite easy to picture. Because of this, an imponderable number of women made unexpected and at times rather inconvenient calls on missionary wives all over the Pacific.

Aitutaki in the Cook (then called 'Hervey') Islands was one such, and Mary Brewster (again) was one of the pioneering visitors. She went on shore on 24 October 1847, and found 'the Ryols [sic], the missionaries, who welcomed us with a cordial reception.' Mrs Royle 'was glad to see a female. Mrs Greene [of the *Ontario*] was here some two weeks ago and spent the day which with myself was all she had seen for a long while.'

The hospitable Mrs Royle was fated to see many more whaling sisters. The *Moctezuma* called at Aitutaki the following year, 4 December 1848. 'I went on shore with my husband,' wrote Betsy Tower. 'He went to trade got some fruit and hogs and fowls I went to the house of the English missionary Mr Royal [sic] found them to be very pleasant people.'

'We arrived to Whytootaki Sat. Dec 17,' wrote Charlotte Dehart. She was on board the *Roman*, which was on a Christmas cruise after the 1859 North Pacific season. 'We got a few recruits of fruits and other necessaries,' she noted. Next day they were joined by the *Reindeer*, Captain Edward and Adra Ashley. The women were old acquaintances, for they had spent the northern summer together in Hilo, Hawaii, while their husbands whaled in the Arctic.

## Abram and Charlotte Dehart

'We have had a very fine day, and I have had a very pleasant gam with Mrs Dehart, this afternoon,' wrote Eliza Williams on 16 April 1860, in the Sea of Japan. Eliza had 'met with Capt. D. several times, but I had never had the pleasure of seeing his Wife. I was much pleased with her visit,' she decided.

Charlotte Weeks Sherman was born in September 1829, and 'Abram' (in the shipping papers and the census records his name is given as Abraham), her husband, was five years her senior. He became a whaling master in Honolulu on 21 September 1853; Captain Edward T. Sherman died of palsy, and Abram took over the command of the *Coral*. His next command was the bark *Roman II*, and when he took her out of New Bedford on 24 August 1857, Charlotte sailed with him.

It was a poor, unprofitable voyage – when they arrived in the Arctic in May 1858, the

ship was still 'clean', having taken no oil, but Charlotte coped remarkably well with the vicissitudes of sea life. She was not even seasick: 'We have got in most all her sails and she pitchy now,' she wrote in her first rough sea; 'I have not seen such seas before but I am not sick      I think I am quite a sailor      we are all well and harty.' The birth of a son early in the voyage did cause a tremour or two, but, like other women who had babies to care for, Charlotte found the pleasures and problems of bringing up an infant on board a sure remedy for boredom.

'My darling babe is in bed asleep,' she wrote in August 1858; 'what would I do without him he is such company his father has to be aloft nearly all the time.' That 'darling babe' was nameless, 'for we have not got a whale yet'. Then, on 16 September, when he was eight months old, the first whales were taken (Dehart was so desperate that he took that most unusual prey, orcas, two of which made only 15 bbls), and 'this afternoon the Capt. Christened the baby and gave him a name Alex C.'

'It was quite an unexpected pleasure to me meeting with Mrs Dehart,' wrote Adra. The two women renewed their friendship 'up to Mr Reals [sic] the Missionarys, and the only white family on the Island'. The Royles had four daughters: 'The girls said never a word. Their ages ranged from sixteen to twelve and you may imagine how they looked all dressed in pink calico made from the same piece and made after the same style.'

Helen Jernegan visited Aitutaki on the *Oriole* in 1866, and found the Royles pleasant, too: 'They lived in a thatch hut on a high hill,' she wrote in her memoirs, 'and it was a delightful situation, with a broad view of the Pacific. They had not left the Islands for 25 years and were very glad to see us. 'They cooked their food in an oven made of stones in the yard,' she added. The Jernegans gave them a bale of calico, perhaps for dresses. Then Lucy Smith called at Aitutaki in January 1876, and found Mr and Mrs Royle still there, still labouring away. She accepted their invitation to 'come on shore' on the 12th.

> 'There are 1500 inhabitants on the island and at least 1000 were on the shore to see us land. They filled the road leading to Mr Royle's house and as we went up the native police took little whips and whipped each way to make room for us to walk and all that could get to the edge of the road held their hands to shake hands with us sometimes three extended their hands and caught mine at the same time. There are 600 children that attend school regularly    Mr Royle has charge with 70 native teachers under him    he is also assisted by his wife and daughter Alice they gave us a very cordial welcome and we enjoyed the day very much. We visited the schoolhouse and church large buildings built of Adobe with thatched roofs the pillars and rafters all covered with cloth made from the mulberry tree and painted with black figures. We stopped until about four and when we came away brought a number of curiosities presented by Mr Royle and family.'

Aitutaki's larger sister island, Rarotonga, was equally popular; the provisions were excellent, and there was a well-established mission, too. The *Lexington* recruited at Rarotonga in March 1854 and Eliza Brock 'stoped at the Missionary's house, Rev Mr Buzzacotts [and] had a very pleasant visit stayed there two days found them to be very fine Folkes, very pious people'. Their daughter Sarah, 'a very amiable young Lady; was Educated in England. . . plays well on the piano'. Two of the daughters of the Reverend Mr Hardie of Upolu were there as well, 'came there to be educated'.

Eliza went to Mr Buzzacott's 'new Church; just finished built by the Natives a very nice one [though] not quite equal to the Churches in America'. She also met the Queen, 'shook hands with her. She was dressed in a white Robe, with a wide long red belt around her waist.' The weather was 'extreem warm' and the mosquitoes were abundant, but the visit was well worth such minor inconvenience.

'Rarotonga is a beautiful island,' she wrote on March 11; 'a complete forest of Trees loaded with all kinds of Fruit.' In July 1870 Rachel Beckerman went on shore there, too, and 'spent two days with the missionary's family, Mr Chalmers. This is a very pretty Island,' she decided, 'the climate is very mild, the natives are exceedingly kind to strangers who visit them, the productions of the Island, are cocoanuts, vees [mango], pineapples, Breadfruit, Bananas,

Plantains, Limes, Oranges, Coffee, Cotton, Mummie Apples [pawpaw], Yams, Sweet Potatoes, Tarro [taro] and many other Tropical fruits.'

Emma Thomas called on the Chalmers family, too, in August 1873. 'Oh Mother,' she sighed in a letter, 'I do wish you was here with us so you could see this beautiful place. . .It is a very healthy place and so much fruit all the time.' Emma stayed only five days and would have loved to stop longer, and it seems very likely that the mission women would have liked her company for longer, too. Back in October 1847, at Aitutaki, Mary Brewster wrote, 'Seldom have I passed a day in more agreeable manner' — and it seems evident that mission wives must have found the visits most agreeable too. It must have been very soothing when a decent, pious woman took such a flattering interest in all they had done: in that respect little had changed since Abby Jane Morrell visited the mission at the Bay of Islands in January 1830.

In December 1849 Sarah Taber called at Huahina, one of the Society Islands, and her experience seems just as satisfactory. 'We passed two weeks,' she wrote; 'got accomidated in the family of the Rev Charles Barff while they [the crew] were imployed on board in wooding and watering the ship.' Missionaries provided comfort, too, in times of stress. The *Gazelle* put into 'New Nantucket' (in modern Kiribati) 22 July 1858, for the rather grim purpose of burying the steward, who had died in a fit. 'How uncertain is life!' Eleanor Baker, the captain's wife, penned. However: 'It was a great consolation to think we could give him a burial on shore on an Island that is covered with birds and the earth is composed of guano which will probably preserve him for years in this state.'

In June 1860 Eleanor arrived in 'the harbour of Pangopango', Samoa, on a more personally tragic errand. She went 'to church after which we went to the missionary's house and was kindly received'. Mrs Baker needed their kindness badly: her first baby had died, just ten weeks old, and she had brought the small corpse to them for Christian burial. 'At times it seems as though I could not endure it,' she grieved. 'I cannot wish him back in this world of sin, for he is doubtless in Heaven for he knew no sin. To beautiful for earth, Eleanor N. Baker.'

Of all the exotic South Seas islands, Pitcairn was considered by the wives to be about the most romantic, for this was the fabled place where Fletcher Christian had set up his colony after the mutiny on the *Bounty*. There was no mission, but John Adams, one of the leaders of the mutiny, had repented of his wicked ways, and had instilled Christian practices into the lives of the island families.

Susan Veeder called there in April 1850, and found the landing difficult, but the inhabitants were 'the kindest people I have ever met with'. She visited the Fletcher Christian house, and 'had the pleasure of naming a little one while their. Son of henry and Albina Young, the number of Residents is 164.' In 1852 'Admiral Moresly, of HBM Pacific fleet' wrote to the *New Bedford Whalemen's Shipping List* that Captain and Mrs Weeks of the *Adeline Gibbs* 'were living on shore. It would be a happy circumstance,' he added, 'if a person like her could be found to reside among them.'

Two Nantucket whaling wives did reside at Pitcairn Island for a few months in 1850. Charles Grant of the *Potomac* left his wife Nancy on shore, and Mrs Palmer of the *Navigator* stopped there, too. Both women were in delicate health, Mrs Grant with a pregnancy and Mrs Palmer with 'the consumption'. Nancy Grant bore a baby boy on 24 December, but in the meantime Mrs Palmer's condition had proved fatal. The log for the *Navigator* of 2 October 1850 reads, '...heading for Pitcairn's Island at 5 O'clock PM Capt Palmer went on shore at 6 spoke ship *Robert Edwards* of New Bedford and heard of the death of Mrs Palmer middle part strong breezes...'

George Palmer had arrived just a few days too late to be at the side of his wife as she died. Instead he found a grave — and a poem, dedicated to his name, which his wife had composed on her deathbed.

Both the poem and the tale behind it were considered extremely romantic, certainly appropriate for such a setting as Pitcairn Island. It became a kind of whaling bestseller, copied into the backs of countless journals. 'Farewell my husband,' it began,

> 'The cold hand of death
> So long extended now arrests my breath
> I feel the impervious mandate and comply
> For not today have I just learned to die
> My days of suffering and my nights of pain
> I thank my God have not been sent in vain
> My faith is strong in Jesus I confide
> I know that I shall live, for he hath died
> Yes, my dear Husband, though that wasted form
> Must mingle with the dust and feed the worms...

And so on...and on, it ran, until the last triumphant line —

> '...Farewell, beloved — until we meet again!'

And how did Captain George Palmer feel when he read this remarkable dying effort? The imagination quails.

# 8
# Around Cape Horn

'In fact, I asked a little boy
If he could tell where he was born
He answered with a mark of joy
"Round Cape Horn".'
                    – old Nantucket song.

**W**HILE it may seem rash to take a wooden windjammer into the Pacific via the westward Cape Horn route, many whaling skippers did it, and had no compunction about taking their wives on that uncomfortable passage as well. It is little wonder, however, that those wives grew somewhat nervous as Tierra del Fuego was neared. 'The ship steering for Staten land which reminds me we are nearing Cape Horn, the only place I have dreaded to reach,' Mary Brewster meditated on 27 January 1846, on the *Tiger*, 'having heard so much relative to the winds which prevail and storms.'

'I shall be glad to get around the Cape,' confessed Almira Gibbs of the *Nantucket* on 27 November 1855. 'That seems to trouble me about as much as anything at the present.' The men had work to occupy their minds, even if the conditions were grim. The women were trapped below, where, as Almira Gibbs put it, all was 'dark and lonesome enough', and where there was little to do but brood on about discomfort and probable dangers. The days must have dragged for those women, heightened by fear, worsened by sickness, made dreadful by the dark and damp. 'The weather cold and no stove up dead lights all closed and calked to keep the water out,' wrote Mary Brewster on 30 January 1846.

'Quite cold, have to stop below in the cabin altogether it is so dark that I can't see without a light,' Almira Gibbs penned almost precisely nine years later, and then added, bracingly, 'but this is Cape horn weather so they tell me and suppose it is.' And so it was — and it seemed to go on for ever. Because the prevailing gales blew from the west, contrarily ahead for the ships, that passage went on...and on. 'We are now near the Falkland Islands,' wrote Harriet Swain on the *Catawba* on 6 April 1853, 'but make no headway which is rather discouraging, as our passage has been prolonged beyond all their expectations and all are anxious to get round the Cape where the weather is more even.'

'All we (who have our watch below) can do is to set on the floor by the stove and talk of friends at home, hoping for better days,' she sighed on 21 April. Better days were a long while coming. On 13 May she penned, 'Have been sick 12 days, vomiting up everything I took down. During the time it has been a continual succession of gales of wind with rain hail and cold. We have made no headway in the time but have instead drifted back which is very discouraging to all.'

'This is off Cape Horn,' noted Mary Brewster on 4 February 1846, 'here we are thumping about wind ahead and like to be, hard old place. . . A small chart of Cape Horn hangs up before me and never was a chart so often looked at as this by me. Every day the distance we made is pencilled out but instead of advancing we go backwards.' Staring and pencilling did little good: sixteen days later the old ship *Tiger* was still off the Cape, doing her utmost to double the Horn:

> 'But oh the sea is dreadful; keeps the ship laboring so hard trying to get along but alas we make but little progress and the motion is so bad I am sick all the time. My room dark and most of the time keep a light burning I am to sick to read think or do anything save roll from one side to the other. Lat. 54.21 Long 80.58.'

However — as she wrote another time — all things come to an end, and so did Cape Horn passages. Then, once the wide Pacific was reached, the ships dispersed according to the grounds they cruised. The nor-westmen like William Brewster steered north for the Hawaiian Islands to reprovision before sailing to the right whaling grounds off north-west America. The sperm whalers, like Captain Obed Swain's *Catawba*, sailed the 'Off-shore' and 'On-shore' grounds off Chile and Peru, recruiting at exotic South American ports like Talcahuano, Tombez and Paita.

> 'For the first time I am at Paita I cannot describe it as being a very pleasant place, not a tree nor spot of grass have I seen      sandy enough. . .the next day was one of there grate days with the church they had a prosesion out with their saints parading about the streets dancing and music it was quite a sight to me      we went into the church in the afternoon and looked about with silent wonder to think that there was so many poor deluded creatures that were kept in darkness by the crafty priests      poor things they sin and then confess and all is right with them. . .' — Almira Gibbs, 3 October 1856.

Predictably, the non-conformist Yankee women, with their Calvinist philosophy of hard work, meditation, piety and pre-destination, found Paita, Tombez and Talcahuano quite scandalous. Henrietta Deblois arrived in Talcahuano, Chile, on Sunday 8 March 1857, expecting 'to go to church, but find there is no Protestant church here. . .Could see the Ladies returning from church with black mantillas over their heads and thrown gracefully over their shoulders,' she recorded. 'They all wore sandals with wooden soles which make a clumping noise on the sidewalk. . .I should never have supposed it was Sunday, stores open Fruit selling music playing, and altogether it seemed like some holiday instead of the holy Sabbath.' The other popular Sabbath occupations, of gambling and cockfighting, were (if possible) even more reprehensible than the music and dancing.

The ports were unequivocally exotic, in both squalor and scenery. 'Paita is nothing but sand not a green thing to be seen,' wrote Sarah Cole on 13 March 1860; 'the houses are nearly all built of bamboo with thatched roofs.' Paita was surrounded by massive sand dunes, and the land was so dry that water was brought in from the hinterland springs in calabashes slung from donkeys, and then sold from door to door, as milk was sold back home in the States. Fresh provisions were brought by coastal sloops as the recruiting whalers arrived. Henrietta Deblois went to market there, in April 1857. 'Here was every variety of costume under the sun,' she observed. 'Black ladies in pearls, white ladies in jet ornaments. Many children perfectly nude; some women almost as bad. Everything from wood to cloth could be obtained here, but in decidedly small quantities.' Somewhat nauseatingly, she found that 'Little nudgets of Dog's meat' were exhibited for sale.

The overriding poverty horrified the wives. Sarah Cole found it upsetting that people slept on the pavements at night, or — if they could afford them — hung hammocks from any handy eave and awning. 'Oh such degraded people as are these poor Peruvians,' wrote Henrietta Deblois in 'the *beautiful* city of Paita', April 1857. 'The houses are in a most tumble-down condition, roofs thatched, narrow filthy streets, houses as dirty, or more disagreeable.' They were as bad as the 'ranchos' she had already observed in Talcahuano, Chile, which were made of 'poles driven into the ground, then covered with boards, and thatched with grass and straw'.

In January 1849 Susan Veeder was 'confined with a fine daughter' at the house of the consul, Mr Crosby, in Talcahuano, and then was left there to convalesce. 'I feel quite feeble to be left among strangers,' she confessed. She did manage to get out to visit Mrs Munkley of the *Emerald*, who was stopping at a boarding house run by a Captain Finch. 'Capt Finches house is very Pleasantly Situated and nicely Furnished,' she described; 'it is A bout the best house hear but not like our houses we have at home. It has two Front rooms two large bedrooms An entry that goes through the house into the back yard and all of the horses mules cows and everything they want their is Carried through the hall.'

The sanitary arrangements were barbaric to match, and not improved by the passing of the years. 'Right opposite our [hotel room] door, is a hennery and two water closets, *well ventilated*,' wrote Lucy Ann Crapo in Talcahuano in April 1879; 'and a yard full of turkeys & hens, which may or may not be served up for our digestion. On our way to the dining room, we have occasion to see where our meals are prepared. Some of the Captains declare that it takes away their appetites, but the ladies are *stronger* and the last to complain.' They were lucky to have any toilets at all, as Lucy Ann testified in October 1880, in reply to a letter from her sister, Ruth Ellen Mosher.

'Wms says if you are coming on this coast one of the most necessaries, is a *house with a hole* in it, as the nearest approach to one he has met with, was a 100 lb Butter keg with a board laid over it. But there was *one* at Paita and three that I know of in Talcahuano. But the women in either place wouldn't go to one if they had a dozen, they all use the *Jimmys* right in their rooms, and think it so strange that we don't.'

The ever-present filth meant that disease was ever-present, too: the wives were very aware that 'yellow jack', 'black vomit' and smallpox lurked in wait in every port. In June 1880 'the smallpox was raging fearfully in Talcahuano', as Carrie Turner recorded. 'I hope it wont break out aboard of the ship I feel somewhat alarmed for fear it might,' she confessed, 'for it is a terrible disease.' At that same time the *Linda Stewart* came into port with four sick men on board. As it turned out, they had a harmless rash and not smallpox at all, but it killed them all the same — because the doctor sent them into isolation in the smallpox ward, where they contracted the disease from the men who were already there. 'The want of *knowing one* [kind of rash] from the *other*,' Lucy Ann Crapo wrote, 'has made a sad chapter in our voyage.'

Wives died, too, many with 'childbed fever' as well as more exotic diseases. Maria Kelley of the *Robert Edwards* died at Talcahuano in January 1856, leaving an infant daughter three days old; 'truly a sorrowful sight,' as Almira Gibbs wrote on 25 February, 'a little babe without a mother and in a strange land.' While she was in port Captain Kelley's ship arrived and he came on shore 'to meet his wife and child and found it motherless, truely his trouble was great'.

## Charlotte and Samuel Wyer

Samuel Wyer, born in 1810, was known firstly as a mariner, and secondly as a 'distinct character': according to the genealogy of the Nantucket Wyers, he was very short and very stout, and, it seems, flamboyant. He married twenty-year-old Charlotte Coffin in August 1844, and in November the following year their first daughter, Charlotte Elizabeth (the 'Charlotte E.' of Charlotte's journal) was born.

In December Samuel was given the command of the whaleship *Enterprise*, and, while there is no evidence that Charlotte and their infant daughter accompanied him on that voyage, her journal later, on the *Young Hero*, is that of a seasoned mariner: 'quite like old times', she wrote more than once. The *Enterprise* arrived home in January 1850, and in October their second daughter, Harriet Amelia, was born. Samuel took out his new command, *Young Hero*, in November, and Charlotte and the girls stopped at home.

Harriet Amelia died just after her second birthday, in October 1852, and this may be the reason Charlotte packed her trunks and took passage to join her husband, leaving Boston on the merchantman *Harriet Irving* in March 1853. It was a long, slow journey, and, considering the poor communications of the time, it must have been a nervewracking wait for her husband. He took his whaler into the port of Valparaiso, Chile, where they had arranged to meet, hung around, sent the ship out, and waited on shore...but still the merchantman failed to arrive. The *Young Hero*

So many Americans died in Talcahuano that a parcel of ground was purchased for an American cemetery, and Maria Kelley was one of the first to be interred there. Her grave became a place of pilgrimage for many of her whaling sisters. Henrietta Deblois went there in March 1857. 'It seemed sad indeed,' she wrote, 'to see her lying so far from home and kindred.'

A preoccupation with death was typical then, but at times it became rather ghoulish. When Sarah Cole was in Tombez in September 1860 she went to a doctor with a swelling in her neck, and was given a virtual death sentence: he diagnosed scrofula (tuberculosis of the glands), an incurable condition at that time. Instead of returning at once to the boarding house she went to the Tombez burying ground, and noted with remarkable calmness that the local custom was to mark each grave with a cross and a heap of skulls.

Even more gruesomely, in March 1862 Sarah viewed an 'angelito' in Talcahuano. This was exactly three months before she died herself, at the age of twenty-eight. When a child died, the Chilean custom was to dress up the body in hired finery. Then the small corpse — or 'angelito' — was taken to a hall and arranged as a kind of centrepiece, around which the family and guests played music and danced, to celebrate the entry of a pure soul

came back, Samuel gave up, and was just setting out when — as he wrote in the log on 9 June — 'saw the ship going in with my wife on board, sent the ship to sea and returned on shore myself'.

'Valparaiso, 13th June,' wrote Charlotte in the journal-letter intended for home, 'enjoying myself beautifully at the House of the Ewer.' Four days later the whaleship came back for them, and Charlotte arrived on board to find that Samuel and the crew had been making great preparations for her arrival. 'I should admire for you to see how beautiful my accommodations are,' she wrote to her older sister; 'they worked all of last season to get ready for us, built a house upon Deck, with a wet sink where I wash and I have a [stove] that I burn Charcoal to heat my Water, and Flat Irons, and do not have to go to the gallery [sic] for anything.'

Charlotte Elizabeth had a berth in her parents' room and, 'Samuel has built a nice Sofa in the Transom, which is just the thing, and together with the Carpet, and Rocking Chairs, makes us look comfortable and I am perfectly happy.' And happy she was — until January 1854, when she began to feel queasy: 'took an Emetic,' she wrote on the 8th, 'to see if it would not remove something that made me feel half sick all the time.' Then, on the 27th, she developed an unaccountable craving for oyster soup. Samuel indulgently made her some, but by then the truth must have started to dawn.

In March Charlotte and Charlotte E. were left on shore at Talcahuano, Chile, to pass away a tedious day-to-day existence in shopping, paying calls and taking Spanish lessons. 'Very lonesome,' wrote Charlotte, but did her best to feel reconciled to it, 'and try to think it's all for the best.' She had a long wait: a note in the log of the *Young Hero* reads, 'Harriet Amelia Wyer [the second] born Wednesday September 27 at 5 PM.'

to heaven.

> 'The dead child,' Sarah wrote, 'was dressed very prettily, and trimmed with flowers, it was standing on a table, with candles burning before it, over it was a sort of canopy, trimmed with flowers, on the floor in front of the child sat a company of men playing cards, and laughing and talking very loudly, and so were the people seated around the room...

'It made me feel very solemn,' she meditated — which was not surprising, for Sarah had left her little girl Lizzie at home, and she missed her greatly. 'Oh how I wish my darling Lizzie was here,' she wrote once, in June 1860, after gamming with the David Baker family on the *Ohio*. 'I wish so more than ever since I have seen children on board other ships. I feel homesick this evening, but am not sorry I came.'

Sarah had the rare and fortunate quality of being able to see the best in most of what she saw — and she was particularly delighted with the town of Tombez (now spelled 'Tumbes'), which was reached by rowing up a beautiful but alligator-infested river.

'It was delightful going up the river,' she wrote in October 1861. 'I enjoyed it much. The Plantations along the banks of the river looked beautifully, saw several alligators and Iguanas, and a great many beautiful birds.' She visited the doctor again while in the town, but even the news that her disease had progressed to her lungs didn't dampen her enthusiasm: 'we came back across the river in a canoe by moonlight, had a delightful time.'

Her only complaint was made (predictably) on a Sunday: 'Oh that I was in a Christian land today,' she sighed. Others were much less charitable. When Susan Veeder arrived in Tombez in September 1849, 'about all that is to be seen is A few bamboo houses and a lot of half naked Children,' she recorded in disgust. The passing of the decades did not improve this picturesque scene. In September 1878 Lucy Ann Crapo observed in a letter to her sister, Ruth Ellen, that the houses in Tombez 'are mostly built of reeds or bamboo which are put together with interstices between so that everyone may see you...[and] yet they are not backward about showing their breastworks...the heat is intense and sacks worn in the morning are discarded at midday and doors (very broad) are thrown open while the fair or unfair (as the case may be) occupants are exposed to the view of those who run or less wise stop and stare.'

During the 'fifties many of the captains and their wives were hosted by some Spanish settlers in Tombez, a family called Somonte who owned a large plantation, and this gave the women the chance to observe, at first hand, a most disturbing contrast between the obvious poverty of the many and the blatant wealth of a few. Henrietta Deblois visited the Somonte plantation in September 1857, and wrote a vivid description of the elaborate occasion that the family made of the sabbath. When she arrived the Somonte women were wearing 'sky blue satin dresses, with three rows of deep fringe around the skirts, very low neck, very short sleeves, with no collar or undersleeves, but their arms covered with magnificent bracelets. Immense mantillas of blue satin...Then such large black lace veils thrown over their heads and trailing on the floor...No gloves, but fingers literally covered with rings.'

Somewhat to her embarrassment, the Spanish women insisted on lending her 'one of their elegant green and black shawls and also one of their parasols. I selected one of the plainest,' Henrietta recorded. 'It was white silk embroidered with every color of the rainbow, and having a large bow on top.' Thus adorned, she and the women proceeded to church, the hems of their shawls held up by servants. They arrived to the accompaniment of bells, cannon, the 'firing of small arms, and the music of fifes, drums and fiddles', and then Henrietta was given 'some very sweet smelling flowers cut up very fine' to put in her handkerchief, to counteract the smells from the commoner part of the congregation.

Then, after mass, the family and guests returned to the house for breakfast, a huge repast served at noon, 'consisting of stews, soups, rice dressed several ways, fried eggs garnished with onions and garlics, and roast beef flavored with the same'. Callers came and tarried and went, and at five in the afternoon there was another grand feast, which 'lasted until church time. In the meantime the ladies had changed their dresses several times. This evening they wore pink satin dresses with pink crape shawls so large that they swept the ground as did also their dresses.' During the service a baby was presented for baptism:

> 'It wore a white satin dress with bands of gold about four inches wide around the skirt "stiff as a poker". Then such a head-dress! Shaped like the Witch of Endor's cap and loaded with trimming. . .The priest stopped every few minutes to interpret for me. . .He was very pleasant and sociable but I pitied the poor baby so much that I am afraid I did not rightly appreciate his condescension. When all this was over and I had put on the baby's hideous cap and shaken hands with the priest, behold a babe of a few hours was presented for the rite. It was brought in by a servant (the mother being too ill to admit of the father's leaving her) who positively did not know the sex of the child. Here was a dilemma not easily got over. But the priest ordered the young lady (Godmother) to raise its garments and the assistant put his hand under and in a loud voice pronounced it "un hombre".'

That over, Henrietta found that 'it was expected of us to make our compliments to the parents of the baptised child, and it would be against religion to refuse as they [were] very poor.' She and her husband John arrived at the new parents' abode, to find an elaborate charade in progress in the street: there was a feast of 'Fowls all trimmed with crimson ribbons, and equally as tough, cakes, pies, cordials, wines' which had been 'loaned' by the wealthy Somontes and the 'Commodore' of the port. All the guests were expected to give money to the new mother – and so Henrietta discovered the form of one kind of South American charity.

And so, too, the day progressed, until at last 'they concluded the Sabbath with dancing, singing comic songs, and playing the guitar'. Over a year later, in November 1858, Henrietta took part in yet another baptism, in Paita this time, and this time as godmother to a Yankee whaling infant. This was a second daughter born to Mary, the wife of Captain James Cleveland of the *Seconet*.

Mary's first child had been born in Talcahuano, in traumatic circumstances: the doctor was drunk, the midwife was filthy, and a man shot himself to death in the next-door room. That second baby arrived in Paita in 1858, in a more civilized manner, and was baptised on 21 November. 'Henrietta DeBlois Cleaveland behaved admirably,' wrote the proud godmother, Henrietta Deblois, 'as she slept throughout the entire ceremony.' And, what's more, there was no confusion this time about the gender of the infant!

While the wives of the 'Off-shore' whalemen experienced such adventures, the wives of the Nor'westmen, like Mary Brewster, explored the exotic scenes of Hawaii. The Sandwich Islands — named thus by Captain Cook after the Earl of Sandwich — formed the logical recruiting base for the American whaling fleet, because so many of the American ships whaled in the North Pacific during the northern summer.

Mary Brewster arrived at Hilo, on the Island of Hawaii, on 20 April 1846. 'Arose early this morning and found the prospect charming,' she wrote.

> 'As far as my eye could see the Island was green and even down to the shore were trees. A large number of canoes were off, fishing quite near whilst many were paddling round the ship examining the *Tiger* with great interest. All of course were novelty to me both land and inhabitants and after 5 months sailing on the Ocean a less beautiful land would appear pleasant...At 3 I got into the boat and we were soon on shore and a distance of some miles to walk...when we arrived at Mr Coan's where I was very cordially received having been previously invited to stop with them...[I] enjoyed myself exceedingly well and esteemed it a great privilege to be with such a dear family and with christian society and trust I had a thankful heart that...I was once more permitted to dwell where prayer and praise was heard.'

## Mary Carlin Cleveland

Mary and James Cleveland were legendary figures in his home island of Martha's Vineyard, Massachusetts. He was a tough and resourceful specimen who was once challenged to a duel (or so the story goes) by a drunken and touchy Englishman. James (as laid down by duelling etiquette), was given the choice of weapons. 'Harpoons at ten paces,' he growled. He kept the appointment; his challenger did not.

Mary Carlin, an Irish girl from Sydney, met him in Honolulu in 1851. She was a small, dark girl with a lovely singing voice, just sixteen years old and on her way to join her sister in San Francisco. That was an appointment she did not keep, for she married James in the Seamen's Bethel at Honolulu instead, and he took her home to live with his mother Mary Ann Cleveland (who had a fearsome reputation of her own) while he went off on a whaling voyage.

As an arrangement, it did not work out.

Both females, it seems, were strong-willed, and the fact that Mary was Catholic would not have helped. When James arrived home, in 1854, Mary was living elsewhere; his mother had locked her out when she'd gone off one evening to the Baptist meeting house for singing classes. The only solution, obviously, was to take Mary along on voyage — which he did, on the *Seconet*, in 1855.

Mary, being a trailblazer in the petticoat whaler business, was a refreshing novelty to the Reverend Mr Titus Coan and his wife Fidelia as well — a novelty that was soon to wear off as the wife-carrying fad took on momentum, for so many more wives came along in her wake. 'A week, or rather 9 days since, we had but two ships — Since then some have come every day, & we now have about 50,' wrote Dwight Baldwin, missionary at Lahaina, on 22 October 1852. 'Many of the Capts have their wives & children with them. Scarce a day but some of these families are with us.'

However, the kindness of the missionary people was not stretched to the extent of having to find beds for the whole flood of visitors. In all three Hawaiian ports enterprising settlers went into the business of providing suitable accommodation for decent women. In Hilo, Betsy Morey of the *Phoenix* stayed in a house that belonged to 'Mr Pitman A native of Boston Mass...he has A verry nice house furnished as neatley as ours at home'. When Mary Lawrence of the *Addison* arrived in Lahaina, Maui, in April 1857, she went on shore and lived for a week 'in a straw cottage on the shore, surrounded by trees, with walks laid out bordered with flowers', which was owned by a bachelor, Mr Gilman. 'He has a native cook and native women to take care of the house,' she continued:

> 'The house contains four rooms, a sitting room, two bedrooms, and a dining room. The sitting room extends the whole length of the house...with a door opening at either end, four windows with crimson and white drapery, straw matting upon the floor, Chinese chairs and lounges, sofa, a whatnot filled with Japanese curiosities, a secretary and library, center and side tables, and the walls hung around with paintings and engravings.'

For a 'straw cottage', such opulence was remarkable indeed and much appreciated, for while the women were enjoying the exotic scenes, the men were preparing the ships for a 'summer season' of grappling with ice and fog in the North Pacific and Arctic Ocean.

It all began in the northern summer of 1848. 'NEW WHALING GROUND' ran a banner headline in the *New Bedford Whaleman's Shipping List* for 6 February 1849. 'The whaling bark *Superior*, Capt. Royce [Roys], of Sagharbor, arrived at Honolulu on the 4th of September last, with 1800 bbls of whale oil, which she took in the Arctic Seas.' Since 1835 whalemen had been hunting right whales off the northwest coast of America, and from the year 1843 whaling vessels had been cruising the Russian coasts of the Kamchatka Peninsula. Other ships had ventured into the Ochotsk Sea. However, whaling in the ice- and land-locked western Arctic was a new prospect altogether, and most certainly very dangerous.

It was rumoured that Roys only ventured through the scarcely charted Diomedes Islands because he'd been made reckless by the death of his young wife in August 1847. According to at least one account, he kept the frightened crew in order with a pistol. The venture was profitable, for he found a new kind of whale there, the 'Bowhead', an immense and sluggish species. However, the last thing he would have expected, surely, was that a woman should follow in his wake, but — considering the slow way news got about then — Mary Brewster, the first American woman in the Western Arctic, did it with remarkable celerity.

Her husband, William, informed her on 29 April 1849 that he was carrying her there. He had what probably seemed to him to be a very good reason: he was doing very badly in the Sea of Japan. 'The Arctic seems a long look,' Mary mused, 'but from all accounts there are plenty of whale so perhaps we shall get the ship full and I am willing to go anywhere if it will only shorten the voyage.'

'Anywhere' she went indeed. On Thursday 12 July the *Tiger* arrived in the Arctic in a 'fog so thick dare not run...At PM cleared up...found we were close to land — and in Beering's Strait. Saw the Diomedes islands high rocky land covered with snow also both continents *Asia* & *America* and I thought I was the first civilized female who had passed through the straits and probably shall be the only one this season.'

She might have been the first 'civilized' woman in the western Arctic, but she was certainly not the first in the Ocean itself. Whaling masters on the Atlantic side had carried women there, and that for quite some time. In August 1775 one Captain Warrens, commander of an English whaler, found himself becalmed near Greenland, in ice that was on the move. He and his men struggled all night to save their ship, and then when the weather at last cleared up, they found another vessel nearby.

Evidently the ship had been carried towards them by the ice. There was no movement on deck, so Warrens boarded the stranger. In the first cabin he discovered a man at ease in a chair, pen in hand, logbook on lap...mould in his eyes and his hair. In the next cabin a young woman lay on a bed, 'in an attitude of deep interest and attention'. She seemed fresh as life, but was as dead as a rock. A young man sat frozen on the floor beside her, and seamen lay equally rigid in the forecastle.

The last entry in the logbook read, 'We have now been enclosed in the ice seventeen days. The fire went out yesterday, and our master has been trying ever since to kindle it again without success. His wife died this morning. There is no relief.' The entry was dated 11 November 1762.

Surely this kind of yarn was sufficient disincentive for any woman to travel anywhere within the Arctic Circle, but Mary Brewster was by no means the last 'civilized' female to do so. In fact she was as much a pathfinder for her whaling sisters as Captain Thomas Roys was for his whaling brethren — and the women arrived in their dozens.

The ships congregated off the Sakhalin Peninsula in May, waiting for the ice to break up. On 29 May 1854 Betsy Morey counted six ships from the deck of the *Phoenix*. Three weeks later there were thirty. 'Fifty-seven ships at anchor here,' wrote Eliza Brock less than a month later, 25 June 1854, 'and but four out of this large Fleet Boiling.' Captain R.M. Hathaway reported 'from one to two hundred ships' in plain view from his whaler *Congress* in the Ochotsk Sea that same season. While the ships waited for the ice to go and the whales to come, the captains entertained each other. The tables groaned: on 19 June 1859 Mary Lawrence gave a visiting captain 'some very nice biscuit, coffee, mince pie, and for dessert preserved peaches, pineapples, and quinces'.

## Captains Adams, Keenan and Baker

Towards the end of the century there were great changes in whaling. Wife-carrying was almost accepted, many of the ships had auxiliary engines, and most of the whaling was done in the icy Arctic – but that did not make the skippers any less flamboyant.

The wife-carrying, for instance. Captain Joshua G. Baker, the fellow on the right, carried his wife on the *Reindeer* the same year that this picture was taken. However, she seems to have been a shy and shadowy figure. Sallie Smith, another wife, recorded that in 1878 her husband's ship, the *Ohio*, encountered the *Reindeer*: 'Capt Baker and wife and child came on board and spent the day we tried hard to get them to stay all night but Mrs Baker would not stay.'

In 1893 Baker was given command of one of those new-fangled steam whalers, the *Beluga*.

'New Bedford,' he penned on the flyleaf of the diminutive book he used for a log;

'bet Capt Whitesides
would beat him
steaming in new
steamer $5.00
viz that the *Beluga* would beat *Navarch*.'

They sailed alternately under sail and steam-engine – which he nicknamed the '*jingle bell*'. The engine, he considered, was an overrated thing, but he didn't let it beat him. In May a cake of ice broke a blade off the propellor, so he ordered the men to build a coffer dam to hoist the stern out, and then they fixed the screw. The snow came down, so they built an igloo on the deck and skippers, mates and crew alike made themselves suits out of seal skins. Baker and his brother captains passed away the lagging hours with 'quiet games of draw' poker...and the *Beluga* did not beat the *Navarch* to the whaling ground, so Captain Whitesides won the bet.

The competition for whales was less friendly. 'More craft than whale,' Mary Brewster remarked on the northwest coast on 23 May 1846, and within a few short seasons the Arctic whaling ground was no different. 'There cannot a whale poke his head out of water unless there is about 20 Boats after him,' noted Sam Morgan of the *South Boston*, 1 June 1852. 'The Bowhead is no longer the Slow and Sluggish Beast he was at first found to be,' wrote Eliza Brock on 25 July 1854; 'they are not so numerous as in Seasons past and are more Dificult to strike; how can it be otherwise, by day and by night the whale is chased and harrassed the only rest they have is when the Ice is thick and the wind high.'

The ice was thick and the wind was high often enough, and the sails of the clustered ships became thin and luminescent in the fogs. 'There is no depending on the weather here, two hours at a time,' Elizabeth Waldron noted. The summer was so short that flowers developed very fast, and many of the wives recorded their surprise when presented with bunches of blossoms by the men. 'I have A verry Pretty Beaucai of wild flowers that Mr Hussey

## Captain Penniman, wife & bear

'SHIP CAPTURED BY BEAR,' ran a headline in the *Boston Globe*, 'Thrilling Experience of Capt. Penniman and Crew.

'Whole Watch Took to the Rigging for Safety,' the banner ran on in the flourishing style of the time. 'The writer has heard a number of white bear stories in his time,' the journalist confessed in the body of the article itself, 'but Captain Penniman tells one which beats them all.'

Captain Penniman was in command of the *Minerva* at that time; he departed from New Bedford on 12 October 1864, and Mrs Penniman sailed with him for a summer cruise in the Arctic Ocean. As was usual, they arrived in the Arctic rather early for the whale migration and had some time to fill in, which the men spent (also as usual) in gunning. One of Penniman's victims was a large female polar bear which he had discovered on a cake of ice. She had a cub, which Penniman was also going to kill, but then he changed his mind and decided to take the young bear on board his ship instead.

Now this was not one of your small cuddly cubs: it was a half-grown male with a full complement of talons and teeth. However, the boat's crew tangled him up with rope and somehow manhandled him into the boat. But

gave me,' commented Betsy Morey in July 1855; 'it is singular to see the snow and flowers together.' Back in July 1849 Mary Brewster was equally startled. 'I had no thought that there was such a thing as a flower [here, for] from the ship I can see only snow but the snow has disappeared in spots and these bloom shortly after they appear above ground,' she recorded, and then noted that 'they have no fragrance'.

When the fog lifted the women talked their husbands into taking them to the beach to pick fruit, which was also very forward and correspondingly tasteless. On 27 July 1855 Eliza Brock went on shore at one of the Shantar Islands with Betsy Morey: they 'had a pleasant walk around on the green Grass, picked some beautiful flowers found Blue Lilies here saw a plenty of bumble Bees and Butterflies very large high trees Pine, Hemlock, Maple and Cedar...saw two beautiful springs of water running down from the high mountains.'

Betsy had 'A pleasant time' too, but she also remarked that the women 'Did not walk far into the forest for fear the Bears would Devour us for we have heard that they are verry numerous and Wolfs also and Raind Dears'. The hordes of mosquitoes were a more immediate menace. During the previous season, in August 1854, Betsy had 'wanted verry much to go and walk in [a] Beautiful Grove but could not the Tormented Musketoes wer so numerous that it did appear to me they would eat us alive. [The] Poor

once they pulled away the bear started to disentangle itself, and gnawed through a few thwarts in the process. As Penniman told it, the men in the forward part of the boat did not dare go aft, while those in the stern did not dare move a whisker. Somehow, incredibly, they hoisted him up onto the deck of the ship and secured him to a ringbolt. Then Mrs Penniman had a good long look at the bear, from a good safe distance.

'Ed,' said she, 'I'm not at all certain that that there bear should be on the same ship as your children and me.' Her husband merely grinned at this, but when night fell the young bear set up a most unearthly howling.

'Ed,' said his wife with a shudder, 'that bear has to go.' At midnight the uncanny noise had worn even Penniman down, so he sent up orders that the bear was to be dropped over the side and allowed to swim free. A lull in the howling followed, and, as Penniman remembered it, he had 'felt sure that the bear was being made ready for his plunge.

'Then was heard overhead on deck the hurried patter of feet,' he recounted. For a moment Penniman was at a loss to guess the reason for this, but then he heard the

unmistakeable sounds of 'the bear clawing along aft'. Then Penniman heard a loud yell as the man at the helm deserted his post and scrambled up the mizzen rigging. The ship 'commenced to act strangely, as if under no control' and Penniman dashed up the companionway stairs. He arrived at the top and threw the door open – just in time to see the bear arrive in the deckhouse. He shut the door again rather smartly.

The bear, as he told it, 'had taken possession of the ship, while the mate and entire watch had fled to the rigging for safety.' Penniman waited until he heard the bear snuffle off, and then he went onto the deserted deck with a rifle in his hand. The mate and watch took a lot of persuasion before they'd consent to come down from the rigging: Penniman's account gives the strong impression, in fact, that the rifle was needed more for that than for his own protection. At length, however, they shivered down the shrouds, and once the ship was put on the right tack the bear was easily shoved over the open gangway. 'It was Captain Penniman's first and only experience of taking a live bear aboard ship,' the reporter concluded – which is not particularly surprising.

little strangers wer so glad to see us that they met us on the Beach and was verry loth to part with us but we wer glad to leave,' she added dryly.

Other 'strangers' were glad to see the whaling wives, too. These were the inquisitive and friendly Inuit (whom the whalemen called 'Indians') and the first Yankee woman they saw was (of course) Mary Brewster, on 30 June 1849. She found them not only attractive in appearance but also well-dressed, 'in seal skin trouzers and a coat made from deer skin made loose and belted round them. The women dressed the same save their hair is long and braided.' It was a style she admired, and it is interesting that when a pastel portrait was made of her in later years, Mary braided her thick black hair in the same Eskimo fashion.

The men, by contrast, shaved 'a place smooth on the top of their heads about the size of a tea-plate, and are always bareheaded, which seems a singular idea, in this cold climate,' as Clara Wheldon recorded in a letter of 8 June 1868. 'They take their hair off from the very place where our men take the greatest care to keep it,' she joked. The Inuit people swarmed onto the decks of the ships, overwhelmingly inquisitive, but intent on trade as well. Elizabeth Waldron remarked on 11 July 1853, that 'they bring off furs and walrus teeth to trade for rum, tobacco, files, knives and almost anything'.

As far back as August 1849 Mary Brewster foresaw that the trade in rum would bring tragedy to these otherwise happy and self-sufficient people. 'I think if the whaling continues good here they will not be the happy people they are now,' she meditated; 'they will naturally learn many ways which will not be for their good      liquor will only cause them to quarrel      it is a great pity that they should ever get accustomed to the use of it.' Nine 'Indians' called on the *Bowditch* on 4 July 1853, and, 'they wanted to trade walrus teeth for *rum*, poor creatures,' Elizabeth Waldron wrote; 'what a pity that that accursed stuff should ever have been brought among them.'

The treacherous climate was a more immediate menace. '. . .it has snowed and blowed and thawed and frozed,' wrote Elizabeth Waldron on 12 May 1853, 'but without joking we have had very disagreeable weather. . .the days are long now, it is not dark more than four or five hours in the night, it looks curious to me to see it so light evenings.'

The sounds were uncanny, too, especially when muffled by all that mist. The ice groaned and wrenched back and forth in the giant Ochotsk tides, and birds honked and cawed ghostily in the milky skies. 'Dreary and lonesome, boisterous breezes and Rough Seas are our position,' wrote Eliza Brock on 20 September 1854; 'a shrieking Bird now and then glides dismally past as if to remind us that these Cold regions are not altogether devoid of life; the time is sad and dreary in the extrem.' Worst of all, however, was the noise of the ice, the constant grind of the shifting floes.

On 25 June 1849 the *Tiger* dropped anchor, 'it being a thick fog. The ice cannot be far off though,' Mary Brewster worried, 'for it is very smooth and calm and we can hear it at a distance surging & splashing sounding like the sea breaking against the shore.'

'Wensday July the 4th [1855]', wrote Betsy Morey, and rimmed this page of her journal in black. 'This Day begins with A Gale of wind At four oclock

# Clara and Alexander Wheldon

Clara Wheldon sailed with her husband Alexander on the bark *John Howland* on 25 June 1864, and she wrote sensible, forthright letters home throughout the next seven years, over two voyages. Because she wanted to reassure her friends and relatives, the letters are cheerful as well, even when 'the wind blew furiously and the sea rolled in wildest tumult'. Any woman, one would think, would be frightened, but, she wrote, 'Capt. tied me to the side of the ship where I had a splendid view.'

Like most of her whaling sisters, Clara had to learn to cope with incompetent, surly cooks and stewards – 'Life at sea has its servant troubles and vexations as well as life on land,' she admitted, 'in fact, an undesirable cook on land is more easily disposed of than one at sea.' The ship's steward was not too bad a cook, as it happened, 'having been connected with a hotel previous to engaging with us, but he has proved himself to be a miserable specimen of a man, besides extravagant and wasteful. We were obliged to banish him.' Even seasickness didn't wear her spirit down. 'Ship cooking, sea-sickness, rolling and tumbling about does its work in process of time,' she philosophised, 'and one grows calm, then contented, and finally happy.'

She kept herself busy to keep monotony away, and even in the Arctic managed to impart a rare sense of domesticity. 'We have a little tea-kettle that supplies us with hot water,' she wrote. That very homely little instrument 'sings merrily at times, and the tea-pot sends forth its fragrant odor after the fashion of well regulated teapots.'

She was not equal, however, to the friendly curiosity of the 'Siberians'. A noisy party of Inuit people invaded the decks, and, 'They no sooner caught a glimpse of me than they surrounded me,' Clara penned with most unusual agitation. 'Captain was not within call and none of the men seemed disposed to come to my relief.'

Wheldon was a stern disciplinarian who had no time for such frivolous luxuries as heating in the icy forecastle: the men, no doubt, were having a quiet laugh at Mrs Wheldon's expense. She tacked back and forth, doing her best to escape the natives, but one man 'caught hold of my arm,' she related, 'and pulled me along saying over and over again as fast as he could speak, "me wyena, me wyena" ["my woman, my woman"].'

Clara managed at last to escape. 'I was thankful when I got safely into the cabin,' she tremulously wrote – but even then she couldn't avoid ardent attentions, for the Siberians crowded about the skylight and sent her long and languishing glances.

AM the Ice came Down upon us taking all the advantage of our ship that it possibly could. Husband went on Deck immediately and that left me alone in Gloomy Meditations for it was Dreadful to listen to the Different sounds on Deck for the Ice would Roar and the Sound was like a Mighty Cateract, and it would strike the Ship and Jar it so hard that it would Shake the Cabin windows I could not stop in Bed anny longer I arose and in A Minute the Steward came into the cabin saying that Husband said I must put up some of our clothing and be Ready for anny Emmergency and these wer fearful Momments to me and yet I tried to compose myself as much as Possible for I knew verry well that anny one Must have Great Presence of Mind in such A time as this, and with the Steward's help we had about got our task completed when Husband came down below and Spoke to me in A calm firm Manner and says be Reddy Elizabeth for My Ship is gone I am afraid and with A sad careworn look he turned and went on Deck...'

As it happened, the *Phoenix* was spared by a shift of the wind. Other ships were less lucky. In September 1871 almost the whole of the northern whaling fleet was lost. Eliza Williams was one of the women who fled south across floes and over fast-freezing water, to the safety of seven small ships that waited beyond the ice. Then, more than a thousand men, women and children were carried to Honolulu, 'pushed together, as bad as any Irish

## Leander and Jane Owen

Leander Owen was a Martha's Vineyard man who went on 16 voyages, beginning in 1848 as cabin boy of the *Valparaiso*, when he was just fifteen years old. His first command was the *Contest* in 1870, and he took his wife Jane with him, along with their little son William (who, in later years, was the man who sold the 'victrola' gramophone to the world, and whose little dog, Nipper, was the fox terrier featured in the *His Master's Voice* logo). This wife-carrying venture could not have been more badly timed, for the *Contest* was one of the 34 vessels lost in the 1871 Arctic disaster.

When the fleet arrived off Cape Thaddeus in May the ice was heavier than usual, and even in the 'mid-summer' of August the ships were still beset by drifting floes. An abrupt change of wind caught some of the skippers unaware: on 2 September the brig *Comet* was crushed, and then, on the 7th and 8th respectively, the *Roman* and the *Awashonks* met the same fate. Except for seven ships lying to the south of Blossom Shoals, the entire fleet was trapped by rapidly closing ice. On the 12th the decision was made to abandon the fleet, and on the 14th the exodus – of 1,219 men, women and children – began.

By rowing and sailing, the flotilla of whale boats made Icy Cape by nightfall. A tent was put up on the beach for the women and children, and great fires were lit to cook food for the multitude. All night it sleeted and snowed; the seamen upturned their boats and crouched underneath them, and the women huddled together under the flapping canvas. Then, in the morning, they hauled the boats out and started again.

Once they reached Blossom Shoals the seven ships that had escaped could be glimpsed five emigrants', and glad indeed Eliza must have been to set foot on Hawaiian shores again.

> 'Yes blessed Ochotsk we leave thee
> All thy seens we loved thee well
> And until my memory fails me
> In my mind you will always dwell
>
> And ere long we hope to Greet thee
> To view these Beautiful seens again
> In hopes to find the Bowheads plenty
> And then A good voige obtain
>
> Then far away the winds will Blow us
> Let the Breeze the Canviss swell
> Glad we leave the lovely Ochotsk and in full chorus
> With God's blessing we do say fare well, fare well.
> E.H.M.
>
> Ship Pheonix [sic] 1854
> Arrived in Hilo
> Nov the 17th 25 days from Cape Elizabeth.'
> — Betsy Morey.

miles out on a gale-tossed sea. The distance the men had to row was quadrupled, however, by a huge tongue of ice projecting out from the land, which had to be skirted. In the lee of that outcrop, the weather was tolerable, but once around the point and into the wind, the boats were tossed about sickeningly, and within moments every shred of clothing was saturated with icy brine. However, by four in the afternoon every single refugee was safely aboard one of those seven ships, and then the slow, overburdened passage to Honolulu began.

They straggled in at the end of October. Not a single life had been lost, but the loss of the fleet was a blow from which New Bedford whaling never recovered. Back in the Arctic the Inuit people were ransacking the abandoned vessels. The skippers had taken care to destroy all liquor supplies before they left, but some of the natives drank fluids from the medical chests and became sick. A few died, and ships were burned in retaliation. Other vessels were crushed by the ice; when the whalemen returned in the spring of 1872, only one ship — the *Minerva* — could be salvaged.

The saddest aspect of the whole affair was that the wind changed again shortly after the fleet was abandoned, and the ships could have been saved if the exodus had been delayed by just a few days. The owners blamed the wife-carrying skippers for the premature decision, saying that they had been panicked by fears for their women and children. Leander Owen, despite damaged sight caused by snow-blindness during that trek to Blossom Shoals, took other ships to the Arctic — but the owners refused to allow him to take Jane on those northern voyages. Instead she waited each season in Honolulu or San Francisco, along with Lucy Smith and dozens of others.

# Herbert and Mary Colson

Mary and Herbert Colson married on 7 December 1875, and that was the start of her voyaging life, of 'years with a great many changes and variations,' as she noted herself, on the second anniversary of that wedding, in the journal she kept on the *George and Susan*. 'Herbert came home [and] we were married,' she remembered; 'went our [honeymoon] journey and spent the winter at home. In the spring went to San Francisco sailed from there on the *Java* had a year at sea in her then I came home Herbert going to the Arctic.'

In 1876 the *Java* was lost, along with 12 other vessels, crushed by the ice in an episode reminiscent of the big Arctic disaster of 1871. This time lives were lost as well as ships, for several men died in the trek across the ice to the ships that waited to rescue the survivors. Herbert returned home safely, and 'in a little while' he and Mary were at sea again. 'I have so much to be thankful for, that I have such a good loving husband and that we are spared to each other and can be together,' wrote she.

They were certainly a loving couple: once, when there was a particularly beautiful rainbow, Herbert carried Mary in his arms over the streaming deck so she could see it, 'a most perfect bow and such briliant colors.' Never, despite constant seasickness throughout the three-and-a-half year voyage, did Mary hint that she would have preferred to stop at home.

They arrived back in New Bedford in May 1881 and then went to San Francisco to join the growing whale-fleet there, for Herbert was given command of the *Sappho*. That voyage was not so lucky: he lost that ship too, near Lawrence Island. However, Herbert Colson's reputation remained undamaged. A San Francisco syndicate – the embryo Pacific Steam Whaling Company – had embarked on a revolutionary plan to build three new whaling steamers. One of these was the *Orca*. She was ready for sea and standing at the Vallejo Street Wharf on 14 December 1882, and Herbert was given command of her.

The year 1883 marked the beginning of the predominence of San Francisco in the whaling industry. California was as handy to the Arctic as the Hawaiian Islands, and competition with the sugar planters for labour had made Honolulu an expensive proposition; the famous

thrift of whaling masters, allied with the bustling prosperity of California, turned San Francisco into the New Bedford of the Pacific. Petroleum wells pumped busily all over the States, many in California itself, and hardly anyone used whale-oil lamps any more, but in the 1880s a spirit of optimism prevailed. The invention of spring steel was twenty years away, and fashion decreed that women cinched their waists to unlikely slenderness. Whalebone was still gratifyingly profitable, and each November the wharves were lined with ships unloading the valuable stuff. In 1884 the *Orca* was one of them: Herbert Colson justified the owners' faith by returning with a cargo of more than 30,000 lb.

When the conditions in the north are considered, it is little wonder that many captains adopted the custom of leaving their wives in Hilo, Honolulu or Lahaina for the summer, instead of taking them along to the Arctic or Ochotsk. The practice made sense, for not only were the wives and children safer on shore, but the captains themselves could take more risks without their women being reproachful about it.

Indeed, after the 1871 disaster, most captains were ordered to leave their wives behind in the islands. This was the cause of a great deal of heartbreak. On 3 April 1873, when the *Nautilus* arrived in Honolulu to recruit for the northern season, Lucy Smith recorded that her husband George had had a letter from the owners, 'saying I must be left at the Islands. I was very angry but supposed what can't be cured must be endured,' she wrote, and resigned herself to long months of waiting about for the ship to come back in the autumn. In future years she was to do it again, and dozens of her whaling sisters with her.

In September the ships drifted back into port, some in worse repair than others. The wives waited anxiously to hear what kind of season their husbands had made — what Sarah Taber of the *Alice Frazier* called 'the yankee privilege of gessing what they are about up North this season and how they have prospered the time'. Then, in October, the wives looked forward to the 'between seasons' cruise.

This Christmas cruise was spent in warm latitudes, and, while the hunt for whales was as grim as ever, it was considered by the wives as something of a holiday. It could take the form of bay whaling for 'devil fish' in the lagoons of lower California, or it might be the more tranquil pursuit of sperm whaling along 'the Line'. This latter cruise, in windjammer parlance, meant sailing south-west on the north-east trades to join the New Zealand and New Holland whalers who were steering north-east in that season. It was a time for gamming often, and recruiting at various tropical islands and visiting exotic ports — up to and including Australia.

# 9
# *More decency and order. . .?*

'Whaling masters in these days must go well-armed, and, expecting no favors at home, must exercise their own judgement for the maintenance of order, the preservation of peace, and protection of life.' — *New Bedford Whalemen's Shipping List*, 12 July 1859.

**W**HEN the *Harrison* first dropped anchor in Sydney, in the month of February 1847, it had been an unlucky and unhappy voyage thus far for Captain Abner Sherman — and particularly so for his young wife, Mary Ann. Miserable voyages were common enough. Despite all the hellraising and adventure the Pacific ports offered, a whaling voyage wasn't fun, and on top of everything else the captain had the responsibility of a ship and a crew — not to mention trying to satisfy the demands of the agents and owners back home. 'I long to see my husband free from this vexacious business,' penned Mary Brewster in a sentiment that was echoed by many of her whaling sisters: However, the *Harrison* voyage was worse than most, for Sherman seems to have been an uncommonly brutal and incompetent commander.

In January 1846, after leaving the Great Australian Bight, Abner Sherman had decided to bypass both Tasmania and New Zealand, and had proceeded instead to Tahiti, arriving in March. It was not a good decision. On 7 March Sherman 'put the steward inn the rigin & flog him give him 1 duson for sassey' — or insolence, surely a minor demeanour to warrant such punishment. Then three men deserted. Sherman caught the runaways and vented his anger on their hides: he 'flog them give them 12 blose a pice'.

After that he put them 'in irons' — which meant both handcuffs and leg-cuffs with chains — and the ship set sail for the Hawaiian Islands. On 14 April 1846 the *Harrison* arrived at Lahaina, and the flogged men were still dragging the chains that had weighed them down for more than a month. Sherman recruited for provisions and then they sailed, for a 'summer' a-whaling in the chilly fogs off the northwest coast of North America.

The ship took 1,100 bbls right whale oil, and 500 pounds of whalebone, not a bad season at all. However, that was no indication that the voyage had improved. The ship arrived back in Lahaina on 14 September 1846, made Honolulu on the 26th, and twelve of the men mutinied, a large number out of a crew of thirty. They 'refused to do duty' – according to the report in the *New Bedford Whalemen's Shipping List* – 'alleging bad provisions and incompetency'. Sherman put down the uprising with the help of the United States consul. As a result some of the men were imprisoned in the fort, while others were 'put in the rigging [and] flogged'. Three of the four boatsteerers demanded their lawful discharge from the ship, and Captain Sherman was forced to allow them to go. Then at last the anchor was weighed, and a course was set south-west, for the 'Port of Sydney New South Whales'.

It was not a peaceful passage. On 19 December 1846, mid-Pacific, another mutiny was staged. Sherman had tied up a man ready for a whipping for some unstated crime, and 'the men all com aft to stop it; but they dint make it out,' the journal-keeper added. Sherman put down that uprising with a pistol and another spate of flogging, and so the dissension continued, while all the time the unhappy ship *Harrison* jogged her way towards Port Jackson.

Most whaling wives were forced, at some time or another, to witness some kind of dissension on board ship. Whalemen were rough and many captains little better, especially if the luck of the voyage was bad. Given the overcrowded conditions and the tedium of the cruise, undignified ructions were almost inevitable.

Captains stamped and swore when roused, and devised all kinds of strange punishments, such as setting men to scrubbing out the trypots with bricks, sitting on the end of the spanker boom for hours, slushing down the topmasts with fat, holystoning the deck and tarring head rigging, and – as Sylvanus Robinson did, when he carried his wife on the *Bartholomew Gosnold* in 1876 – forcing a culprit to wear a notice on his back, proclaiming to the world that he was a 'Thief & liar' (or whatever).

'Today. . .the steward made known to the Capt that there was Onions missing,' Abram Briggs, third mate of the *Eliza Adams*, related off Stewart Island, New Zealand, in March 1874:

> 'the Capt requested the 1st & 2nd Officers to proceed into the forecastle & diligently search for the Onions missed, while down their the Capt let his tongue loose on the crew fore & aft he called them the lousiest thieving buggers that ever was collected in a ship. . .he said they should go with him another season then they could all go to Hell. . .

'It is a good way to keep a crew,' Briggs observed then; 'no wonder they run away.' To Captain Caleb Hamblin's credit, however, there is no record of him flogging anyone – for flogging was a very different matter.

Susan Brock, who spent part of her childhood on the merchantman *Midnight*, always remembered her revulsion when one of the seamen was flogged. 'The captain was ashore,' she related in her memoirs, 'or his little girl would never have been allowed to witness such a scene.' The young sailor had come on board a trifle drunk after his day of liberty, and – like Sherman's steward – he had been saucy to the second mate. The boy was tied up in the rigging by the thumbs, so that he dangled with his toes just brushing the deck. Then his bare back was whipped with some handy piece of rope.

The young sailor who was flogged was a favourite, for he was the best singer in the ship, 'and, as the blows fell on his bare back, and my friend cried out in pain, my heart was nearly broke,' Susan remembered. Mary Ann Sherman must have felt some of the same repugnance, surely, as she sat in the transom and listened to the awful noises filtering down from deck. Worst of all, however, must have been the knowledge that she could do little or nothing to stop her husband from behaving like a tyrant.

After all, the so-called moderating influence of women was one of the stated advantages of taking one's wife along on a whaling voyage. As the

## Charity Norton

Back in New Bedford, Martha's Vineyard and Nantucket, the romantic stories of the women who stood between the poor sailors and the wrath of the Jehovah on the quarter deck were often told, eagerly received, and — it seems — believed as well. Lucy Smith featured as the heroine of one of these yarns, when she undertook a second voyage, in 1882, on the *Abraham Barker*. According to the tale, as told by George 'Fred' Tilton, who was a seaman on that ship, Lucy arrived up on deck just as Captain George Smith was set to clap him in irons for some trifling misdemeanor.

'Please, George, I wish you would not do that,' said she.

This quiet and reasonable request (according to Fred Tilton's recollection) sent the captain perfectly puce with rage. 'Mutiny on my ship?' he roared.

'Yes, George,' agreed Lucy with perfect equanimity, and was promptly sent below. She went without argument...but somehow in the meantime the irons had mysteriously disappeared.

Another of these heroines was Charity Randall Norton of New Bedford, a formidable woman who doubled the Horn six times in all. She sailed with her husband John Oliver Norton on every one of his voyages, the first being on the *Luminary* of Warren, in 1848.

According to the legend, she went at the behest of the owners: she had to (or so the tale went) or John Oliver would never have returned alive, as the men would have risen and murdered him. 'There were some hard tickets among the whaling captains in those days' — or so the yarn (as told by another seaman, Theodore Wimpenny) went — 'and John Oliver Norton was one of the hardest of the lot. She had to go with him on his voyages.' The owners, in fact, begged Mrs Norton to go, for

she so often interceded between her husband's wrath and the men.

At Talcahuano — the story continues — a number of the men deserted. John set sail and pretended to depart, but instead sneaked back and caught them all. Then, once properly under way, he triced those men up, all set for a flogging. No sooner had he hefted the lash, however, than Charity hove up onto deck. 'John,' says she, 'what is thee doin'?'

'I'm givin' 'em a few licks,' said he.

'John,' she said firmly, 'thee is not.' And he didn't.

New Bedford merchant Charles W. Morgan optimistically put it, when Captain Prince Ewer took Mrs Ewer on the 1849 voyage of the *Emily Morgan*, 'There is more decency on board when there is a woman.'

Apparently this sentimental notion was justified here, for the Ewers made most successful voyages. One of the crewmen called Mrs Ewer 'an agreeable, intelligent women, well fitted to be the wife of such a man' as Captain Prince W. Ewer. On a later voyage – bark *Henry Taber* 1855-9 – the vessel returned home with 'all her original crew except one man discharged owing to ill health, since deceased' and in a state 'of neatness and orderly arrangement vieing with that of a tidy housewife ashore,' according to the shipping paper. All New Bedford lauded Ewer, who was 'in all respects a model ship master', and Mrs Ewer, surely, could have been forgiven for quietly claiming a part of the credit. . .But would she have been justified in doing so?

Many folk would have said, yes. Nathaniel Taylor of the *Julius Caesar*, for instance, thoroughly approved of Mrs Morgan's presence on board ship in 1851: she restrained, he believed, rowdy or bad-tempered behaviour.

Another sailor, Harry Chippendale, shipped on the *Greyhound* some time in the 1880s, when the skipper was Joseph Enos and Mrs Enos was on board. He, too, was highly approving (though he could have been prejudiced by the fact that he himself was born on board a petticoat whaler, the *Alice Knowles*) and declared that the practice had 'a great effect on the crew's morale. . .

> 'Even though a sailor had the reputation of being rough and tough, still there was something under that rough exterior that made him want to put his best foot forward in the presence of the captain's wife. Where ordinarily he might come back to the ship drunk and reel down the dock singing a bawdy song, and then maybe cause trouble when he got aboard, if he thought Missis Skipper was apt to be about he would stop singing before he made the ship.'

What's more, Chippendale declared, if the skipper 'was the hell-rip-roaring type the little woman was usually able to keep him in check'. Chippendale would have been sadly disappointed, then, if he'd shipped on the *Hannibal* back in 1849. Captain Gray – whose tongue often set the tar in the deck seams a-bubbling, despite Mrs Gray's pleas to stop – flogged his wife's cabin boy on that voyage.

On 21 August 1861, one of the officers of the unlucky and unhappy bark *E. Corning* flogged a seaman, and Elizabeth Stetson wrote, '*Sylvia flogged Jose Solas for getting the ship aback I do not think it was right,*' and underlined the entry in her impotent fury. Even though she was the captain's wife, she was unable to prevent such brutish behaviour. Another sufferer was Viola Fish Cook. Her husband John was a bully by nature – what they then called 'bucko' – and his sadism disgusted and appalled her. One day in the Arctic, after he'd carried out a multiple flogging, Viola's sense of wifely duty finally snapped. She locked herself up in her cabin, and didn't come out for *nine whole months.* When they got home John told everyone she'd had a nervous breakdown (on account of going down with scurvy, he said), and Eugene O'Neill wrote a play about it.

In the face of such evidence, it seems very likely that Mrs Ewer and Mrs

# Viola Cook

'MRS COOK'S CHRISTMAS IN THE ICY NORTH,' ran a headline in the *Boston Globe* for Christmas Eve, 1905. 'The Wife of Capt John A. Cook of Provincetown is With Him 160 Miles North of the Arctic Circle – There is No Surety of Their Safety, but in Any Case They Cannot be Released Until Next July.

'At a point approximately 160 miles north of the Arctic circle. . .' the item elaborated, 'in latitude 70° north and longitude 130° west, a cultured white woman is at this moment, doubtless, bending over the shuttle of her sewing machine in the lamp-lit cabin of a ship, about whose sides glass-clear ice of great thickness is welded by frosty bonds that must remain unbroken until mid-July of 1906.'

Overwintering in the Arctic was yet another development in the history of whaling. On 4 July 1860 Eliza Williams met Captain Washington Walker, who had deliberately set out to over-winter the *Alice Frazier* in the Ochotsk Sea. 'His object was to be there when the ice broke up in the spring, hoping to get a large quantity of oil,' she recorded. His ship was crushed by the ice in January 1860, and the crew spent the winter with the Russians instead. However, the competition for whales had become so brisk that other captains adopted the same proposition, and by the 1890s overwintering at Herschel Island in the Beaufort Sea had become routine.

Instead of leaving the Arctic in September, the ships were anchored together in so-called 'winter berths'. Shelters were built over the decks and banked up with snow, and so a strange community grew up. Eskimos set up their igloos about the ships, so that a sizeable village was established. The Arctic foxes became so tame that they hung openly around all the garbage dumps.

It was a strange, long winter, and a boring one, too, but the captains and crews gritted it out gamely until spring came along and brought the whales. Being there waiting for the thaw and the migration was logical enough. What is amazing is that men like Captain John Atkins Cook decided to take their wives along to help pass the long boring winter away, and women like Viola Cook agreed to go. . .or perhaps they were given no choice.

When Viola first sailed Arctic-bound on the

*Navarch* in 1893, the official story given out was that she travelled for her health. At the start of that voyage Viola Cook weighed 93 pounds, and when she returned on 23 November 1896, she weighed 130 – which says much for the effects of enforced inactivity.

After that the newspaper reporters liked to believe that she went along 'to please her husband – cheerfully abandoning the pleasures of home life to give companionship to her husband and to share and brave all dangers to which he might be exposed'. The truth, however, was that John Atkins Cook was a tough old customer with strong views on the duties owed to men by women.

During that first winter in the Arctic, 1893-4, Viola did have the company of other women. One was 29-year-old Sophie Porter, of the *Jesse H. Freeman*, who had her five-year-old daughter Dorothy with her. Others were Mrs Albert Sherman and her two-year-old son on the *Beluga*, Mrs Green and her niece Lucy on the *Alexander*, and Mrs Weeks on the *Thrasher*.

It was a weird existence. The wives went sledding, played whist and staged dinners with elaborate menus. The courses for one such feast included 'Lobster salad & olives, Oyster Pate with French Peas', and, 'Bartlett Pears, with citron & sponge cake'. They had a grand ball on the *Alexander*, and a birthday party for Bertie Sherman on the *Beluga*.

The captains filled in the time by trading for ivory and furs with rum and tobacco. They traded in arms, too, if they could get away with it. Cook was warned repeatedly by the Consul at Unalaska about smuggling guns and powder, and in the end that exasperated official boarded the ship and bonded the goods. The crews formed concert parties: one was called 'The Herschel Island Snowflakes' after the name of the island where the ships were iced in.

The men went hunting as well, so that there was often fresh venison on the menu, and some supplied excitement by trying to desert (perhaps with some vague idea of joining the Yukon goldrush) and coming back instead with their toes all black and dropping off.

Captain Charles Weeks blighted the season somewhat with a fatal fall into a hold. His body was kept in an ice cellar until they were able to salt him down, ready to take him to port. However, life went on. On 8 June 1894 Mrs Sherman gave birth to a daughter, with all of the other wives in attendance. On the 12th they had a christening party and the baby, in true seafaring style, was named Helen Herschel Sherman.

However, in future winters Viola Cook had no female Yankee companionship at all. On this, the 1905 season (her ninth), the ships were not able to get out of the ice and were forced to spend one winter longer in the Arctic than intended. She suffered dreadfully with scurvy (and more), and when she reached her home in Provincetown Viola mutinied at last. She declared her firm intention never to sail again.

This, obviously, did not suit John Cook. He was scandalised and shocked at such disloyalty. Viola proved impervious to argument, so he resorted to stealth instead: he built a brig and named her *Viola*, and Viola fell for the 'compliment' and relented. She voyaged again – and sickened with beriberi, another food deficiency disease. When she got home she reverted to her original decision; Viola Fish Cook never voyaged again.

It was fortunate for John Cook that Viola remained adamant. In September 1917 the command of the brig was given to Captain Joseph Lewis, who sailed with his wife and five-year-old daughter. In 1918 the *Viola* disappeared, lost with all hands. The popular theory was that the brig was sunk by a German submarine.

Enos (while being admirable women) deserved little of the credit, if any. They didn't need to moderate the skipper's nature, because that skipper was moderate already. Mrs Enos was certainly useful about the ship, for she was the one who did the navigation (it was also rumoured that the captain could not read). However – as Chippendale admitted – Enos was 'a good skipper to sail with'; he had the knack of running a happy ship. It seems reasonable to guess that the crew of the *Greyhound* would have been just as contented a set (though maybe lost) if Penelope Enos had happened not to be there.

It seems very likely, in fact, that Captain Prince Ewer would have run a clean, pious ship even if Mrs Ewer had opted to stop at home. Benjamin Morrell ran a clean and pious schooner, but his smug account certainly indicates that a competent ship's master would never allow himself to be influenced by a mere female encumbrance. All any woman could rightfully expect on board of his ship was to be a useless, bored and frequently seasick passenger.

Abby Jane, on the other hand, was romantically certain that the voyage would provide many opportunities for her to demonstrate 'what my sex can do if called to act' – and she had her first chance in February 1830, when the *Antarctic* was nearly wrecked at one of the Philippine Islands.

A remorseless tide was driving the *Antarctic* towards the reef, and the air was filled with the whistling of the winds and the howling of the lofty combers. 'Keep the helm hard a-port!' Morrell hollered in the midst of the din; 'Brace the head-sails aback!' The canvas flapped, the schooner yawed...and Abby Jane came up, looked around, and asked with tender solicitation, 'Dearest, shouldn't you be wearing a hat?'

As Morrell recorded, 'Happily for her, she knew not at that moment that we were all tottering on the extreme verge of destruction's precipice.' Happily for Abby Jane, too, her husband was too busy to slay her. 'My reply,' he reminisced, 'was short and *not* sweet.' Then, not long afterwards, Abby Jane was treated to an even more galling demonstration of just how irrelevant her presence was to the voyage. It all began in March 1830, when the *Antarctic* anchored at Manila, and Abby Jane made the acquaintance of the American consul.

Consuls were often a suspect lot, as they were usually adventurers intent on making a 'pile' out of the job. However, Abby Jane thought that this fellow (unnamed) seemed 'courteous and friendly'. Then, a few days before Morrell was due to leave the port for the *bêche de mer* grounds of Fiji, official permission for the ship's departure was withheld...unless Mrs Morrell stayed behind at Manila. According to the consul, the Spanish governors were quite happy to let the ship go, along with Morrell and his men, but had stipulated that Mrs Morrell must stop behind in port. It was all very puzzling. As Abby Jane remarked, 'There was something extremely suspicious in it.'

It did not take long for realisation to dawn: the 'next time I saw the consul all was as plain as day,' she wrote. To put it broadly, the consular gentleman lusted after Mrs Morrell's plump body, and his evil intention was to get her all to himself.

It was the stuff of the most lurid kind of melodrama. At first Abby Jane declared she dared not tell her husband, 'for fear of the consequences from his quick sense of injury, and his high spirit as a brave man. And then, again,' she added thoughtfully, 'my youth and ignorance of the world made me fear that I had put a wrong construction upon the consul's demeanour.'

Those doubts were soon dissolved. 'From every appearance, I was fully satisfied that the consul had scattered slanders about...' she passionately declared, 'in order that I might feel myself so shunned and ruined as to fly to him for protection.' Abby Jane then declaimed (like any proper heroine) that she'd die before she'd succumb to this 'villainy and gross falsehood'. Morrell, however, neglected to play the part of hero. He blithely and ungallantly sailed away, and didn't even bother to mention the fuss in his journal.

He didn't appear to miss her company, either. By mid-May, while the consul in Manila was harassing Abby Jane with notes that she 'never deigned to answer', the *Antarctic* was cruising the 'Young William's Group in 5°12' N, 153°27' E', and Benjamin Morrell, along with the rest of the crew, was getting acquainted with the local damsels:

> 'These girls were about sixteen or seventeen, with eyes like the gazelle's, teeth like ivory, and the most delicately formed features I have ever met with...with small hands, feet, and head, long black hair, and then those eyes, sparkling like jet beads swimming in liquid enamel! They had small plump cheeks, with a chin to match, and lips of just the proper thickness for affection's kiss...Their limbs were beautifully proportioned, and so were their busts. Imagination must complete the bewitching portraits; I will only add the shade – their skin was a light copper colour.'

It is impossible not to wonder how Abby Jane felt when she read this, but it is most unlikely that she would have dared to complain. After all, she had sailed 'at my own solicitation' and when Benjamin had finally consented to take her along, he had made her agree to certain conditions.

> 'Viz: that she must expect no attentions from me when duty called me on deck; that she must never blame me, if things were not agreeable or pleasant, at all times, during the voyage; and that she must not expect that there would be any extra living on board the *Antarctic* on her account.'

Perhaps Abby Jane took comfort in the belief that she'd influenced her husband in the matter of grog. When the *Antarctic* sailed from New York on 2 September 1829, the ship carried – according to Benjamin – '*no ardent spirits on board*'. 'He was the first captain, I believe, that ever shipped a crew for so long a voyage on such terms,' his wife wrote with perceptible complacency. Within days one of the seamen took a fit and died. According to Abby Jane, the fatal apoplexy was 'brought on by having drunk too freely of ardent spirits in the early part of his life, and now leaving off suddenly'. Neither her faith nor her husband's determination were shaken in the slightest, however.

Many people (though perhaps not including the sailors themselves) would have heartily agreed with the Morrell stand, for the evil effects of drunkenness were so very obvious. Captain Worthing Hall of the whaleship *Natchez* (who carried his wife and his little girl Mary on voyage) spoke a British steamer, the *Brisbane*, in March 1855. The steamer was 62 days from Glasgow and on the way to Sydney, he reported, but he wouldn't have liked to hazard a guess about how much time would elapse before the *Brisbane* finally got there, 'the captain having been drunk all the time, no steam on, chronometer broken...and was drifting 10 or 15 miles to leeward every day'.

The very notion of his valuable property drifting about at the mercy of the waves and a drunk was enough to set up a shudder in any owner's breast. Here was a potent reason for encouraging a shipmaster to carry his wife. Women, despite feminine frailty, were (like the missionaries) supposed to be a powerful force in the war on demon grog. And not only did the ship-owners believe it, but many of the women did, too.

Mary Lawrence certainly trusted that this moderating influence could be hers. At the first good opportunity she filled her daughter Minnie's doll's buggy with Bibles, and sent the little girl forward to give them out to the men. The good books were all taken; she felt filled with optimism...and then, in April 1857, the ship made port in Lahaina.

> 'Saw several of our sailors,' she noted on the 22nd. The men reported 'that one of our number had been taken to the fort for drinking and being unruly in the street. It made me feel badly; I had hoped there would be no such doings among our crew. I thought better things of them, but my husband has always told me that sailors would be sailors and that after we had been in port, my eyes would be opened. I am fearful that it is so.'

Mary's eyes were well and truly 'opened': five days later she went back onto the ship and 'found a state of affairs on board which made my heart ache'. Four of the crew were in irons for various misdemeanours. 'This is the beginning of trouble to me,' Mary mourned, and then admitted that she had been foolish in believing that the men would behave. She was certainly not the first or the last woman to learn that prohibition on board was not enough, that grog – like women – could be readily obtained on shore, and that 'sailors would be sailors' whether there was a wife on the ship or not.

Back in 1841, when the New London whaler *Chelsea* made port in the Bay of Islands, the groggeries were doing an excellent trade. At least some of the crew were excellent customers, and this despite the so-called moderating effect of Mrs Franklin Smith and her infant daughter. 'William Miner drunk before breakfast, not Capable of any duty,' noted her husband in his huge canvas-bound log. 'Belongs to the temperance Society Norwich (Connecticut),' he added. In the end he was forced to send for the consul: 'The Consul talked to several of the crew and Merrels he Called a verry Saucy Boy and all that prevented him from giving him a floging was his being so young.'

Even if Mrs Smith had wanted to remonstrate with the men, she would have been hampered by the simple fact that she happened to be of the female gender. 'I *do* feel sorry about *Louis*,' wrote Harriet Allen agitatedly after one of the men deserted from the *Merlin* on 19 June 1870. 'He would not have deserted if he had kept from drinking. I regret now that I never got courage to speak to him upon this subject. If it were not for that one failing he would do well anywhere – I might have spoken when he called to see

# Mary Lawrence

The six sons of Thomas Lawrence of Falmouth, Massachusetts, became whalemen, and of those three were wife-carrying skippers. Thomas jr took his wife Mercy to the Pacific on the *Anaconda*, 1852-6, and then, in 1857, on another Pacific voyage on the *Alto*. In September Elizabeth Marble, on the *Kathleen*, wrote home saying that they had spoken a ship which 'proved to be the Bark *Alto* of New Bedford the mate has charge of the Ship now and is out on a cruse the Capt is at Fayal wating for his wife to be sick they are the Capt Lorance and wife I wrote to you were stoping where I stoped they have a little girl with them now that was born on the last voyage she is 3 years and a half old and they have another at home 8 years Old Mrs L told me she expected to stay there about 2 months more and then they were bound to the Indian Ocean.'

Another brother, Lewis, carried his wife Eunice on several voyages of the *Commodore Morris*, despite the fact that he did not have the knack of managing a contented crew. Once, when he left Tahiti, for instance, he had the wheel lashed when the pilot left the ship, and counted off his crew just to see which men were missing, for so many had been left behind, imprisoned in the fort. One, Jim Macoudry, 'was rather Contrary and spoke uncivil to the Captain,' the logkeeper tersely noted; 'put him irons again and sent him off.' Despite all this Eunice presented Lewis with children as well, giving birth in Tahiti, Norfolk Island and Honolulu.

Samuel, the third Lawrence skipper to carry a wife, married Mary Chipman on 20 July 1847. On 27 December he set off on the *Lafayette* to the Off-shore Ground, but did not take her along with him on that particular voyage, even though it was his first command. As it happens, it was fortunate she did not go. The *Lafayette* was wrecked on the reef at Albemarle, the Galápagos Islands, in June 1850. The *Nauticon*, with Susan Veeder on board, was one of the first ships on the scene. Together with Captain Sisson and the crew of the *Callao*, Charles Veeder and his men dismantled the wreck and salvaged the oil. Though Captain Lawrence had been rescued along with some of his men, thirteen of the crew were still on shore, in a starving condition. Veeder shipped four of them, and took three to another island in the group, Charles.

This made quite a blot on Samuel Lawrence's record, and after that he could only get a berth as first mate (of the *Eliza Adams*, 1851-4), and when he was offered the command of the *Addison* in 1856, it was because the appointed captain had defaulted on his contract. However, it is little wonder that he, like his brothers, opted then to carry his wife and their little girl, Minnie, for it was obvious that if he did not make a profitable voyage (which, in the event, he did not manage) this would be his last command. Mary Lawrence responded well to the challenge. 'It is a life of hardship,' she gallantly decided, 'but it is a life full of romance and interest.' She missed the 'privileges' of sabbath worship, but she gained a new respect for her husband. 'I never should have known what a great man he is,' she wrote, 'if I had not accompanied him.'

me at Mahé but he was so well informed and seemed so much a *man* I could not.'

The liberty crews were not the only ones to kick up their heels in port. 'We have quite lively times, there are so many here [in Talcahuano, Chile],' wrote Lucy Ann Crapo on 17 April 1879, 'and I am sorry to say that some of our brothers in the business do not behave as well as they ought. But I think,' she added, 'it is only when they get overburdened with liquor.' Surely, the reader would think, the captains' portside behaviour should be restrained by the presence of decent Yankee women — women, what's more, who would gossip back home. Sad to say, however, some of the 'frail sex' were frailer than others.

'Captain Smith of the *Lucretia* cannot take even a small dram without getting hilarious,' Lucy Ann reported, 'and the others, some at least will get him tipsy if they can, to make sport of. Some of the ladies joined in it, and I said to them the other evening, when they had him dressed up with a ruche and tie around his neck, and was urging him on to say and do things for the sport of the company, how would you feel if it was your husband in his place. . .?'

'They call me the quakeress,' Lucy Ann went on, 'so I pin on a white silk hand'k'f and put Wms' specs astride my pug, and appear to them in the parlor when they get too noisy, and try to check them.' However, it seems, she seldom succeeded. The ladies even indulged in flirtatious sport. 'Ther is some ladys round here that will kiss me' John Deblois wrote to Henrietta from Talcahuano, 20 June 1861. It was a new kind of fun, this kissing game, and it was all to do with hoops.

Hoop-skirts were a very popular fashion, especially in hot climates, because they dispensed with the need to wear a multitude of petticoats. However, they did have one disadvantage: when the wearer bent over, or tried to sit in a chair, the hoops swung up at the back and displayed a large view of what was commonly known then as 'the lower works'. 'You know how hard it is for ladys to set down at a table with ther hoops on,' John wrote. 'I saw that the Capts did not take eny notes of it, so I wold shove the chire under them, they wold say how kind and tender.'

At that the 'Capts' did indeed take notice, and seating the ladies turned into a competition in gallantry. The men who missed out on shoving the chairs would pretend to sulk, and the ladies would kiss them to restore their spirits. One cannot help but wonder how Henrietta Deblois felt about the fun when she eventually received John's letter. Lucy Ann Crapo was certain that the women would not have behaved thus back home in New England, and no doubt she was perfectly correct.

However, even the demure Henrietta had not been exempt from at least one encounter with the demon grog. One day in March 1857, in Talcahuano, one of the Chilean seamen, Lewis, invited the captain's wife to his house to see his new baby. 'His house consists of one room,' she recorded.

'In it is a small bed, over this hangs a canvas cradle with a string which is pulled to make it rock. In this curiosity lays the fattest little chubby dark boy that I ever had the pleasure of seeing. Before we came away Lewis insisted on giving 'ma'am" some sweet drink. I at first declined but he insisted and seemed hurt at my refusal, so I accepted. He put a little lemon syrup into a not very clean tumbler, then filled the tumbler nearly full of water from an exceedingly dirty pitcher. I tasted, but could hardly swallow a spoonful. He then took a bottle from the shelf and poured something from that and then begged me to try if it was not better, but it was the most execrable drink that I ever attempted to swallow. I turned to see if there was any place where I could pour it out unseen, when, by the open door, directly in front of me, were several sailor boys in whose faces I could plainly see astonishment at seeing the captain's wife making free with a bottle.'

This story, obviously, would entertain the tavern set of Talcahuano for weeks. Henrietta met Captain Clarke of the *Chili* on the way back to the boarding house, 'and told him my adventure,' she related. 'He made himself very merry at my expense and said it would hardly be credited in the States.' She tartly told him she would keep his secrets if he kept hers, and he went off chortling to himself.

The attitude towards drink was more complicated then, than it may appear from today's perspective. 'Temperance' meant 'moderation', not 'abstinence', and despite the Morrells' claim that there were no ardent spirits on board, the crew was given 'switchel' (a slightly alcoholic mixture of fermented molasses, vinegar and water) twice a day, and 'shrub' after any unusual exertion. Shrub was a kind of cordial that was most definitely intoxicating: it was made to the ratio of one part sour (lemon juice or vinegar), and two parts sweet (molasses or sugar) plus three parts strong (rum or whisky) to four parts water.

Even the strict wives enjoyed a mug of toddy or a glass of wine. Elizabeth Stetson drank ale at night to help her sleep on the bark *E. Corning*, and when her husband Charles went on shore in October 1861 he brought her back a present of '12 bottles of brandy & 12 bottles of Port, also 2 barrels of Ale'. When visitors came on board Elizabeth served them wine.

At times, however, the hospitality was over-done, as Susan Veeder found out when the *Nauticon* spoke the brig *Agemoria* of Hobart on 1 November 1849. The Colonials were an affable and generous lot: 'the Captn gave me Jar of plums a tin of soup a Cheese a few bottles of wine,' she recorded. Then she added that 'while our boat was on board of the brig some of our Crew got Intoxicated and brought Liquor on board of the Ship with them and got more of them drunk and by their bad conduct two of them got punished.'

Colonial hospitality at the Bay of Islands was just as openhanded. 'There *may* have been "temperance" people in Russell,' Louisa Worsfold mused, 'but I never heard of it; it was much later that a wave of the "horrors of drink" came to the place.' Dr Ford medicated his surgical patients with 'lots of gin' and on the upper shelves of his cupboards 'there were many things to drink. There must have been some party on,' she meditated, 'or I would not have been there at lamplight – for I saw him making something in a big bowl – sliced lemons and lumps of sugar, and he told us he was making "brandy punch", and the hot water made his spectacles misty. . .'

His parties were held in a drawing room, 'with all that old-time furniture

— heavy and thick carpets, and hanging lamps with dangling glass drops that tinkled — Candles were a great feature in lighting arrangements — This room had one wall that was all doors, folding and sliding back to bring the next room into it for the purpose of dances. . .There was quite a lot of musical talent in Russell and many who played good dance music. . .and he taught some of the young people to play "square" dances, as these were called — lancers and quadrilles.'

It is easy, then, to imagine the scene, Eliza Brock and Mrs Nickerson, Mrs Fuller, Rachel Beckerman, Nancy Grant and all the other pretty Yankee women who had been cruising the various whaling grounds of New Zealand, tapping a foot to the lively music and watching the young ones dance, flushed like the good doctor with candlelight and the warmth of the occasion, sipping at hot brandy punch. The picture this inspires is an engaging one indeed, but nevertheless rather odd when one remembers that many of the wives might have been persuaded to ship along in order to encourage sober habits in the men.

The crews of their husbands' ships were almost certainly not hanging about wistfully while their skippers and those skippers' wives were having all the fun. They were patronising the grog-shops — and the passing of decades made no difference to the boozing. 'Third mate Engineer and some men forward full of firewater,' wrote Gertrude West on the *Horatio* in 1898.

So those who, like Mary Lawrence, sailed in the happy belief that they could play 'the gentler sex's role' on board the ship, were, like Viola Cook, sadly disillusioned. Then, in 1859, a contemporary observer went to some trouble to make the wives' lot even less rewarding, by pointing out to the world that the presence of the captain's wife made little difference, if any, to the whoring that went on, on the decks of their husbands' vessels.

This tactless fellow was Luther Gulick, missionary at Ponape (Caroline Islands) from 1852 to 1859. In August 1857 he published a most inflammatory letter in the *Boston Journal of Missions*:

> 'You may not be fully aware,' he wrote to his audience of whaleship owners, 'that most of the ships which you are sending to this ocean are the most disgusting of moral pesthouses. Not only are the sailors given to every crime, but the captains with nearly all their officers practise in these seas vices similar to those which brought destruction to Sodom and Gomorrah.'

The furore that ensued can be vividly imagined. *The New Bedford Whalemen's Shipping Paper*. . .for 5 January 1858 described it as 'an amazing attack on whaler captains'. As Gulick himself wrote later, 'The letter excited indignation both in America and the Pacific Ocean. . .I was told,' he added resentfully, 'that a missionary had nothing to do with such matters, and that it was especially amiss to state such things to the American public where the character of the seafaring world was not known.' Gulick wrote another letter in defence of his views, and sent it to Samuel Damon's paper, *The Friend*.

It arrived in Honolulu in November 1858, but Damon did not publish it. He reportedly remarked, 'Perhaps the less said on this subject the better.' This fanned Gulick's righteous wrath to explosion point, so he published the letter, along with lists of damning statistics, on his press in Ponape.

He did admit that some shipmasters were pious and righteous; he apologised if the innocent had been offended by his first letter. However:

> 'Having said this much, let me now give a fact. . . Seventy-four vessels have visited the two harbors of the tribe in which I live, since Sept. '52. Ten only of them have not been the public residences of native females during the whole time of their stay in port, some of them always finding their homes in the cabin, while others live in the steerage and forecastle.'

Then, in merciless detail, he presented lists of vessels that had arrived in port while he or his brother Theodore (another missionary) were in residence, *along with an indication of whether the captain's wife was on board or not.* Thus we find that prostitution was allowed on the decks of the Fairhaven vessel *Arab* even though Mrs Grinnell was in residence in the cabin, but Mrs Drew of the *Frances Henrietta* was made of sterner stuff, for the girls were allowed on the decks only when she was not on board the ship.

It was ungallant and scurrilous, for Luther Gulick must have been perfectly aware of the moral character of the great majority of captains' wives. As it happened, the lists were not even accurate. While the ships he listed were in the islands at the time, many more made port there without being noted. Similarly, some wives were named, while other wives were allowed to pass unmentioned. However, his motives were plain: among other things, he wished to prove that the presence of a wife on board made little or no difference to the morals of the ship.

Unfortunately, he was right. The undeniable fact was that whatever the wife believed or did made no difference at all to her husband's moral stand — on any issue whatsoever. Captain John Deblois, for instance, ran a strict ship, but he ran it the same whether his 'dear wife' was on board or not. At Easter Island in 1861 he wrote to her that the native girls swam out to the *Merlin*:

> 'I wated for them to come up with the ship, ther was a quite a nomber of young Girls they wanted to get on board very much but the *Ugly Capt* wold not let them com on board. I let ropes hang over the rail so that they cold rest them some as thay had to swim a bout 4 miles to get back thay had nothing to cover them sylfs with[out] *the hair on their head* was very *long* thay went a way very much disappointed good many on board thought the Capt might let the girls come on board to *rest* a little while.'

John was undoubtedly trying to impress Henrietta with his moral stand, but in effect all he accomplished was to point out to her that she couldn't, in all honesty, take any of the credit for the moral fibre of the previous voyage.

A righteous female could still let her feelings be known, however, if she felt strongly enough about the issue. When, in early 1847, the ship *Tiger* was anchored in a secluded Baja California bay, along with four other vessels, Mary Brewster was scandalised to learn that three of the captains kept strumpets in the cabins. These men, what's more, were neighbours back home, and their wives were Mary's acquaintances.

It was always difficult for Mary to restrain her opinion, for she was blessed with a tart temper and a devastating tongue. However, she managed to control herself until, one day, when she was sitting at the table, and had just commenced operations on her favourite meal – 'a dish of oysters' – one of those reprehensible skippers had the sauce to pay her a call. Her feminine role was one of reticence, but this was too much: Mary determined to take a strong stand. So she rose, '*so prim*', as the captain came in, and with a haughty toss of her head she quit the cabin.

And was the erring skipper embarrassed, did he stammer and flush? Not on your tintype. He grinned; he rubbed his hands together; he sat down; he ate her oysters.

'Remarks Wednesday March the 17 1847 Commences with fine weather and fine brese from the NNE at 5 oclock Capt com onn board brou[gh]t the cook and the boat steer[er] in irons...PM took in all sail but 2 reef [double-reefed] main topsail wind from the North had vary sharp liting [lightning] at 4 oclock PM sout [shook out] 2 reefs topsail in the morning made all sail sout the fore top mussstunysail [fore topmast studdingsail] 4 PM took the irons off the boat steer went to his duty.' – log kept on *Harrison*, on departing from Sydney.

After sailing from Sydney the *Harrison* steered north to try for whales in the Ochotsk Sea and off the Kamchatka Peninsula, Russia. Sherman's fortune, however, merely worsened: the anonymous seaman's journal is a misspelled litany of dissension, missed whales and hurt men from that date on. Then it ends, abruptly, mid-whaling – 'loard 3 boats dint git onn Pm spoke the ——' – on 20 August 1847. The next record of Mary Ann's voyage is a newspaper report of the arrival of the *Harrison* in Honolulu on 4 November 1847.

'We have now 37 whale ships in port and outside, and others arriving daily...' recorded the *Polynesian* of 20 November. 'Most of them report bad weather...Quite a number have lost spars and sails, but the saddest scene of all, is the number of seamen we see carried through the streets to the hospital painfully afflicted with the scurvy...

'The *Globe*, *Harrison*, *Isaac Hicks* are among the greatest sufferers,' the report continued; 'the sick have been taken to the hospital and provided for. Two men have died since getting into port.' Obviously, there was still a problem with provisions on the *Harrison*. The crew had suffered a great deal, and yet had taken only 500 bbls of oil. While in Honolulu Sherman put 500 pounds of whalebone on a New Bedford-bound ship, the *Maria Helena* – and the *Maria Helena* promptly wrecked on Christmas Island, with the loss of the whole of her cargo.

It was by no means the end of bad luck. After recruiting the *Harrison* steered sou'sou'west. The intention was to cruise for whales on the way back to New South Wales. Instead the ship struck on a reef at Upolu in the Navigator Islands, now called Samoa.

The *Harrison* finally arrived in Sydney on 8 June 1848. 'She has come on to Sydney for repairs,' the *Shipping List's* correspondent reported, 'having been driven ashore in Apia Harbour, in April last, during a heavy NW gale of 36 hours duration. At the time she drove she had two anchors out, topmasts struck and yards down. When got off again, it was found her false keel had gone, rudder unshipped, and that the vessel was leaky; also that the oil was leaking from the casks.' Abner Sherman was forced to stay three months in port, for the ship had to be 'hove down' and recoppered.

The *Harrison* departed from Sydney in September 1848, 'bound two years sperm whaling'. Instead of steering for the Equator, however, Abner kept to the right-whaling grounds east of New Zealand, and the reports he sent to both Sydney and New Bedford are a testament to the fact that he was incapable of making up his mind. January 1849 found the *Harrison* whaling off the Chatham Islands, and Sherman was telling the skippers of all the ships he spoke that he intended to steer for Sydney, sell his oil and refit for the Sea of Japan.

April found the ship still whaling off New Zealand, recruiting at Akaroa and with the captain ruminating aloud over the profitable possibilities of the Californian gold rush. Then finally, in August 1849, Abner took the ship into Sydney and put his oil on the *Mary Catherine* for London. He made rough alterations to the hold, putting in a mixed cargo and then covering the cargo with a level floor of planks. Then a long table was built down the middle and berths were nailed up about the bulkheads, turning the hold into extempore passenger quarters. The *Harrison* made sail on 25 October bound for California. Her passengers were Mrs Sherman and 28 others, presumably all Australians. The passengers' motives for sailing are easily guessed: they had embarked at Sydney for San Francisco and the syren gold. Perhaps Abner Sherman had good reasons for steering for California, too...but his wife had just ten weeks of life left.

On 9 February 1850 the *Alta California* reported the arrival of the 'American ship, *Harrison*, Sherman, 107 days from Sydney'. The passengers disembarked and disappeared, most into the hills, undoubtedly – and Abner Sherman put that mixed and private cargo up for sale. As advertised in the 9 February issue of the *Pacific News*, it consisted of:

200 tons Newcastle coals
33,000 bricks
30,000 shingles
1 wooden house 12 by 24 feet
6 extra large stalion [sic] horses, with carts and harness, [which] will be landed on the north beach today
72 setts horse shoes
8,000 horse shoe nails
48 pairs boots
12 pairs wheelbarrows
135 bbls pork
50 cases chairs
Lemon syrup, tar, pitch, washboards, ploughs, Manilla cigars &c.

It is a list that is irresistibly evocative: here are the ingredients (bar, perhaps, the cigars, boots and chairs) for a house and a farm – and it is traditional that every sailor's greatest ambition is to buy a farm and swallow the anchor. Abner Sherman had so nearly accomplished it, too. All that had been needed to make the picture complete was the land and a housewife...and death had cheated him of that last article.

The makings of that farm and homestead were sold, and Abner Sherman, recent widower, failed whaleman, left the *Harrison*. The ship sailed from port on 29 May under the command of a replacement master, Captain Savage, and Sherman never went whaling again. What he did, in fact, is unknown. The census reports for 1855 described him as a seaman, and he never remarried. Then, on 1 September 1893, his death was reported in the *New Bedford Daily Mercury*.

'FATAL ACCIDENT' — the headline read — 'Capt. A.D. Sherman Thrown From His Carriage and Killed.

'Capt. Abner D. Sherman, a well-known resident of South Dartmouth,' the report went on, 'was thrown from his carriage on Shawmut Avenue, near Austin Street, shortly after 6 o'clock last evening, receiving injuries from which he expired a half hour later.' Captain Sherman, it seems, had been to Evergreen Park to try out a frisky young mare 'that he alone had driven and one that he was fond of speeding'. Speeding the mare he was indeed, despite the fact that he was on a public thoroughfare: his 'light carriage collided with another carriage going in the same direction'. In a word, Abner Sherman, despite his advanced age, was racing.

And so the old whaleman died, in a violent and competitive manner that seems strangely appropriate for one of his trade. And so, too, the story is finished. Abner Sherman was a shabby kind of man to have as the *de facto* hero of a book, brutal in a trade that was brutal to start with, unlucky in a business that depended so much on good fortune. His story, however, demanded the telling, if only because he, like William Brewster, was one of the first to carry a wife; like William and Mary Brewster he and Mary Ann helped set off the remarkable wife-carrying fashion.

It was a passing fad; in that year of his death it was very nearly over. Wife-carrying was a custom that had cost Abner Sherman his own wife and, as we have seen, had accomplished very little in its sentimental aims. Looked at analytically, it was no more than an eccentric episode in the story of windjammer whaling. But — and this must also be allowed — the legendary wives who came to Lahaina, Honolulu, Samoa and Sydney, and who stopped on shore in Albany and Russell, Hobart Town and Mangonui, played a colourful part in the story of the Pacific. And, because of that wife-carrying fad, Hobart, Vasse, Mangonui and Russell are remembered in America — as fascinating footnotes in the genealogies of New England.

# Chapter notes

Specific references, published, unpublished and illustrative, are given in order of appearance in the chapter, to make further study as accessible as possible. Each chapter is treated as a separate essay, so sources are repeated when necessary. If the manuscript can be found on microfilm, as part of the Pacific Manuscripts Bureau project, then the number of the PMB reel is given as well as the name of the repository. Abbreviations are as follows:

Baker – Baker Library, Graduate School of Business, Harvard University, Boston, Massachusetts 02163.

Brown – John Hay Library, Brown University, Providence, Rhode Island 02912.

Cold Spring – Whaling Museum Society Inc., Cold Spring Harbor, Long Island, New York 11724.

Dixson – Dixson Library, State Library of New South Wales, Sydney, NSW 2000, Australia.

Dukes County – Dukes County Historical Society, Edgartown, Martha's Vineyard, Massachusetts 02539.

HMCSL – Hawaiian Mission Children's Society Library, Honolulu, Hawaii 96813.

Houghton – Rare Books and Manuscripts, Houghton Library, Harvard University, Cambridge, Massachusetts 02138.

Huntington – The Huntington Library, Art Gallery and Botanical Gardens, San Marino, California 91108.

IMA – International Marine Archives microfilm collection, held at New Bedford Whaling Museum Library, New Bedford, Massachusetts 02740.

KWM – The Kendall Whaling Museum, Sharon, Massachusetts 02067.

Mariners – Mariners' Museum Library, Newport News, Virginia 23606.

Mystic – Manuscripts Collection, G.W. Blunt White Library, Mystic Seaport Museum, Inc., Mystic, Connecticut 06355.

NBFPL – Melville Whaling Room, New Bedford Free Public Library, New Bedford, Massachusetts 02740.

Newport – Newport Historical Society, Newport, Rhode Island 02840.

NHA – Nantucket Historical Association, Nantucket, Massachusetts 02554.

ODHS – Whaling Museum Library, Old Dartmouth Historical Society, New Bedford, Massachusetts 02740.

PMS – Phillips Library, Peabody Museum of Salem, Salem, Massachusetts 01970.

PMB – Pacific Manuscripts Bureau microfilm collection, Department of Pacific and South-East Asian Studies, Australian National University, Canberra ACT 2601, Australia.

PPL – Nicholson Whaling Collection, Providence Public Library, Providence, Rhode Island 02903.

Sag Harbor – Sag Harbor Whaling and Historical Museum, Sag Harbor, New York 11963.

### Chapter 1: 'A disgraceful drinking riot'

John Randall's journal on *California* 1849-51 is held at ODHS, PMB 294. The correspondence of the Reverend Dwight Baldwin of Lahaina (a most lively and perceptive missionary) is held by the HMCSL, Honolulu. Daniel Wheeler's scandalised opinions are quoted in Ernest S. Dodge, *Islands and Empires: Western Impact on the Pacific and East Asia* and in *Europe and the World in the Age of Expansion vol. VII* (Minnesota: Univ. of Minnesota, 1976), pp. 74-5. This chapter (5, *Whalers Ashore*) also has much of interest on whalemen in the Bay of Islands.

The anecdote behind the title comes from Francis E. (Frank) Tod, *Whaling in Southern Waters*, (Dunedin: priv. pr. 1982). The typescript of Dan Baldwin's journal on *Charleston*, 1844-7, is held at ODHS, PMB 287. The log kept on ship *Balance* of Bristol, Rhode Island, captain unknown, is held at PPL. First mate Eldredge's testimonial to Captain Bonney's drunkenness is held at Cold Spring Harbor, PMB 689. The racy account of Captain Reuben Swain is told by another Reuben, Reuben Delano, in *Wanderings and Adventures of Reuben Delano, being a narrative of Twelve Years' Life in a Whale Ship!'* (Boston: Thos Drew, Redding, 1846).

John T. Perkins' personal journal on the *Tiger* was published by Marine Hist. Assn., vol 1, no. 8, Mystic. The *Dauphin* rhyming log is held at PPL, PMB 772. Alfred Peck's retrospective account is held at PPL, PMB 797.

The observations of Captain Sawtell's second mate are quoted in Clement Sawtell, *The Ship 'Ann Alexander' of New Bedford 1805 1851* (Mystic: Marine Hist. Assn Inc. No. 40, 1962). William Wilson's highly illuminating but difficult-to-read journal on bark *Cavalier* is also held at Mystic, log No. 18. The log of the *Globe* 1850 is held at ODHS, PMB 720.

The journal kept on the *China* 1843-5 is held at NBFPL, PMB 363. Rhodes' log was published as C.R. Straubel (ed), *The Whaling Journal of Captain W.B. Rhodes 1836-1838*, (Christchurch: Whitcombe & Tombs 1954). The journal kept on *Emerald*, by Eagleston, is held at PMS, PMB 225; that on the *Columbus*, 1837-9, is held at KWM, PMB 805.

The observations made by John B. Williams and John Dyes are quoted in Robert W. Kenny, *Yankee Whalers at the Bay of Islands*, in 'American Neptune' 12 (1952): pp. 39-40. Kenny also edited *The New Zealand Journal 1842-1846 of John B. Williams*, (Salem: Peabody, Brown Univ. 1956), from which the conversation with Mrs Busby is taken.

The photograph of the whaling captains is held at ODHS, reproduced by permission. James Willis's journal on the *Rambler* 1856-60 is held at KWM, PMB 816. The pictures of the men in the yards and on the foredeck (of the *Charles W. Morgan*) are held at NBFPL. Captain William Phelps' letter written on the *Alert* (which is the same vessel described in Richard Dana's classic, *Two Years Before the Mast*) is held at the Harvard College Library, PMB 737, and George Pomeroy's equally charming journal on the *George Howland* is held at Mariners, PMB 776.

The advertisement calling for whalemen and the two photographs of mid-century New Bedford were supplied by Joseph D. Thomas of New Bedford, and the early history of the city comes from Judith A. Boss and Joseph D. Thomas, *New Bedford: A Pictorial History* (Virginia: Donning Co. 1983) pp. 12-17 and 22-41. The anecdote about Rodney French is on page 53 of this book. My material on Prince Edward Sherman was supplied by Thea Meenagh of Kerikeri, and I thank Greg Bowen of Hamilton for the Henry Davis Snowden anecdotes, and also for the photograph of Prince Sherman.

### Chapter 2: 'To preserve unbroken the ties of domestic life'

Mrs William Swain's poem is in the log of the *Clifford Wayne*, 1855-8, NHA No. L79, PMB 374.

The anecdotes about Captain Abraham Russell, his ship and his sweetheart come from *Bartholomew Gosnold* 1840-43, PPL, PMB 575, and Cochran Forbes, *The Journals of Cochran Forbes, Missionary to Hawaii 1831-1864* (Honolulu: Hawaiian Mission Children's Society, 1984) p. 122. Susannah Holden's background comes from *The Holden Genealogy*, compiled by Eben Putnam, Boston 1926, v.2, pp. 368-6, 466-8. Horace Holden's account is called *Holden's Narrative*, in *A Narrative of the shipwreck, capture, and sufferings of Horace Holden and Benjamin H. Nute, who were cast away in the American ship 'Mentor' on the Pellew Islands in the year 1832, and for two years afterward were subjected to unheard of sufferings among the barbarous inhabitants of Lord North's Island*, (Boston: Russell, Shattuck & Co., 1836). I thank Elizabeth Hamlin-Morin of the New Hampshire Historical Society for her invaluable assistance in collating this material.

Nathaniel Morgan's journal on the *Hannibal* 1849-50 is held at Mystic, log No. 862. The seafaring career of Abner D. Sherman was taken from the catalogue of crew cards held at NBFPL.

An account of Mary Hayden Russell's voyaging can be read in Edouard A. Stackpole, *Whales & Destiny* (Univ. of Mass.: 1972) pp. 366-370. The description of Eliza Williams comes from Harold Williams (ed) *One Whaling Family* (Boston: Houghton-Mifflin 1964) *passim*, partic. pp. 391-2. The Williams material, originally held privately in Hawaii, is now held at PMS. The story of Mrs Brown and the *Flying Fox* is told in J.E. Philp, *Whaling Ways of Hobart Town* (Hobart: Walch, 1936) p. 41.

An account of Benjamin Gibbs' birth is in the *Evening Standard*, Nantucket, 5 Dec 1903, p. 10; also see W.B. Murdock, *The Murdock Whaling Voyages* (New Bedford: Reynolds, 1938) p. 13.

The memoirs of Capt. Benjamin Morrell Jr. are published as *A Narrative of Four Voyages to the South Seas, North and South Pacific Ocean, Chinese Sea, Ethiopic and Southern Atlantic Ocean, Indian and Antarctic Ocean from the Year 1822 to 1831...* (New York: J & J Harper, 1832); also see the account written by said wife: Abby Jane (Wood) Morrell, *Narrative of a Voyage to the Ethiopic and South Atlantic Ocean, Indian Ocean, Chinese Sea, North and South Pacific Ocean*, (Upper Saddle River, NJ: Gregg Press, 1833, repr. 1970).

Charles Gelett's memoir of his whaling career was published as, C.W. Gelett, *A Life on the Ocean* (Honolulu: Hawaiian Gazette, 1917). The account of his wife's seasickness is on p. 51, and of his own conversion by Barker is on p. 41.

The Baldwin letter about Barker and the crew of the *Roman* was written on 5 September 1841 to Samuel Castle — Baldwin letters, HMCSL.

Mary Wallis's account of the goings on, on Nauru, is contained in Mrs (Mary Davis) Wallis, *Life in Feejee, or, Five Years Among the Cannibals* (Boston: William Heath, 1851), p. 202.

The trio of hurried weddings is documented in the *Vineyard Gazette* for 15 June 1855, under the intriguing headline 'GREAT EXCITEMENT — One hundred Ladies in full chase after a Methodist Minister' and also in the 'Dukes County Intelligencer' Vol. 28 No. 3, February 1987, pp. 126-7. The weddings were held at dawn so the couples could catch the 6.45 AM ferry to New Bedford for the start of their honeymoon trips. Betsy (Morse) Morey was born on 7 Feb. 1810 in Thompson, Connecticut. Her husband died 4 years after they returned to Nantucket, aged 49. She lived to the age of '83 years, 8 months, 13 days' (Nantucket Vital Records). The Nantucket yarn is retold by Susan Wolf in a paper titled *Women and the Sea*, submitted at Mystic, Spring 1978, held there as ms No. RF 327. Benjamin Wing's letters to his wife from the *Good Return*, 1851-5, are held at PPL.

The Blackmer and Post letters are quoted from Genevieve M. Darden, (ed), *My Dear Husband*, (New Bedford: Descendants of Whaling Masters, Inc., 1974), pp. 18 and 47, by kind permission of Ms Darden and the society.

The picture of Harriet Peirce and daughter Harriet comes from the Robert E. Van Dyke collection, and I am grateful to Mr Van Dyke for permission to use it. Some of the details in the caption are recounted in MacKinnon Simpson and Robert B. Goodman, *WhaleSong* (Honolulu: Beyond Words Publishing Co. 1989) pp. 104-5. I also thank Mac Simpson for his interest and assistance.

The photograph of Mary Brewster is held at Mystic, used by permission. © Mystic Seaport, Mystic, Connecticut. The details of her birth and marriage come from Joan Druett, *Our Charming Diaress* (Mystic: Marine Publications 1991).

The death of Almira Gibbs was recorded by another whaling wife, Elizabeth Stetson, in February 1865: Mrs Stetson wrote, 'Mrs Gibbs dead, died three months ago in Valparaiso [Chile].' Almira was 49 years old at the time of her death.

A short ms account of Marianna Almy Sherman's life, marriage and voyaging is held at PPL. The somewhat mysterious genealogy of Mary Ann (Zoeth) Sherman is listed in Roy V. Sherman, *Some of the Descendants of Philip Sherman* (Akron, Ohio, priv. pr. 1968) p. 502, which also states that she died in 1845. Zoeth's genealogy is listed on p. 504; it does not include Mary Ann. I am grateful to Paul Cyr, New England genealogist, NBFPL, for advice on extrapolation from these scarce and dry details.

The photograph of Charles and Rachel Chase is held at KWM, used by permission. The crew list can be seen at NBFPL. Much of the material for the caption comes from, Lisa Norling, *Contrary Dependencies: Whaling Agents and Whalemen's Families, 1830-1870*, in, 'The Log of Mystic Seaport' vol. 42, No. 1, Spring 1990, p. 10. I am indebted to Lisa Norling for her constant encouragement and generous access to her findings.

### Chapter 3: 'This Floating Prison'

The John S. Deblois letters are held by Newport, Vault A, Box 113, Folder 6. I am grateful to the Society for much help and material, including illustrations. A full and fascinating account of the loss of the ship *Ann Alexander* can be found in Clement C. Sawtell, *The Ship 'Ann Alexander of New Bedford, 1805-1851'* (Mystic: Marine Hist. Assn. Inc. 1962), pp. 70-90. Also see Joan Druett, *"My Dear Wife": the Story of John and Henrietta Deblois*, in 'Newport History, Bulletin of the Newport Historical Society' vol. 60, Part 1, Winter 1987, No. 205, pp. 4-12. The Jenkins material and the captain's account of the loss of the *Kathleen* come from Captain Jenkins' great-grandson Ralph E. Jenkins of New Dartmouth; I thank him for his generosity.

The story of Anne Joseph and the bed on chains is told in Pat Amaral, *They Ploughed the Seas* (St. Petersburg: Valkyrie Press 1978). A charming monograph, W.B. Murdock's *The Murdock Whaling Voyages* (New Bedford: Reynolds 1938) has the description of the transom cabin. Another interesting and detailed description of accommodations is given in John F. Leavitt, 'The Charles W. Morgan', (Mystic: Marine Hist. Assn. 1973) pp. 32-7.

Abram Briggs' journal on *Eliza Adams*, Caleb O. Hamblin, is held at ODHS, PMB 911. The journal kept by Perkins, seaman on the *Tiger*, is published as, *John T. Perkins' Journal at Sea, 1845*, (Mystic: Marine Hist. Assn., 1934) pp. 119-150.

The comment about Jane Worth is contained in Irwin Shapiro, with Edouard A. Stackpole, *The Story of Yankee Whaling* (New York: American Heritage 1959), within the section on whaling wives and children, pp. 94-107. The photograph comes from Dukes County, and material for the caption was found in E.M. Whiting and H. Beetle Hough, *Whaling Wives* (Boston: Houghton Mifflin 1953) pp. 99-114.

David Baker's reminiscences to his daughter, Lilian Baker Fenton, including the anecdote about the rat, are held in typescript at Mystic. The ms is catalogued as *Whaling voyage 1858-1862, on board Bark OHIO, David Baker*, and headed *Mary's Adventure*.

The yarn about the medical bottles is related in B.A. Botkin, *A Treasury of New England Folklore* (New York: Brown, 1937) p. 372. Swift's log on the *Good Return* is held at ODHS, PMB 267. A typescript held at NBFPL, by Arthur C. Lipman and George E. Osborne, *Medicine and Pharmacy Aboard New England Whaling Vessels* has several such ghoulishly amusing anecdotes, including some reminiscences told to the authors by Reginald Hegarty, who spent his childhood on various whalers, and was curator of the whaling collection there at that time.

Also see Joan Druett, *Rough Medicine: Doctoring the Whaleman*, in 'The Dukes County Intelligencer', Vol. 30, No. 2, November 1988, pp. 3-15. For a discussion of another aspect of the business, see Honore Forster, *British Whaling Surgeons in the South Seas, 1823-1843*, in 'The Mariner's Mirror', Vol. 74, No. 4, November 1988, pp. 401-415. I thank Honore Forster for her lively and informative correspondence on this fascinating topic.

The photographs of Helen Jernegan and her daughter Laura are held at Dukes County. For details of her marriage and the journey to meet her husband, see Arthur Railton, *Jared Jernegan's Second Family* in 'The Dukes County Intelligencer', Vol. 28, No. 2, November 1986.

Susan Brock's anecdotes of her childhood years on the *Midnight* are held as a privately printed monograph — *Doubling Cape Horn* — at the NHA Research Center, Nantucket. An interview with Jamie Earle forms the basis of an article by Patricia Biggins, *Doughnuts in the Tryworks: A Child's Life Aboard the 'Charles W. Morgan'*, in, 'Log of Mystic Seaport' No. 27, May 1975, pp. 8-16.

The photograph of Mary McKenzie is held at KWM, used by permission. The *Platina* voyages were 1892-6, 1896-7, 1898-1901; logs all held at NBFPL, PMB 358; and 1901-3, 1903-4, 1904-6, 1906-8, 1908-10, also at NBFPL, PMB 359.

Obed Swain's photograph is held at NHA, used by permission. His log on the *Catawba* is also held at NHA No. L34, PMB 374.

## Chapter 4: 'Blood, grease, sweat and oil'

For a contemporary view of the 'desecration of the Sabbath' by whalemen, see Rev. W. Scoresby (a whaleman himself), *The Whaleman's Adventures* (London: Darton & C. 1861) pp. 104-5.

The engraving made by Joel S. Polack in 1838, 'Whaling off the North Cape', is held at the Alexander Turnbull Library, National Library of New Zealand, Wellington, used by permission. The log kept on board the schooner *Alfred* is held at KWM, PMB 801. The journal kept on the *Harrison*, 21 May 1845-21 August 1847, is held at ODHS, IMA No. 931. That kept on the *Mechanic* 1846-51 is held at PPL, PMB 880.

Ellsworth West, with Eleanor Ransom Mayhew, published his reminiscences as *Captain's Papers — A Log of Whaling and Other Sea Experiences* (Mass: Barre, 1965).

The anecdote re trying out comes from, E.K. Chatterton, *Whalers & Whaling* (London: T. Fisher Unwin 1925) p. 81. I am grateful to Joseph D. Thomas and the NBFPL for the pictures of cutting in and trying out.

An informative and entertaining account of nineteenth century fashion, including details of the 'Bloomer costume', can be read in Charles N. Gattey, *The Bloomer Girls* (New York: Coward-McMann 1968).

The photograph of Charlotte Jernegan is held at Dukes County, and the anecdote comes from E.M. Whiting and H. Beetle Hough, *Whaling Wives* (Boston: Houghton-Mifflin 1953); Maxfeld's entertaining journal kept on the 1852 voyage of the *Niger* is held at Houghton, PMB 736.

The photograph of Lucy Smith is held at PPL, and the one of Sallie Smith is held at Mystic, while the picture of Lottie Church comes from KWM, all used by permission.

Dan Lincoln's journal kept on the *Coral* is held at KWM, PMB 834, in a book which also includes his journals kept on *Tacitus, John, Josephine*, all made in the years 1844-9; Dan was a restless fellow who moved from ship to ship. 'I might as well be spoiling paper and wasting ink as doing nothing,' he wrote — and he was by no means the only man to fill in the lagging hours by keeping a journal. See Joan Druett, *Those Female Journals* (which covers male books as well), in 'The Log of Mystic Seaport', Vol. 40, No. 4, Winter 1989.

The story of the captain who shaved his head is recounted by Jones, 'The Roving Printer', in, *Life and Adventure in the South Pacific* (New York: Harper & Bros. 1861). Abram Briggs' journal on the *Eliza Adams* is held at ODHS, PMB 911. Nancy Grant's exploits are described in, Nancy S. (Grant) Adams, *My Grandfather — Captain Grant*, published in, "The proceedings of the Nantucket Historical Assn.', July 1924.

### Chapter 5: 'About the Cape of Good Hope'

The photograph of Annie Ricketson is held at ODHS, used by permission. Many of the details of her biography come from the introduction to Philip F. Purrington (ed) *Mrs Ricketson's Whaling Journal* (Mass.: ODHS 1958).

I am grateful to T. Moore Holcombe 4th, of Levittown, Pennsylvania, for his generous present of a print of the photograph of the Corvelho family on the *Greyhound*. An account of the bloodless mutiny can be read in Walter Hammond, *Mutiny on the 'Pedro Varela',* (Mystic: Marine Hist. Assn. No. 30, June 1956). In some parts veracity has been sacrificed for entertainment, but it is valuable reading nonetheless, with excellent descriptions of cutting in and trying out. The true story of Antonio Corvelho is contained in Pat Amaral, *They Ploughed the Seas* (St. Petersburg: Valkyrie Press 1978).

The anecdote about James Henry Sherman and his wife Phebe comes from Genevieve Darden (ed) *My Dear Husband*, (New Bedford: Descendants of Whaling Masters 1980) pp. 61-9.

The photograph of Desire Fisher comes from Dukes County, and material for the caption was found in E.M. Whiting and H. Beetle Hough, *Whaling Wives* (Boston: Houghton Mifflin 1953).

The incomplete diary kept (by an almost-illiterate seaman — perhaps the blacksmith or carpenter) on the *Harrison* during Mary Ann Sherman's voyage is held at ODHS on microfilm, IMA No. 931. When microfilmed, it was the property of Gale Blosser, and I thank him for permission to use it. The diary begins on 21 May 1845 on departure from New Bedford, and ends on 21 August 1847 at sea near Petropavlovsk, a town on Kamchatka Peninsula, Russia, book full. The tone is tough and experienced; the spelling is startling, at times so eccentric it seems almost like a private code. Captain Abner D. Sherman is usually referred to as 'ADS'; Mary Ann Sherman is not mentioned at all, but it was by no means unusual for the captain's wife to be ignored in the men's logbooks and diaries, particularly if she was quiet and retiring.

Lucy Smith's remininscences — *My Adventures Afloat* — are held in ms form at Dukes County. Napoleon's body was not, of course, in that grave (his remains had been returned to Paris in 1840) but the notion of taking geranium cuttings from plants that grew where his corpse had mouldered would have appealed to the ghoulish kind of sentimentality popular in Lucy's time.

Nellie Allen's essay is called *When I was Seven*, or *Sea Memories*. It is a ms memoir held at KWM (log No. 402a) under her married name of Bradford (see appendix of women's writings). It is based heavily on her mother's journal, and also on her own partial diary (also held at KWM).

Harriet Allen sailed on an earlier voyage, *Platina*, 1857, to the same grounds. There is no surviving journal from this one. Her shore journal, 1863-7, is also held at KWM, reel No. 47.

The story of the 1863 *Brewster* voyage is related in Captain John A. Beebe, *The Ocean from Real Life*, in 'The Century Monthly', a Nantucket magazine, December 1891. The Nantucket paper 'Zion's Herald' of 31 August (year not given on the clipping held at NHA) relates the hoop-frame story about Lydia Beebe. All this material is held in the Vertical File at NHA, under the heading 'John A. Beebe'. Other books of that same voyage are an official log, kept by Beebe himself, NHA No. L237, PMB 373; another, kept by the first officer, NBFPL, PMB 313; and an informal journal kept by the third mate, Marshall Keith, PPL, PMB 577.

George Cook's comment about his remarkable mother Hannah (Fawkes) Cook is recorded in Kay Boese, *Tides of History* (Russell: Bay of Islands County Council 1977) p. 378. The description of Mrs Joseph Chase comes from Scherzer, *Narrative of the 'Novara'...*, Vol. 3, pp. 255-6.

An account of Mary Hayden Russell's voyaging can be read in Edouard A. Stackpole, *Whales & Destiny* (Univ. of Mass.: 1972) pp. 366-370. I am grateful to Mr Edouard Stackpole and Mrs Jacqueline Haring for material relating to Mary's journal-letters.

Abram Briggs' caustic journal on *Eliza Adams* is held at ODHS, PMB 911.

The log of the *Islander* 1871-3 is held at KWM, PMB 811. The reminiscent account of 96-year-old Bertha Hamblin Boyce, who was one of the children on board during that voyage of the *Islander*, was published as *Bertha Goes Whaling: Personal Memoirs of a Voyage aboard a Whaling Bark, 'Islander'* (Falmouth, Mass.: priv. pr. 1963).

William B. Whitecar's account of his voyage (on the bark *Pacific* of New Bedford, Capt. John W. Sherman, 1855-9) was published as *Four Years Aboard the Whaleship* (Philadelphia: Lippincott 1860); it is entertaining reading because of his startling observations on Australia and New Zealand.

Georgina Molloy's letter is quoted in Lady Alexandra Hasluck's book, *Portrait with Flowers*, (London: Oxford University Press 1955) partic. pp. 210-1.

I thank Ellen Howland, President of the Descendants of Whaling Masters Inc., for the story of her grandmother, Ellen Scott Howland.

The log of brig *Harvest* is held at PPL, PMB 768.

The notice of Captain John Hempstead's marriage can be found in *The New Bedford Whalemen's Shipping List...for 1 February 1853*.

The description of the New London whalers at Desolation Island comes firstly from Barnard Colby, *New London Whaling Captains* (Mystic Seaport: 1936), in Marine Historical Assn. Inc. Publications Vol. 1, No. 1-12 1930-38 (which includes brief biographies of John Potter Rice and Benjamin Nelson Rogers — who also took their wives on voyage — as well as an account of Franklin F. Smith), and, secondly, from Howard Palmer, ed., Nathaniel W. Taylor, *Life on a Whaler* (New London, Conn.: New London County Historical Society, 1929). Also see, Barnard L. Colby, *Whaling from Southeastern Connecticut, 1647-1909*, in 'The Log of Mystic Seaport' Vol. 41, No. 3, 4/Fall 1989-Winter 1990, pp. 75-90, partic. p. 86. The anecdote about the *Offley* comes from W.J. Dakin, *Whalemen Adventurers* (Sydney: Angus & Robertson 1934) pp. 123-5.

The account of the wreck of the *Strathmore* and David Gifford's rescue of the survivors is documented in Ian Church, *Survival on the Crozet Islands* (Waikanae, NZ: The Heritage Press 1985); the photographs of David and Eleanor Gifford are from the W.H. Tripp Collection, Mystic, used by permission.

### Chapter 6: 'Steering in for the Bay of Islands'

Abby Jane Morrell's account of New Zealand can be found on pp. 33-40, 120 and 224-5 of her book; Benjamin Morrell's version is on pp. 367-9 of his.

For an inspiring discussion of the peculiar frustrations of the mission wives, see Patricia Grimshaw, *Christian Woman, Pious Wife, Faithful Mother, Devoted Missionary: Conflicts in Roles of American Missionary Women in Nineteenth Century Hawaii*, in 'Feminist Studies' 9, No. 3 (Fall 1983) pp. 489-521.

While, as explained by the title, the setting is Hawaii, the problems were those of mission women all over the Pacific. Sandra L. Myres, of the University of Texas at Arlington, has also carried out most interesting research on women and the frontier experience (including in New Zealand); I thank her for sharing this with me, via a copy of her 'Report on Research in Progress' for a forthcoming book, *Victoria's Daughters*: pages 14-16 of this were particularly relevant.

Also see A.E. Woodhouse (ed) *Tales of Pioneer Women* (Hamilton: Silver Fern Books 1988), Chapter 2, 'Mrs Henry Williams, Paihia', esp. pp. 12-17.

The major resource for the background and events in the Bay of Islands about the time of the Morrells' visit is Jack Lee, '*I have named it the Bay of Islands...*' (Auckland: Hodder & Stoughton, 1983) majorly pp. 117-148; Edward Markham, *New Zealand, or Recollections of it* is quoted on p. 120. The log of *Samuel Robertson*, 1837-40, is held at ODHS, PMB 287. The McNab letter is held at NBFPL.

Charles Wilkes' comment comes from p. 377 of vol. II of *Narrative of the US Exploring Expedition...* (Phila.: Lee & Blanchard, 1845). The bulk of my material on Caroline and William Mayhew comes from a transcript ms held by Dukes County, originally handwritten by Ruby Holmes Martyn. Mayhew's letter to the U.S. Government is quoted from this, but is held by the National Archives in Washington. Contributory details come from Jack Lee, pp. 213, 242 and 250. The photograph of Caroline is held at Dukes County. Captain Jabez Howland's report of the burning of Kororareka was published in the *New Bedford Whalemen's Shipping List* for 22 July 1845.

The Louisa Worsfold reminiscences are in ms and ts form in the Auckland Institute and Museum Library, MS 340. The material used comes from the typescript, pp. 3-12; the account of Charles Fisher's fine for smuggling is on p. 31. I thank Eddie Sun of the Auckland Museum Library for assistance with this material.

The letter written by Lulu Kelly to Parnell Fisher is held at Dukes County; a copy was kindly provided by Arthur Railton. I also acknowledge with gratitude the help and information given to me by Louisa Worsfold's youngest daughter, Dorothy MacGillivray, who allowed me generous access to the wealth of Mair, Greenway and Worsfold material that she holds. Mrs MacGillivray also provided the photograph of her mother, taken at the age of 21, and of Louisa's first son, Dick Kelly, taken when he was a small child. Additional material, including the story of Henry Abbott Mair, came from, J.C. Anderson and G.C. Petersen, *The Mair Family* (Wellington: A.H. & A.W. Reed, 1956), principally pp. 11-27 and 76-83.

The anecdotes about Sarah Luce and Parnell Fisher come from E.M. Whiting and H. Beetle Hough, *Whaling Wives* (Boston: Houghton-Mifflin 1953), pp. 98-9 and *passim*, esp. pp. 241-9. The picture of Sarah Luce comes from Dukes County, as do the pictures of Charles and Parnell Fisher, while Hervey Luce's photograph comes from NBFPL. The photograph of the whaler 'hove down' comes (as do the great majority of ship photographs) from New Bedford, per Joe Thomas and Paul Cyr.

Emma Thomas's experiences in the New Zealand ground are documented in Sylvia Thomas, *Saga of a Yankee Whaleman* (New Bedford: ODHS 1981) pp. 81-123, partic. pp. 96-119. I thank Sylvia Thomas for permission to use the photograph of Emma (and companions) on Pitt Island.

Many of the log-writers and journal-keepers commented about the awful weather on the New Zealand ground: in December 1859 Eleanor Baker wrote with evident passion, 'Oh! New Zealand I hate the sound of it for it is such a rugged place. Hope to one day get home *never more* to come on it [the New Zealand ground] again. *Never!*' (She did return, on the *Northern Light*.)

The account of Elizabeth Brightman's voyaging comes from the *New Bedford Evening Standard* 3 July 1914. My major source for the career of Nancy Grant is, Nancy S. (Grant) Adams, *My Grandfather – Captain Grant*, in 'The Proceedings of the Nantucket Historical Association', NHA, July 1924. Also see the obituary for George Grant, their son – who was custodian of the Nantucket Whaling Museum from its opening (1930) until his passing, May 1942 – also in the 'Proceedings', 27 July 1942. The log of the *Potomac* 1849 is held at NHA No. L204, PMB 384. The log of the *Napoleon*, 1868-72 is held at KWM, PMB 805.

Abram Briggs' journal on the *Eliza Adams* is held at ODHS, PMB 911. The details of the birth and death of the little Hamblin girl come from notices in the *New Bedford Mercury* on the relevant dates.

I am grateful to Captain Wilson's grandson Russ Carroll for the Wilson anecdote: He wrote to me, 'I was named Russell Arnold Carroll, "Russell" from my mother's birthplace, and "Arnold" from the name of the ship, and I am proud of my name and birthplace.'

The log of the *Thomas Pope* 1859-62 is held at KWM, PMB 818. The John States journal on the *Nantasket* 1845-6 is held at Mystic, and I am grateful to Andrew German for drawing this entry to my attention.

The anecdote about the birth of the Nicholls twins on board the *Sea Gull* is told in William F. Macy (ed), *The Nantucket Scrap Basket – being a Collection of Characteristic Stories and Sayings of the People of the Town and Island of Nantucket, Massachusetts*, (Boston: Houghton-Mifflin 1930), pp. 25-6.

The log of the *Abraham Barker* 1871-5 is held at Brown, PMB 772. Mrs Willard's death was reported in the *New Bedford Whalemen's Shipping List. . .* for 17 January 1865. The death of Captain Charles Evans of ship *Arctic* of Fairhaven was first reported in the *New Bedford Whalemen's Shipping List. . .* for 12 May 1857.

The story of Honor Matthews Earle is told in Edouard Stackpole, *Ladies of the 'Morgan'*, in 'The Log of Mystic Seaport', Vol. 13, No. 3, 1961, pp. 17-20. The *Boston Globe* interview with Honor Earle was published in the Sunday edition for 9 August 1906. The photograph of the Earle family, originally from the *Globe* newspaper, is held at KWM, used by permission. The material for the caption came largely from an article by Patricia Biggins, *Doughnuts in the Tryworks: A Child's Life Aboard the 'Charles W. Morgan'*, in 'The Log of Mystic Seaport' No. 27, May 1975, pp. 8-16. The photograph of Marion Smith is at KWM, used by permission.

## Chapter 7: 'Uncharted seas, unknown shores'

The Morrell material comes from Abby Jane Morrell, *Narrative of a Voyage. . .*, (New York: J&J Harper 1833) pp. 55-68, 82, 86, 144, 204; and, Benjamin Morrell, *Narrative of Four Voyages. . .*(New York: J&J Harper 1832), pp. 387-416, 437-452, 466.

The photograph of Alice Henrietta Handy and details of her life were supplied by her American descendants, through the kindness of Alice Henrietta's great-granddaughter, Mimi Smith of La Quinta, California. The logs kept on bark *Belle* 1852-7 were microfilmed at Sag Harbor, PMB 680. Dr Pierson's journal was published in *Missionary Herald*, Vol. 54, No. 3, March 1858, pp. 81-92. I thank Honore Forster of the Australian National University and the staff of the Hocken Library, University of Otago, for assistance with material for the caption.

For an interesting account of early American involvement in Hawaii – including the story of Obookiah — see, Foster Rhea Dulles, *America in the Pacific — A Century of Expansion* (Boston: Houghton-Mifflin 1938) Chapter IX 'Early Contacts with Hawaii', pp. 138-157.

The photograph of curiosities comes from NBFPL. For the fascinating tidbit re Little and his fakes I am grateful to Robin Watt, ethnologist at the National Museum of New Zealand.

The log of ship *Phoenix* (*Phenix*) 1850 is held at NHA No. L245, PMB 399. The log of the *Abraham Barker* 1871 is held at Brown, PMB 772. I am grateful to Paul Cyr, NBFPL, for the anecdote about the *Benjamin Cummings*.

Nat Morgan's journal on the *Hannibal* is held by Mystic Seaport, log No. 862. The illustration for flogging is an etching by J. Halpin, done for the book *Etchings of a Whaling Cruise* (Boston: Harvard Univ. Press repr. 1968), in which the author, J. Ross Browne, tried to bring the plight of the whalemen to the public eye, as Dana had done earlier for the American merchant seaman. Seaman Collins' journal kept on the *Meridian* 1829-31 is held at PPL, PMB 880. The anecdote re Luther Little is told in William Bolster, *The Changing Nature of Maritime Insurrection*, in, 'The Log of Mystic Seaport' 31, No. 1 (1979) pp. 14-21.

The quote from Mary Wallis comes from her book, *Life in Feejee...*, (Boston: William Heath, 1851) pp. 202-3. The journal kept on the *Sharon* (by an unnamed boatsteerer) is held at PPL, PMB 893.

The photograph of Gertrude West is held at Dukes County. The story of the dream comes from E.M. Whiting and H. Beetle Hough, *Whaling Wives* (Boston: Houghton-Mifflin 1953) pp. 263-8. The anecdote about the wife who survived by eating rats comes from J.R. Spears, *The Story of the New England Whaler* (New. York: MacMillan 1908) pp. 265-272.

The material on Abigail Jernegan in Japan comes from the Louise Winter Nolan Huntsman correspondence, held by Dukes County. Also see the journal kept on board the *Eliza F. Mason* by Orson F. Shattuck, ODHS, PMB 956.

An account of the beginnings of whaling on Baja California can be read in David A. Henderson, *Men & Whales at Scammon's Lagoon*, (Los Angeles: Dawson's Book Shop, 1972) pp. 82-3.

The photographs of Charlotte and Abram Dehart are held at ODHS, used by permission. I am grateful to a Dehart descendant, Kinga Spelman-Low, for much kind assistance in researching this whaling wife.

John States' account of Pitcairn is published as *Extracts*, by the Marine Hist. Assn. Inc., Mystic, Connecticut, Vol. 1, No. 4, November 20, 1931. A routine log kept on ship *Potomac* 1849-53, Charles Grant, is held at NHA No. L204, PMB 384; that on the *Navigator* is also at NHA No. L162, PMB 380.

### Chapter 8: 'Around Cape Horn'

The photographs of Charlotte and Samuel Wyer come from NHA, also used with permission.

The story of Mary Carlin Cleveland is told in Dionis Coffin Riggs, *From Off-Island*, (New York: Whittlesey, 1940), and her photograph comes from Dukes County.

For one account of the development of Hawaii as a recruiting place for whalers see Foster Rhea Dulles, *America in the Pacific: A Century of Expansion* (Boston: Houghton-Mifflin 1938) pp. 138-157, partic. pp. 144-6. The Baldwin letters are held at HMCSL. This particular letter was written to his sister Sophronia.

A complete account of whaling in the Western Arctic can be found in John Bockstoce, *Whales, Ice, & Men: The History of Whaling in the Western Arctic* (Seattle: Univ. of Washington Press in assoc. with the New Bedford Whaling Museum, 1986). For the tale of Warrens' ghoulish find, see Cheever, *The Whale & His Captors*,

(London: Nelson & Sons, 1853) pp. 115-9.

Hathaway's comment about the number of ships is quoted in Foster Rhea Dulles, *Lowered Boats*, (New York: Harrap & Co. 1934) p. 266. Sam Morgan's journal on the *South Boston* is held at ODHS, PMB 301.

The photograph of Captains Adams, Keenan and Baker comes courtesy of Joe Thomas. Baker's little log on the *Beluga* is held at PPL, PMB 576.

Penniman's 'thrilling experience' was related in the *Boston Globe* for 19 March 1904. The pictures of the Wheldons are held at ODHS, used by permission.

The story of Jane and Leander Owen was told to the author by the late Doris Coursen Stoddard, of Edgartown, Martha's Vineyard. The pictures come from Dukes County. An account of the 1871 ice disaster can be read in William Fish Williams, 'The Destruction of the Whaling Fleet in the Arctic Ocean in 1871,' being Part 2 of *One Whaling Family*, pp. 221-242.

The photograph of Herbert and Mary Colson is reproduced by kind permission of The Huntington Library. The material on San Francisco as a whaling port comes, firstly, from Lloyd Custer Mayhew Hare, *Salted Tories: the Story of the Whaling Fleets of San Francisco* (Mystic: Marine Publications 1960) pp. 75-82 and, secondly, from John Bockstoce, '*Whales, Ice, & Men*...pp. 173, 213.

## Chapter 9: 'More decency and order...?'

The reports of the *Harrison* were given in the *New Bedford Whalemen's Shipping List & Merchant's Transcript* for 9 February 1847, 2 May 1848, 30 May 1848, 24 October 1848, 28 November 1848, 20 February 1849, 8 May 1849, 14 August 1849, 29 January 1850. The microfilm of the diary kept on the *Harrison* for part of that voyage is held at ODHS, IMA No. 931.

The log of the 1876 voyage of the *Bartholomew Gosnold* is held at ODHS, PMB 247. The journal kept by Abram Briggs on the *Eliza Adams* is held at ODHS, PMB 911. Susan Brock's reminiscences were privately printed in 1926 as a monograph, *Doubling Cape Horn*. There is a copy of this at the NHA Research Center.

For the anecdote behind the title, see Diary of Charles W. Morgan, 25 July 1849, Mystic Seaport Collection 27, Vol. 3. The comments about Mrs Ewer come from Pseud. 'A Roving Printer', *Life and Adventure in the South Pacific* (New York: Harper & Bros. 1861); *New Bedford Whalemen's Shipping List* 25 July 1859. For Taylor's comment see, Howard Palmer, ed., Nathaniel W. Taylor, *Life on a Whaler* (New London, Conn.: New London County Historical Society, 1929).

The Tilton anecdote is related in E.M. Whiting & H. Beetle Hough, *Whaling Wives* (Boston: Houghton-Mifflin, 1953), pp. 217-8, as is the story of Charity Norton. The photograph of the latter comes from Dukes County.

For Penelope Enos see, Capt. Harry Allen Chippendale, *Sails and Whales* (Boston: Houghton-Mifflin 1951) p. 137.

The anecdote about Viola Cook and the flogging is told in Pat Amaral, *They Ploughed the Seas* (St. Petersburg: Valkyrie Press 1978) p. 88. The picture of John Atkins Cook comes from KWM, used by permission. That of Viola comes from the *Boston Globe* article which is quoted in the caption.

The Morrell references come from Benjamin Morrell, *A Narrative of Four Voyages*...(New York: Hayer, 1832) pp. 376-9, 390, 340, 467-8. The italics in all cases are his. Also see Abby Jane Morrell, *Narrative of a Voyage*...(repr. New Jersey: Gregg Press, 1970) pp. 50-1, 53.

Hall's encounter with the steamer *Brisbane* was reported in the *New Bedford Whalemen's Shipping List* for 1 May 1855. I am grateful to Stanton Garner for permission to use the photograph of Mary Lawrence.

The recipe for shrub was found in *Dr Chase's Receipt Book and Household*

*Physician* (Detroit, Mich.: FB Dickerson, 1864) p. 313.

Copies of Louisa Worsfold's reminiscences, *A Social History of Russell*, are held by the Auckland Institute and Museum Library, MS 340. The quotations come from pp. 11-12 of the typescript.

A copy of Luther Gulick's diatribe is held at HMCSL, Honolulu. Also see Joan Druett, *More Decency and Order: Women and Whalemen in the Pacific*, in, 'The Log of Mystic Seaport', Vol. 39, No. 2, Summer 1987, pp. 65-74. The John Deblois letters are held at Newport, Vault A, Box 113, Folder 6.

# *Appendix*

## Logs, journals, letters and reminiscences of the whaling sisters in public hands.

\* published; a 'formal logbook' is almost indistinguishable from one kept by a captain or officer; 'journal' indicates a discursive, personal record; a 'diary' is briefer, more notelike.

HARRIET ALLEN (Mrs David E.) bark *Merlin* of New Bedford, Mass., 23 June 1868–12 April 1872 (journal). – KWM reel No. 47, PMB 847.

ALMIRA (BROWNELL) ALMY (Mrs William H.) bark *Cape Horn Pigeon* of Dartmouth, Mass., 12 June 1854–8 August 1855 (incomplete journal: voyage ended 28 July 1858). – PPL reel No. 10, PMB 580.

ALMIRA (BROWNELL) ALMY, bark *Roscoe* of New Bedford, 9 November 1859–10 April 1860 (formal logbook). – ODHS, PMB 247.

ADRA (BRALEY) ASHLEY (Mrs Edward) ship *Reindeer* of New Bedford, 15 October 1856–23 March 1860 (intermittent journal). – Baker, PMB 730.

ELEANOR BAKER (Mrs Michael D), bark *Gazelle* of New Bedford, 30 September 1857 – 12 June 1860 (intermittent journal). – Loan log ODHS, property of Dietrich American Foundation.

RACHEL (KENDRICK) BECKERMAN (Mrs John A.), bark *Live Oak* of New Bedford, 22 June 1869–14 March 1872 (semi-formal logbook). – KWM reel No. 34, PMB 834.

LYDIA ABBY (JONES) BEEBE (Mrs John), bark *Brewster* of Mattapoisett, Mass., 17 October 1863–1 December 1865 (journal). – NHA No. L237, PMB 395.

LYDIA BEEBE, bark *Xantho* of New Bedford, 1 January 1867–25 June 1869 (incomplete journal: sailed 17 November 1866, returned 28 November 1869). – NHA No. L237, PMB 395.

HARRIET BLIVEN (Mrs George), bark *Nautilus* of New Bedford, 19 July 1865–17 March 1866 (incomplete semi-formal diary; left ship in Honolulu). – PMS log No. 656.

\* BERTHA (HAMBLIN) BOYCE, bark *Islander* of New Bedford, sailed 25 July 1871. – Reminiscences of her childhood on the bark, published as, *Bertha Goes Whaling: Personal Memoirs of a Voyage Aboard a Whaling Bark, Islander,* (Falmouth, Mass.: Kendall Printers, 1963).

HELEN (ALLEN) BRADFORD (Nellie), bark *Merlin* of New Bedford, 1 January 1871–12 April 1872 (child's partial diary plus essays). – KWM, PMB 847.

\* MARY LOUISA (BURTCH) BREWSTER (Mrs William E.), ship *Tiger* of Stonington, Connecticut, 4 December 1845–8 April 1848 (journal). – Mystic, log No. 38.

\* MARY BREWSTER, ship *Tiger* of Stonington, 13 July 1848–19 December 1849 (incomplete journal, abandoned in despair; ship arrived home 7 May 1851). – Mystic, log No. 38. Both journals published by Mystic Publications, Connecticut, 1991, as Joan Druett (ed.), *Our Charming Diaress: the Journals of Mary Brewster on the Whaleship 'Tiger' of Stonington, 1845-51.*

ELIZA (SPENCER) BROCK (Mrs Peter C.), ship *Lexington* of Nantucket, 21 May 1853–25 June 1856 (journal plus poetry). – NHA No. L136, PMB 378.

* AZUBAH CASH (Mrs William), ship *Columbia* of Nantucket, 1850. – NHA log No. 312. Published in Edward Rowe Snow, *Women of the Sea*, (New York: Dodd, Mead, 1962), chapter 8, pp. 71-85.

CHARLOTTE CHURCH (Lottie: Mrs Charles S.), bark *Andrew Hicks* of San Francisco, Calif., 6 December 1905–1 June 1906 (formal logbook). – ODHS/IMA microfilm.

LOTTIE CHURCH, bark *Andrew Hicks* of San Francisco, 1 January 1907–31 December 1907 (formal logbook). – KWM.

LOTTIE CHURCH, bark *Andrew Hicks* of San Francisco, 14 April 1908–5 August 1908 (formal, homeward bound). – Mystic, log No. 156.

LOTTIE CHURCH, bark *Charles W. Morgan* of New Bedford, 27 November 1909–11 September 1910 (formal logbook). – Mystic, log No. 156.

LOTTIE CHURCH, schr *A.M. Nicholson* of New Bedford, 23 April 1914–31 December 1915 (formal logbook). – ODHS/IMA microfilm.

MARIA CLARK (Mrs James M.), bark *Nimrod* of New Bedford, 16 April 1863–25 June 1865 (formal logbook; the bark was captured and burned by the Confederate steamer *Shenandoah* on the date of the last entry). – Mystic log No. 62.

MARIA CLARK, bark *Orlando* of New Bedford, 10 April 1867–6 May 1870 (formal logbook). – Mystic log No. 62.

SARAH (STALL) COLE (Mrs Frederick), bark *Vigilant* of New Bedford, 1 January 1860–5 July 1862 (incomplete journal; voyage began 23 August 1859, Sarah died 18 August 1862, voyage ended 18 June 1864). – PMS, PMB 222.

MARY COLSON (Mrs Herbert), bark *George and Susan* of New Bedford, 26 October 1877–18 April 1881 (incomplete journal; voyage began 16 October 1877, ended 23 May 1881). – Huntington, ms No. HM 26611.

LUCY-ANN (HIX) CRAPO (Mrs Reuben Williams), bark *Louisa* of New Bedford, 1 January 1866–16 August 1867 (incomplete journal: voyage began 13 June 1865; journal ends when a new baby takes up all her time; voyage ended 2 November 1868). – ODHS, PMB 911.

LUCY ANN CRAPO, bark *Linda Stewart* of New Bedford, sailed 27 November 1877, vessel sold at Talcahuano 7 March 1881. – ODHS Mss Coll No. 56 Box 54 Series M Sub-series 4. Letters to Lucy Ann's sister, Ruth Ellen Mosher, and to Ruth's husband Andrew Mosher (whaling in New Zealand), the first dated 15 January 1878, the last dated 11 October 1880.

ELIZA (NYE) DANA, ship *Sylph* of Fairhaven, Mass., 8 July 1847–23 August 1847 (incomplete diary; passenger to Fayal). – typescript, ODHS, PMB 287.

* HENRIETTA (TEW) DEBLOIS (Mrs John S.), bark *Merlin* of New Bedford, 25 June 1856–19 June 1859 (journal, continues as a shore diary). – Newport, Vault A, Box 113; published in serial form in the *Newport Mercury* in the early part of 1885.

CHARLOTTE WEEKS (SHERMAN) DEHART (Mrs Abraham var. 'Abram'), ship *Roman* of New Bedford, 24 August 1857–2 May 1861 (intermittent diary). – ODHS loan log, property of Mrs Kinga Spelman Low.

CYNTHIA ELLIS (Mrs William B.), bark *Ohio* of New Bedford, 18 September 1877–7 July 1878 (diary). – KWM, Log No. 544.

* SUSAN FISHER (Mrs Nehemiah), bark *Cowper* of New Bedford, sailed 10 September 1851, arrived home 6 May 1855. Letters to her cousins, describing events in the Ochotsk Sea, dated 12 June–7 October 1854, published in *New Bedford Whalemen's Shipping List and Merchants' Transcript*, 27 March 1855.

* JANE (RUSSELL) GELETT (Mrs Charles E.), ship *Uncas* of New Bedford, sailed 27 August 1846, arrived home 11 May 1849. Extracts published in her husband's book,

*A Life on the Ocean*, (Honolulu: Hawaiian Gazette, 1917).

ALMIRA (AMES) GIBBS (Mrs Richard), ship *Nantucket* of Nantucket, 14 June 1855–3 August 1859 (journal). – Nantucket Athenaeum, Nantucket, document No. 328, microfilm also held at NHA, reel No. 166, PMB 227, 391.

JERUSHA (BLAKE) HAWES (Mrs Jonathan C.), ship *Emma C. Jones* of New Bedford, 1 September 1858–5 December 1859 (incomplete diary; sailed 10 August 1858, arrived home 28 August 1860). – typed transcript, NBFPL.

HELEN (McCLELLAN CLARK) JERNEGAN (Mrs Jared), bark *Oriole* of New Bedford (joined ship in Honolulu, arrived home 2 September 1866, bark *Roman* of New Bedford, sailed 29 October 1868, ship lost in the Arctic 1871). – Reminiscences of crossing the Isthmus of Panama 1865 to join the *Oriole*, shipboard life on the *Roman* with her first two children (Laura and Prescott), written for her second son Marcus, held at Dukes County.

* LAURA JERNEGAN, bark *Roman* of New Bedford, sailed 1868. Child's partial diary on board ship, published as, Marcus W. Jernegan, ed., *A Child's Diary on a Whaling Voyage*, in, 'The New England Quarterly', II pp. 125-39.

* ANNA (STOTT) KING, ship *Northern Light* of Fairhaven, Mass., sailed 18 November 1851, arrived home 14 April 1855. – Reminiscences of childhood years on board ship, published in 'Old-Time New England' 48:2, 1957.

* MARY (CHIPMAN) LAWRENCE (Mrs Samuel), ship *Addison* of New Bedford, 25 November 1856–13 June 1860 (journal). – PPL, PMB 572, 772, published in Stanton Garner (ed), *The Captain's Best Mate – the Journal of Mary Chipman Lawrence on the Whaler 'Addison' 18561860*, (Providence, Rhode Island: Brown University Press 1966).

ASENATH (TABER) McFARLIN, bark *Alice Frazier* of New Bedford, 3 December 1854–2 September 1855 (child's intermittent diary; ship homeward bound, sold oil in Australia). – Mariners, PMB 775.

EMMA McINNES (Mrs John), bark *Josephine* of San Francisco, 16 December 1891–22 June 1892 (journal). – KWM, PMB 824.

SUSAN (STIMSON) McKENZIE (Mrs James), bark *Hercules* of New Bedford, 1869-1871 (intermittent journal, begins in Honolulu 23 October 1869). – ODHS Mss Coll No. 56 Series M Sub-series 4.

SUSAN McKENZIE, ship *Europa* of New Bedford, sailed 14 December 1871, arrived home 17 April 1876 (intermittent diary begins 22 January 1872 – many entries undated, much retrospective material). – ODHS Mss Coll No. 56 Series M Sub-series 4.

ELIZABETH MARBLE (Mrs John), bark *Kathleen* of New Bedford, 25 August 1857–2 January 1860 (journal-letters, some lost). – Marble Papers, KWM.

ELIZABETH MARBLE, bark *Awashonks* of New Bedford, 6 September 1860–8 April 1862 (journal, becomes diary soon after death of husband, 23 October 1861). – Marble Papers, KWM.

MALVINA (PINKHAM) MARSHALL (Mrs Joseph), brig *Sea Queen* of Westport, Mass.; ship sailed 15 October 1851, Malvina joined ship after crossing the Isthmus of Panama in 1852, arrived home 26 April 1855. – ODHS/IMA microfilm No. 934. Two lengthy letters, written home to her Nantucket Pinkham family, the first dated 4 October 1852, the second 22 June 1853.

ADALINE (HEPPINGSTONE) MATTHEWS, bark *Fleetwing* of San Francisco, 14 February 1882–5 November 1882 (diary of the captain's daughter). – ODHS, PMB 914.

ELIZABETH (MORSE) MOREY (Betsy: Mrs Israel), ship *Phoenix* of Nantucket, 2 September 1853–13 August 1855 (journal, ends when book is full; voyage ended 13 May 1856). – NHA No. L207, PMB 385.

HARRIET PEIRCE (var. Pierce), bark *Emerald* of New Bedford, 20 July 1857–23 October 1857 (child's diary, kept on passage to Honolulu). – KWM.

SOPHIE PORTER (Mrs William, P.S.), steam bark *Jesse H. Freeman* of San Francisco,

8 March 1894–29 March 1896 (detailed journal of overwintering in Arctic). – ODHS.

ADDIE POTTER (Mrs Sylvanus), ship *Emma C. Jones* of New Bedford, sailed 1 June 1875, arrived home 21 July 1879 (semi-formal logbook entries: filled in the captain's formal logbook while her husband was ill, four days only, 20-23 June 1879). – ODHS, PMB 956.

\* ANNIE (HOLMES) RICKETSON (Mrs Daniel), bark *A.R. Tucker* of New Bedford, 2 May 1871–17 October 1874 (journal). – KWM, PMB 802. Published as Purrington (ed), *Mrs Ricketson's Whaling Journal*, (New Bedford: Old Dartmouth Hist. Soc., 1958).

ANNIE RICKETSON, schr *Pedro Varela* of New Bedford, 5 April 1881–13 October 1883 (journal). – KWM reel No. 16, PMB 287, 816, 887.

ANNIE RICKETSON, schr *Pedro Varela* of New Bedford, 13 January 1885–20 November 1885 – journal, begins on the *Lottie Beard*, en route to join her husband in St Helena (schooner sailed 21 May 1884), continues on board the schooner, becomes a shore journal on Barbados during husband's illness, resumes on passage home (arrived 6 August 1885), sailed again 5 September; journal ends 20 November 1885 (voyage ended 22 November 1886, abandoned after Captain Ricketson's death). – KWM log No. 168, PMB 287, 816, 887.

\* MARY HAYDEN RUSSELL (Mrs Laban), ship *Emily* (English). Begins 11 February 1823, ends 10 March 1824, at Guam. Letters to her daughter, Mary Ann Mount, held by NHA as 'Sea Letter', Collection 83, Folder 1, extracts published in, Edouard A. Stackpole, *Whales and Destiny*, (Amherst: Univ. of Mass. Press, 1972).

MARIANNA (ALMY) SHERMAN (Mrs Wanton), ship *Nimrod* of New Bedford, 23 September 1848–3 December 1849 (daily diary on passage to Hawaii. Ends in Honolulu 12 May 1849, starts again 3 December 1849 for one entry only, no reason given; voyage ended 1 July 1851). – PPL reel No. 44, PMB 884.

SARAH JANE SLOCOM (Mrs George W.), ship *Mary & Martha* of New Bedford, 28 November 1851 'bound round Cape Horn' – 21 March 1852. (Formal logbook, ends prematurely, no reason given; the voyage ended 11 April 1855. The rest of the book is a routine log beginning 17 August 1857, on the *Abraham Barker*, in a different hand). – Mystic log No. 99.

LUCY (VINCENT) SMITH (Mrs George A.), bark *Nautilus* of New Bedford, 20 October 1869–21 May 1874 (journal). – PPL reel 43, PMB 883.

MARION S. SMITH (Mrs Horace P.), bark *California* of San Francisco, 1 December 1898–16 November 1899. (Routine logbook, brief formal entries, mentions herself in the third person: 'Capt. and Lady'). – ODHS, PMB 252.

SARAH (SALLIE) (WORDELL) SMITH (Mrs Frederick H.), bark *Ohio* of New Bedford, 6 July 1875–17 October 1878 (diary). – Mystic log No. 399.

SALLIE SMITH, bark *John P. West* of New Bedford, 7 June 1882–11 May 1884 (diary). – Mystic log No. 78.

ELIZABETH STETSON (Mrs Charles), bark *E. Corning* of New Bedford, begins 15 November 1860, ends at Talcahuano,Chile, 18 February 1865, book full (journal; voyage ended 24 May 1866, the ship having taken only 744 bbls sperm oil). – KWM.

MARY STICKNEY (Mrs Almon), bark *Cicero* of New Bedford, 12 December 1880–4 August 1881 (diary). – PPL reel No. 14, PMB 794.

HARRIET (MYRICK) SWAIN (Mrs Obed 2D), ship *Catawba* of Nantucket, 25 December 1852–13 May 1855 in New York, after crossing the Isthmus of Panama (journal). – NHA No. L33, PMB 374.

SARAH (PARKER) TABER (Mrs Daniel C.), ship *Copia* of New Bedford, 25 September 1848–8 May 1851 (intermittent diary, some poetry, has some retrospective accounting. Arrived at Honolulu March 1849, shore entries interesting but discontinuous. Sea diary resumes 6 December 1850, homeward bound on the *Julian*). – Mariners Museum, PMB 776.

SARAH TABER, bark *Alice Frazier* of New Bedford, 10 September 1851–6 August

1855 (intermittent diary, begins at the start of the passage to the Hawaiian Islands. Then a discontinuous account of voyages and shore life in Honolulu. Ends homeward bound). – Mariners, PMB 776.

\* EMMA (WILCOX) THOMAS (Mrs Albert), bark *Merlin* of New Bedford, sailed 2 July 1872, arrived home 19 June 1876. – ODHS Mss. Coll No. 56, Box 79 Series T Sub-series 12. Letters written on board and in various South Pacific ports, published in Sylvia Thomas, *Saga of a Yankee Whaleman*, (New Bedford: ODHS, 1981).

BETSY ANN (PARLOW) TOWER (Mrs William E.), ship *Moctezuma* of New Bedford, 16 August 1847–13 December 1849 (semi-formal logbook, some poetry: ends in Lat. 19.13 Long 171.57, end of book; ship arrived back 11 May 1850; the dates covering her time in Honolulu 23 September 1848 to 30 October 1848 have been ripped out, probably as a letter home). – ODHS, PMB 302, 692.

CARRIE F. TURNER (Mrs Charles H.), bark *Napoleon* of New Bedford, 1 August 1878–24 June 1882 (intermittent journal; ends one month before arriving home; resumes briefly July 1885 when Carrie was left on shore at St Helena because of her advanced pregnancy: this was during another voyage, on the *A.R. Tucker*, which sailed 26 June 1883 and arrived home 3 August 1886). – ODHS/IMA microfilm No. 763.

ELIZA UNDERWOOD (Mrs S.), ship *Kingsdown* (English) February 1830–24 September 1831 (daily journal, the third one of several, the rest all lost). – Dixson.

SUSAN VEEDER (Mrs Charles A.), ship *Nauticon* of Nantucket, 13 September 1848–23 March 1853 (diary). – ODHS/IMA microfilm No. 366.

ELIZABETH (GLADDING) WALDRON (Mrs Nelson), ship *Bowditch* of Warren, Rhode Island, 17 February 1853–4 December 1853 (intermittent journal: voyage commenced 19 August 1852, journal begins in Hobart after the birth of a baby on shore there, ends prematurely, perhaps because the book was full: there is a list of ships spoken at the end; the voyage ended 20 May 1856). – NBFPL, microfilm.

GERTRUDE WEST (Mrs Ellsworth), bark *Horatio* of San Francisco, 1 January 1898–31 December 1898 (diary). – KWM, PMB 810, 833.

CLARA WHELDON (Mrs Alexander), bark *John Howland* of New Bedford, sailed 25 June 1864, voyage finally ended 29 May 1871 after being interrupted in 1865, when Captain Wheldon and family returned home because he was sick. – Typed transcript of letters, ODHS, Mss No. 56, Box 84 Series W Sub-series 12, PMB 274.

\* ADELAIDE (BAKER) WICKS (Mrs Rodolphus), bark *Coral* of San Francisco, sailed 4 December 1888, left ship in Honolulu 25 March 1889, voyage ended 9 October 1889. – Partial journal published in Genevieve M. Darden (ed), *My Dear Husband* (New Bedford: Descendants of Whaling Masters, 1980) pp. 79-83.

\* ELIZA AZELIA (GRISWOLD) WILLIAMS (Mrs Thomas), ship *Florida* of Fairhaven, 7 September 1858–13 October 1861, nearing San Francisco (journal). – PMS, pub. in Harold Williams (ed), *One Whaling Family*, (Boston: Houghton-Mifflin, 1964).

CHARLOTTE (COFFIN) WYER (Mrs Samuel), ship *Young Hero* of Nantucket, 16 March 1853–1 July 1854 (journal; begins at sea on the *Harriot Irving*, on passage to Chile; ends with no explanation save for a notation in her husband's script, 'Harriet Amelia Wyer born Wednesday September 27 at 5 PM'; voyage ended 27 June 1855). – NHA No. L268, PMB 387.

# Acknowledgments

While many of the individuals who helped in the task of unravelling the story of the petticoat whaleships have already been acknowledged in the chapter notes, some have not – and those who have so materially assisted in the years that have elapsed since the first edition deserve recognition, too. I must again thank the New Zealand–United States Educational Foundation for the award of the Fulbright Cultural Fellowship which enabled me to travel to New England and Hawaii in 1986; and Creative New Zealand, too, for funding that enabled me to take up an Artist in Residency in Orient, New York, and carry out even more extensive research. The original debt that I owed the manuscripts and archives staff at the Alexander Turnbull Library, National Library of New Zealand, has been vastly augmented since: in the intervening years their patience in the face of my endless requests has proved boundless. Rhys Richards remains unfailingly generous with his vast knowledge of whaling history. Harry Morton, who shared so much information at the start of the whaling wives project, is still as interested in my studies of women at sea. The staffs of the Hamilton Public Library, the library of the University of Waikato, the Auckland Institute and Museum (now the Auckland War Memorial Museum), the Wellington Public Library, and the library of Victoria University of Wellington have all been attentive and helpful, and it is a great privilege to be associated with the John David Stout Research Centre at Victoria. Additionally, I owe thanks to the Wellington Maritime Museum (now the Museum of Wellington City & Sea), and to the director, Ken Scadden, in particular.

During a research trip to Australia in 1988, I received much-needed help from the Archives Office, the Crowther Library, and the Museum and Art Gallery in Tasmania. In Sydney, I spent a great deal of time researching Eliza Underwood at the Dixson Library, State Library of New South Wales, the staff of which has fielded many requests since. Over the intervening years, too, I have received interest and attention from the Pacific Manuscripts Bureau at the Australian National University and the National Library of Australia, while the enthusiasm and help that came in the form of personal correspondence with Honore Forster has been a much appreciated boon. In Hawaii, I received invaluable help from the staff of the Hawaiian Mission Children's Society (now the Mission Houses Museum), and the Lahaina Restoration Foundation.

One of the huge bonuses of my association with American maritime museums over the sixteen years of research for the eleven books and many articles that accompanied and succeeded the first publication of *Petticoat Whalers,* is the friendship of staff. At the Old Dartmouth Historical Society, New Bedford Whaling Museum, Richard Kugler, Virginia Adams, Carol Juneau, and Judith Downey were my first guides to their outstanding collection; since my first visit in 1986 Judith Downey and Judith Lund have fielded numberless requests for information with unfailing good humor, expertise, and enthusiasm, while it is always a pleasure to greet both volunteers and staff, Anne Brengle, the Director, in particular. I am also grateful to Paul Cyr and his staff at the Melville Whaling Room, New Bedford Public Library.

At the Nicholson Whaling Room, Providence (Rhode Island) Public Library, Philip Weimerskirch, Special Collections Librarian, the successor to Lance Bauer, has been most attentive in assistance with my ongoing projects. Much gratitude is owed to the Kendall Whaling Museum and Dr. Stuart Frank for the unstinting interest and assistance with materials that I have received over the years. My relationship with Mystic Seaport Museum has also been most rewarding. The staff and volunteers of the Dukes County Historical Society (now the Martha's Vineyard Historical Society) have delighted me with their enthusiasm for my work, particular thanks being owed to Catherine Mayhew, Art Railton, and Jill Bouck. I am also grateful to the staff and volunteers of the Nantucket Historical Society, along with the staff of the Phillips Library at the Peabody Essex Museum (Salem, Mass.), the Newport Historical Society, the John Hay Library, Brown University, the Nantucket Athenaeum, the Baker and Houghton Libraries at Harvard, the library at Mariner's Museum, and the Wethersfield Historical Society, Connecticut. I am very grateful to Peter Blodgett, Western Manuscripts Curator, Huntington Library, for much help and interest over the years. I owe gratitude to Kinga Spelman Low and Deborah M. Rebuck.

On a more personal level, I recognize the friendship, assistance, and interest of curators and librarians in Maine, Rhode Island, Connecticut, and New York: Michele Morrisson, the William Steeple Davis Trust, the Oysterponds Historical Society, the Three Village Historical Society, the Cold Spring Harbor Whaling Museum, the Suffolk County Historical Society, the Sag Harbor Historical Society, South Street Seaport Museum, the Maine Maritime Museum, the Penobscot Marine Museum, the Rhode Island Historical Society, and the many people who have shared their family heritage with me: they had no direct input into *Petticoat Whalers,* but they have vastly enriched my research since.

Thanks are also due to Paul Bradwell, onetime editorial director of HarperCollins *New Zealand,* who made *Petticoat Whalers* such a beautiful and successful book, and to Philip Pochoda and Ellen Wicklum, who have loved it enough to want to see it in the bookstores again. Yet again, I owe eternal gratitude to my husband Ron, who has smoothed the path to many a repository, and somehow managed to provide fine artwork as well. And once again, too, I thank my agent, Laura Langlie: that *Petticoat Whalers* is available again is due most of all to her.

# Selected bibliography

The following list is recommended background reading only. Specific sources, both published and manuscript, are detailed in the notes to each chapter, and are not repeated here.

Everett S. Allen, *Children of the Night: The Rise and Fall of New Bedford Whaling and the Death of the Arctic Fleet*, (Boston: Little Brown, 1973).

Clifford W. Ashley, *The Yankee Whaler*, (London: Martin Hopkinson, 1926). Beautifully illustrated by the author, a famous maritime artist.

Joshua F. Beane, *From Forecastle to Cabin: – the story of a cruise in many seas*. (New York: J.F. Beane 1905). A firsthand account of a voyage on the *Java*, about 1860, and a thoroughly entertaining read.

K.M. Bowden, *Captain James Kelly of Hobart Town* (Melbourne: Univ. Press 1964). A history of Hobart whaling.

Paul Budker, *Whales & Whaling* (trans) (London: Harrap 1958). Valuable because of the wealth of technical detail it contains.

Frank T. Bullen, *The Cruise of the 'Cachalot' Round the World after Sperm Whales*, (orig. pub. 1910) (London: J. Murray, 1928). A bestseller in its time, partly because of the sensational nature of this personal account.

Walter N. Burns, *A Year with a Whaler* (New York: Outing 1913). A racy account of his voyage on brig *Alexander* to the Arctic, with descriptions of his many attempts to desert.

J. Chrisp (Lt Commdr.) *South of Cape Horn* (London: Robert Hale 1958). A riveting account of twentieth century whaling, from the standpoint of a technical observer.

Albert Cook Church, *Whaleships and Whaling*, (New York: Bonanza Books 1938). Excellent historic photographs.

Max Colwell, *Whaling Around Australia* (Adelaide: Rigby 1969).

Geoffrey J. Cox, *Whale Watch: A guide to New Zealand's whales and dolphins* (Auckland: William Collins 1990). A charmingly illustrated guide to species, with a conservation message.

W.M. Davis, *Nimrod of the Sea, or, The American Whaleman*, (New York: Harper Bros. 1874). An authoritative history.

Linda G. De Pauw, *Seafaring Women*, (Boston: Houghton-Mifflin, 1982), chapter 4, women on whalers, pp. 104-161.

George Francis Dow, *Whaleships and Whaling*, (Salem: Marine Reserach Soc. 1925). A collection of historic photographs.

Foster Rhea Dulles, *Lowered Boats*, (New York: Harrap & Co. 1934). A well-sourced history, with plenty of racy anecdotes.

Federal Writers Project, *Whaling Masters*, a gazette of skippers and their voyages, orig. pub. 1938, repr. in, 'Stokvis Studies in Historical Chronology and Thought', no. 8, (San Bernadino, Calif.: Borgo Press, 1987).

Henry Ferguson, *Harpoon* (London: Jonathan Cape 1932). An account of modern

Norwegian whaling, which includes (pp. 128-134) an amusing anecdote about a female stowaway ('a pretty blonde with roguish china-blue eyes' who wanted to be the first woman in the Antarctic) – in this intensely male territory.

Honore Forster, *The South Sea Whaler: An Annotated Bibliography of Published Historical, Literary and Art Material Relating to Whaling in the Pacific Ocean in the Nineteenth Century.* (Mass.: KWM/Edw. J. Lefkowicz Inc. 1985).

R.S. Garnett, *Moby-Dick and Mocha-Dick*, in, 'Blackwood's Magazine', no. MCCCLXX, Dec. 1929. A lively and useful account of whaling and the 'original' white whale, with much animated 'spring to your oars, boys' dialogue.

Frank Gilbreth, *Of Whales & Women* (London: Heinemann 1957). Largely personal comments and reminiscences of childhood holidays in Nantucket, but a lot of fun.

Don Grady, *Guards of the Sea* (Christchurch: Whitcoulls 1978). The story of one New Zealand shore whaling family.

Gordon Grant, *Greasy Luck* (New York: Wm Farquhar Payson/Caravan Maritime Books 1970). A delightful whaling sketch book.

Nelson Cole Haley, *Whale Hunt: the Narrative of a Voyage by Nelson Cole Haley, Harpooner in the Ship 'Charles W. Morgan' 1849-53*, (London: Travel Book Club, 1951). A useful, if somewhat pompous account, with good descriptions of the Bay of Islands at that early time.

Thomas W. Hammond, *On Board a Whaler* (New York: Putnam's Sons 1901). A riotous reminiscent account written by a seaman who was as rough and tough as the rest of 'em.

Charles Boardman Hawes, *Whaling*, (London: Heinemann 1924). A well-resourced account of life on a whaler, with lively quotations from a number of logbooks.

Reginald B. Hegarty, *Addendum to 'Starbuck' and 'Whaling Masters'*, (New Bedford: NBFPL 1964).

Reg Hegarty, *The Rope's End* (Boston: Houghton-Mifflin 1965). Reminiscences of a childhood spent on whalers, the *Alice Knowles* in particular. A hilarious account which gives all kinds of good reasons for *not* taking ones children to sea on a whaleship.

E.P. Hohman, *The American Whaleman*, (New York: Longman Green, 1928). Includes (pp. 156-181) valuable descriptions of whaling and cutting in.

William J. Hopkins, *She Blows! And Sparm at that!*, (Boston: Houghton-Mifflin 1922). Contains a useful description of early New Bedford (pp. 2-7).

Gordon Jackson, *The British Whaling Trade* (London: A & C Black 1978). An aspect of whaling history that is too often neglected.

Robert Jarman, *Journal of a Voyage to the South Seas in the 'Japan'* (Beccles 1838). This was the 1831 voyage of that ship.

Marie M. King, *Port in the North* (Russell: Centenary Committee 1949). A short history of Russell.

Robert Langdon (ed), *American Whalers and Traders in the Pacific: A Guide to Records on Microfilm*, (Canberra: Pacific Manuscripts Bureau, Research School of Pacific Studies, Australian National University, 1978).

Robert Langdon (ed). *Where the Whalers Went: An Index to the Pacific Ports and Islands Visited by American Whalers (and some other ships) in the 19th Century*, (Canberra: Pacific Manuscripts Bureau, 1984).

Robert McNab, *The Old Whaling Days: a history of southern New Zealand from 1830 to 1840* (Christchurch: Whitcombe & Tombs 1913).

Robert McNally, *So Remorseless a Havoc – Of Dolphins, Whales and Men*, (Boston: Little Brown, 1981). A sensitive and well-balanced discussion of the morality of whaling. Excellent bibliography, with helpful comments.

O. Macy, *The History of Nantucket* (Mass: Macy & Pratt 1880).

William H. Macy (Capt.) *There She Blows! or, The Log of the 'Arethusa'* (Boston: Lee & Shepard 1877). Contains much lively dialogue, along with a description of early Sydney.

C. Bede Maxwell, *Wooden Hookers* (Sydney: Angus & Robertson 1940). Anecdotes of Australian maritime history.

Felix Maynard and Alexandre Dumas, *The Whalers* (trans), (London: Hutchinson, 1937).

Samuel Millet, *A Whaling Voyage in the bark 'Willis' 1849-50*, priv. pr. Boston, 1924.

Alan Moorehead, *The Fatal Impact, An Account of the Invasion of the South Pacific, 1767-1840*, (London: Hamish Hamilton 1966, repr. Penguin, 1985). A somewhat unbalanced discussion, which nevertheless gives a good picture of the dire influence of the whalemen on the unwary natives.

Samuel Eliot Morison, *The Maritime History of Massachusetts 1783-1860*, (Boston: Houghton-Mifflin repr. of 1921 edition, 1961).

Harry Morton, *The Whale's Wake* (Dunedin: Univ. of Otago Press, 1982). A most comprehensive account of the whaling trade in New Zealand.

Robert Cushman Murphy, *A Dead Whale or a Stove Boat* (Boston: Houghton-Mifflin, 1967). Sailed on whalers early this century, remarkable illustrations.

F.D. Ommanney, *Lost Leviathan*, (London: Hutchinson, 1871). A well-sourced history, valuable because of the technical detail.

Philip F. Purrington, *4 Years A-whaling* (Mass.: Barres, for ODHS 1972). A hearty account, illustrated by .Charles S. Raleigh.

L.S. Rickard, *The Whaling Trade in Old New Zealand* (Auckland: Minerva 1965).

Capt. Charles Henry Robbins, *The Gam*, (New Bedford: H.S. Hutchinson 1899). 'Being a group of whaling stories': reminiscences of a man who carried his wife on the *Thomas Pope*, in 1859.

Ivan T. Sanderson, *Follow the Whale*, (London: Cassell, 1958). A long look at whaling, from neolithic to modern, with much naturalistic detail, interlarded with semi-fictional whaling yarns.

Charles M. Scammon, *The Marine Mammals of the Northwestern Coast of North America* (San Francisco: J.H. Carmany & Co., 1874). Part III of this learned account is a description of the American whale fishery.

Stuart C. Sherman, *Whaling Logbooks and Journals 1613-1927: An Inventory of Manuscript Records in Public Collections*, revised and edited by Judith M. Downey and Virginia M. Adams, (New York: Garland, 1986).

Bill Spence, *Harpooned* (New York: Crescent, 1980). Includes the story of the British whaling fleets, lavishly illustrated.

Edouard A. Stackpole, *The Sea Hunters*, (New York: Lippincott, 1953). A formidably researched history of American whaling.

Alexander Starbuck, *History of the American Whale Fishery, from its Earliest Inception to the Year 1876*, (New York: Argosy-Antiquarian, 1964 repr.). The indispensable source for dates, tonnages and whaling reports. Best used in combination with Hegarty, Sherman and *Whaling Masters*.

W. Patrick Straus, *Americans in Polynesia 1783-1842*, (East Lansing: Michigan State Univ. Press, 1963).

Harold W. Thompson (ed) *The Last of the 'Logan', The True Adventures of Robert Coffin, Mariner in the years 1854-59*----(New York/Ithaca: Cornell Univ. Press 1941). The *Logan* was wrecked in the Fijis. Includes a lively description of grogshops in Mangonui.

W.S. Tower, *A History of the American Whale Fishery* (Penn.: Univ. Press 1907).

A. Hyatt Verrill, *The Real Story of the Whaler*, (New York: Appleton, 1923). Includes an excellent chapter (VII) on logs and journals, and also an intriguing anecdote about a female who sailed disguised as a seaman.

Ralph G. Ward (ed), *American Activities in the Central Pacific*, (Ridgewood, NJ: Gregg Press, 1966-7). A most useful compendium of newspaper items.

Arthur C. Watson, *The Long Harpoon: a collection of whaling anecdotes*, (New Bedford: William, 1929).

Robert Lloyd Webb, *On the Northwest*, (Vancouver: British Columbia Press, 1988).

A most comprehensive history of whaling on the north-west coast of North America.

Addison B.C. Whipple, *Yankee Whalers in the South Seas*, (London: Gollancz, 1954). Also, *The Whalers* (Time-Life Books 1979).

David Wilkinson, *Whaling in Many Seas* (London: Henry J. Drane, nd.). Includes an account of Capt. Fred Barker, who married Martha Hickton in Russell.

# Index